POSSIBLE WORLDS OF THE FANTASTIC

THEORY/CULTURE

Editors:
Linda Hutcheon, Gary Leonard,
Janet Paterson, and Paul Perron

NANCY H. TRAILL

Possible Worlds of the Fantastic: The Rise of the Paranormal in Fiction

UNIVERSITY OF TORONTO PRESS
Toronto Buffalo London

© University of Toronto Press 1996
Toronto Buffalo London
Printed in Canada
Reprinted in 2018
ISBN 0-8020-0729-5
ISBN 978-1-4875-8500-6 (paper)

Printed on acid-free paper

Canadian Cataloguing in Publication Data

Traill, Nancy, 1953–
  Possible worlds of the fantastic : the rise of the paranormal in fiction

(Theory/culture)
Includes bibliographical references and index.
ISBN 0-8020-0729-5

1. Fantastic fiction – History and criticism. 2. Fiction – Technique.
3. Fiction – 19th century – History and criticism. 4. Possibility in literature. 5. Reality in literature. 6. Dickens, Charles, 1812–1870 – Criticism, interpretation, etc. 7. Turgenev, Ivan Sergeevich, 1818–1883 – Criticism, interpretation, etc. 8. Maupassant, Guy de, 1850–1893 – Criticism, interpretation, etc. I. Title. II. Series.

PN3377.5.F34T73 1996   809.3'8766   C95-932522-0

University of Toronto Press acknowledges the financial assistance to its publishing program of the Canada Council and the Ontario Arts Council.

This book has been published with the help of a grant from the Humanities and Social Sciences Federation of Canada, using funds provided by the Social Sciences and Humanities Research Council of Canada.

Contents

PREFACE vii

1 Fictional Worlds of the Fantastic 3
2 Context and Intertext of the Paranormal Mode 21
3 The Realists: Experience and Inspiration 34
4 Charles Dickens: Tradition and Transition 46
5 Ivan Sergeevich Turgenev: Tentative Beginnings 74
6 Guy de Maupassant: The Scientific Cynic 105
Conclusion 135

NOTES 143
APPENDIX A   Russian Original   161
APPENDIX B   French Original   165
BIBLIOGRAPHY 169
INDEX 193

Preface

It is telling that, as our scientifically and technologically advanced century draws to a close, university students still flock to courses on the fantastic. Leaving aside the matter of reading tastes, something of its popularity must lie in its challenge to common sense and the more rigid kinds of rationality. To their surprise, students often discover that fantastic stories are not merely 'fun' to read – sometimes quite the opposite – and are not always to be recommended before sleep.

The longevity of the fantastic, its persistence through thousands of years of cultural history, is remarkable. Old themes and motifs never seem to go out of vogue, and are renewed in rich and endless variations. The legend of Faust is a good example. Its origins are buried in antiquity; brought to life in popular medieval narratives and poetry, it later found expression in Marlowe's play, *The Tragical History of Dr Faustus* (1604). Calderón adopted it for his 1637 play, *El Mágico prodigioso*, as did Goethe in his renowned *Faust* (1832), and Mann, in a much modified version, *Doktor Faustus* (1947). In a different semiotic system, music, Faust again transcends genre, with Wagner's *Faust Overture*, Liszt's *A Faust Symphony* and his famous *Mephisto Waltz*, and Schumann's production, *Scenes from Goethe's Faust*. Among the vocal works, we have Berlioz's opera, also performed as an oratorio, *La Damnation de Faust*, Gounod's *Faust*, Boïto's *Mefistofele*, and Busoni's *Doktor Faust*. This ability of the fantastic to adapt makes it a cross-generic and cross-semiotic phenomenon that can be harder to explain than many other complex literary phenomena. It is a trait that ensured its survival in the nineteenth century: in an age of science and under the onslaught of positivism, the fantastic, far from disappearing, was transformed by realist writers.

After the middle of the nineteenth century, a new mode of the fantastic, the paranormal, made its appearance. The rise of this mode is, for me, the most interesting stage in the long history of the fantastic, and I am especially struck by the fact that three of the best-known realists of the nineteenth century – the Englishman Charles Dickens, the Russian Ivan Sergeevich Turgenev, and the Frenchman Guy de Maupassant – not only wrote many fantastic stories, but also made the fantastic compatible with the times. A comparative study of the parallel developments in their fantastic works has proved most fruitful.

I have found the concept of fictional worlds, an offshoot of possible-worlds semantics, to be the most appropriate approach to the topic. The theoretical reflections in chapter 1 and the analyses of works by Dickens, Turgenev, and Maupassant in chapters 4 to 6 therefore focus on the semantic and stylistic aspects of fantastic narratives. How these fictional worlds are configured is dependent on the existential status of the supernatural and natural domains. Epistemic and authenticating narrative strategies are the means by which these worlds are constructed, while the interpretations of fictional events offered by the characters and the narrators themselves – the metanarrative – are equally important.

The value of the possible-worlds approach for literature has been proved by the many theoretical and analytical contributions made over the past two decades by such theorists as Eco, Pavel, and Doležel. Even while this manuscript was in preparation, three significant monographs (Ryan 1991, Pozuelo Yvancos 1993, Ronen 1994) have made their appearance, and a special issue of *Style* (1991) was devoted to the subject. Most encouragingly, the possible-worlds approach confirmed its importance for interdisciplinary studies at a gathering of philosophers, humanists, literary scholars, natural scientists, and others at Nobel Symposium 65, the proceedings of which were published in a volume edited by Sture Allén. The vitality of possible-worlds semantics is an encouragement to students of literature to make use of its conceptual tools for the continued enrichment of both literary theory and the interdisciplinary framework.

There is no reason for an approach that focuses on the literary text and the fictional world to ignore the cultural and historical conditions in which the stories were written. Analysis of the stories themselves is preceded by a brief chapter on the intellectual and cultural context that went so far towards shaping the fantastic of Dickens, Turgenev, and Maupassant. It is followed by another, briefer, chapter that links these trends to what the writers thought about art and about spiritualism.

The discourse of the paranormal is the main historical intertext of mid-nineteenth-century fantastic literature. But we ought to bear in mind that the traffic between literary text and extraliterary intertext does not go in one direction only. If spiritualism and psychical research provided authors like Dickens, Turgenev, and Maupassant with a vocabulary, so writers in their turn contributed to and helped to shape the discourse of the paranormal. In developing the paranormal mode, in breaking with traditional forms of the fantastic, they were indirectly presenting an informal set of postulates (not necessarily their beliefs) about reality.

The style of referencing is the author-date system accepted by the 1985 edition of *The MLA Style Manual*. Parenthetical references are to the editions used; the initial date of publication is given in the bibliography. Quotations from Russian and French have been translated; those from primary sources are to be found in Appendix A (Russian, in transliteration) and Appendix B (French), using the system of the U.S. Board on Geographic Names. It is rare to encounter anyone who, knowing the original language, is satisfied with the translations that are available. I am no exception, and the translations from Russian and French are my own. Whatever their merits or defects, I must claim responsibility.

I cannot sufficiently express my gratitude to the many people who were generous with both time and advice: Peter W. Nesselroth, Lubomír Doležel, and Owen J. Miller deserve special thanks. Roland Le Huenen, Jay Macpherson, and Gleb Žekulin gave helpful information in their fields; Thomas Pavel's comments and suggestions were most welcome and useful. I would be remiss if I did not thank the students in my seminar at York University for their challenges and criticisms. Lastly, I would like to offer warm thanks to my friends in the 'Toronto Circle,' a group of graduate students who, under the direction of Lubomír Doležel, met regularly to give criticism, comments, and encouragement to one another in our projects. The fruits of our discussions are to be found in the special issue of *Style*, 'Possible Worlds and Literary Fiction.'

NANCY H. TRAILL
TORONTO

POSSIBLE WORLDS OF THE FANTASTIC

1
Fictional Worlds of the Fantastic

Before the eighteenth century, theorists were not easily captivated by the fantastic, even though it held its appeal for the popular imagination. They dismissed the marvellous as 'the fairy way of writing' – a violation of the principles of mimesis, which required a writer to imitate reality: 'Que la nature donc soit votre étude unique,' wrote Boileau in *L'Art poétique* (1674, Chant III, v. 159). A change came with Baumgarten's theory of heterocosmic and utopian fictions, in 1735, and Breitinger's 1740 typology of marvellous worlds (allegorical, Aesopian, and invisible). Both were modelled on Leibniz's theory of possible worlds. Here, at last, a place was found for the marvellous, which Breitinger, at least, took to be the 'highest achievement' of poetic invention: in the marvellous, the possible of imagination acquires *fictional* existence (Doležel 1990, 43–5).[1]

A taste for the fantastic, especially among the English, had given us the Gothic romances of Horace Walpole, Anne Radcliffe, Clara Reeve, Sophia Lee, and a host of imitators by the close of the eighteenth century. As the fantastic evolved, the Romantics were perhaps the first to try to describe its *kinds* and their characteristics. This interest in defining, in specifying features, has continued into the twentieth century and shows little sign of abating. Much of what has been written recently is pertinent to the typology of the fantastic which follows later in this chapter, since it provides both background and context for comparison. The typology itself is based on the concepts of possible-worlds semantics, and will best be appreciated, I believe, in contrast to other approaches to the fantastic.

4 Possible Worlds of the Fantastic

THEORETICAL BACKGROUND

Thematics concerns itself with cataloguing recurrent themes and motifs; in the fantastic, this means pointing to such supernatural beings as ghosts, werewolves, and vampires, as well as to their transformations. Dorothy Scarborough (1917), one of this century's earliest theorists of the fantastic, noticed how frequently divinities appeared in early religious plays, and contrasted them with the spectral nightwalkers of the eighteenth-century Gothic romances (285).[2] She was well aware, though, that the thematic approach can be haphazard and impressionistic, its lists potentially endless, so she devised a pretheoretical typology of ghosts 'based on the reality of their appearance' (82). With considerable acuity, she understood that such transformations, based as they are on the degree of verisimilitude, have a historical dimension (73, 91). Years later, Louis Vax (1960) and Peter Penzoldt (1965) would avoid heteronomous thematic categories by singling out a universal psychological factor, fear. For Penzoldt, the effect of supernatural stories on the reader follows a gradation, 'an ascending line leading up to the climax' (16). Of course, this is a general plot pattern by no means restricted to the fantastic, but Penzoldt also sees that 'the position and exceptional importance of the climax' distinguish the ghost story from other kinds of short story (16).[3]

Tzvetan Todorov's well-known and influential book *The Fantastic: A Structural Approach* (1975)[4] was a major step in the semantic and structural study of fantastic texts. Todorov established an ideal 'genre,' an invariant which he calls the pure fantastic. Ambiguity is an essential part of the work's structure, rather than a theme, he claims, and causes the 'implicit' reader to hesitate between a natural and a supernatural explanation for the narrated events. Hesitation may become a theme if it is dramatized in the text; that is, if the protagonist shares the reader's hesitation. Texts which do not fulfil the requirement of the genre belong to a 'neighbouring genre,' either the uncanny or the marvellous.

The fantastic is unstable, writes Todorov, only as durable as the hesitation which sustains it. It is an 'evanescent genre' analogous to the grammatical temporal category 'present,' which is the boundary between past and future. Hesitation occurs in the present, whereas an explanation makes it a thing of the past, so that Todorov insists on the irreversibility of the reading: the fantastic narrative emphasizes both the process of 'uttering' and the 'time of reading' (94; 75). Knowing the end of a fantastic narrative before we begin distorts its whole functioning, he says, for the reader can no longer follow the process step by step (94; 75). If we read the fifth chapter of a non-fantastic novel by Balzac before we look at the fourth, 'the loss suffered is not so great as if we were reading a fantastic narrative' (94; 75). But surely the suspense aroused by the complex and sometimes sinister relationships in, say, *Père Goriot* is much more likely to be spoiled by that tactic than the suspense in the 'pure fantastic' *The Turn of the Screw*. Quite simply, the reader *cannot* know the ending of a pure fantastic tale in advance. If the ambiguity must be sustained to the end, as Todorov claims, nothing is there for the reader to know. The notion of the irreversibility of reading becomes meaningless.[5]

The second part of Todorov's theory is less propitious, in part because it is vulnerable to greater abuse by those of a purely intuitive, interpretive bent. With the themes of 'self' and 'other' he hopes to expand his model without destroying its logical structure. Cautiously, he points out that these are general thematic systems or 'networks' (*réseaux thématiques*) of which particular themes are manifestations; the formal determinants are compatibility and incompatibility. There is no signifying relationship between the abstract system and its particular manifestations, he claims. To say, for instance, that 'the vampire *means* necrophilia' is to interpret, to reduce it always to a single meaning regardless of context (151; 143). The vampire (or any theme, for that matter) may in fact belong to both thematic networks, and is therefore polysemantic (151; 143). But Todorov's thematics of the fantastic, though infinitely more organized than other such attempts, is not deduced from his analytical model. Had his secondary classification been based on his theory, it would describe instead the degrees of ambiguity, or the degrees of intensity of hesitation.[6]

Theorists after Todorov have found his model, for all its worth, restrictive and exclusive. Beatrice Chanady wants to distinguish the fantastic from magic realism. She remains close to Todorov's model, yet enhances it with her notion of antinomy, the 'simultaneous presence of two conflicting codes in the text' (1985, 12). And Neil Cornwell, in a recent monograph, recognizes the need for cross-generic concepts. He expands Todorov's linear model to advantage: to the left he places non-realism, faction, and non-fiction, leaving open a potential move towards 'journalism, history and ... scientific literature' (1990, 39); to the right he adds mythology, which in turn 'may shade off into theology and other forms of cosmogony (or the irrefutably absurd?)' (1990, 39).

Others have kept Todorov's model as a framework for their ideas while complementing it with contextual, ideological, and pragmatic factors. For Irène Bessière (1974), Christine Brooke-Rose (1981), and Rosemary Jackson (1981), the fantastic challenges empirical reality. In Bessière's opinion, it uses a ploy to do so: it *pretends* to set up its narrated events as real, whereas fairy tales, with their 'once upon a time,' are candidly unreal; theirs is an autonomous universe cut off from the real world (1974, 36). Realistic and marvellous, or 'thetic' and 'non-thetic' narration, terms which Bessière borrows from Sartre's *L'Imaginaire* (1940), converge in the fantastic. In a sense, the fantastic is a hybrid.

Non-thetic narratives use the unreal to demonstrate historically bound beliefs and ideologies (norms) (i.e., to express absolute values through universals such as good and evil). The fantastic, by contrast, offers several contradictory, mutually exclusive solutions for an event's having happened. Any of them may be right, and all are equally possible. The events become the catalyst for questioning norms. Human concepts are exposed as relative, as fictitious, and the limits assigned to the universe by tradition and convention are challenged. 'The fantastic narrative uses socio-cultural frameworks and ways of understanding which define the natural and supernatural domains ... in order to set up the confrontation of elements that escape the economy of the real and surreal, the conception of which varies according to period' (11).

Brooke-Rose, too, is convinced that the fantastic undermines the standard conception of reality. Insofar as it is represented in a secondary modelling system – that is, in a work of the literary fantastic – reality is meaningless, void, empty. Only its 'utter singularity' can be perceived, its 'idiocy' – a term Brooke-Rose borrows from Clément Rosset's *Le réel – traité de l'idiotie* (1977). The fantastic tries to fill the void, to imbue the meaningless with signification, not by including within reality the unreal (say, in the form of vampires), but by inverting the very notions of real and unreal.

Rosemary Jackson's pragmatics of the fantastic pushes the same issue further. Authors write in a particular social and historical context, so the political, social, moral, historical, and economic determinants of the time should be taken into consideration. 'Literary fantasy' (a term she mistakenly makes synonymous with the fantastic and the literary fantastic) is a kind of writing that recurs in different periods, informed by the author's historical position (3).[7] Through the conventions of realistic fiction, the unreal is introduced (34), articulating '"the unnameable,"' and giving expression to the absent or the taboo (41).[8]

Bessière, Brooke-Rose, and Jackson round out Todorov's model, and yet avoid the pitfalls of thematics. Even so, they overlook some important semantic distinctions. I propose to return to the semantico-structural approach, with a few changes. First, we will exchange Todorov's narrowly conceived model for a theory of the fantastic as a *universal aesthetic category*. In plain language, this means that the fantastic may take any of a number of artistic forms. By broadening the theory in this way, we could include philosophy and religion, but it will be quite enough to concentrate here on prose fiction. If we go along with this for the moment, we can see that the fantastic cannot be called a genre in its own right. It cuts across the genres. It may be a play, short story, novel, ballad; we may find it in the form of a painting or a statue, or perhaps a symphony or an opera. In any of these forms, it surfaces in various period styles, such as Romanticism, Realism, and Surrealism. Once we grant that the fantastic is a universal aesthetic category, we can go on to make two theoretical statements about it: first, it can be distinguished from its non-fantastic counterpart; second, it has clearly differentiated varieties, or *modes*.

Todorov argues that the supernatural/natural opposition is not, and cannot be, the common denominator of the fantastic. To say it is would force us, rather unproductively, to regard as fantastic every work where we find a supernatural event: 'We cannot conceive a genre which would regroup all works in which the supernatural intervenes and which would thereby have to accommodate Homer as well as Shakespeare, Cervantes as well as Goethe' (1970, 39; 1975, 34). His objection follows perfectly logically from his generic approach: any work where the genre feature is observed must be included in the genre. The problems raised will become clearer if we study one example: are we entitled to call *Hamlet* fantastic because Hamlet speaks with his father's ghost? If the simple presence of a supernatural event defined the genre, we would have to allow that *Hamlet* is fantastic, somewhat violating our intuitions about the work. But according to Todorov, a supernatural event or being in itself does not constitute the basis for the fantastic. His genre criterion is reader hesitation, and on that basis *Hamlet* cannot be called fantastic. But we are still left with the ghost unaccounted for. Do we ignore it altogether?

8 Possible Worlds of the Fantastic

THE POSSIBLE-WORLDS FRAMEWORK

It is clear, I think, that a genre theory of the fantastic just cannot account for a work like *Hamlet*. And yet the ghost as a theoretical problem does not 'melt, thaw, and dissolve itself' so easily; at least, not until the theory is grounded in the concept of *fictional world*.[9] This concept will give us a global, or *macrostructural*, view of the work and, with it, an indispensable flexibility. We can now determine whether a supernatural constituent is central or peripheral, functional or auxiliary, dominant or subordinate. The concept is not derived from individual, isolated incidents or episodes of the sort we have found in *Hamlet*. Whether a work is fantastic depends on the *overall* structure (the macrostructure) of the fictional world, on what it is composed of and how its constituents are arranged. And that, in turn, is indeed the opposition of two domains, the supernatural and the natural – terms which will shortly be defined. We now have a theory which can lay the ghost in *Hamlet* to rest while satisfying our intuitions about the work. Undeniably, the ghost is a supernatural entity; but in the context of the fictional world as a whole, it is a fragment, a peripheral phenomenon with a very specific *function*: it serves to motivate Hamlet's actions and thereby trigger the plot.

Most readers will have no trouble finding such episodes in literature. Brontë's Jane Eyre experiences clairaudience when she hears Rochester calling to her in his pain, but it would certainly be straining a point to call *Jane Eyre* (1847) fantastic. In Wilkie Collins's *The Frozen Deep* (1874), Clara, at home in England, has a vision of Richard Wardour about to desert Frank Aldersley on their Arctic expedition. In each case, the supernatural is a device with a limited purpose. Jane Eyre's experience is the means for her reunion with Rochester; Clara's vision heightens suspense, as Jay Macpherson notes (1982, 245).[10]

Within the framework of possible-worlds semantics, we can also define the terms natural and supernatural, something which, in a thematic approach, would require a tediously long, if not endless, list of phenomena, beings, creatures, and events. We will say, simply, that the natural domain is a *physically possible world* having 'the same natural laws as does the actual world' (Bradley and Swartz 1979, 6). It must be borne in mind that 'physically possible' is not restricted to the actual world, but pertains to all the possible worlds where these laws apply. In Nicholas Rescher's words, 'laws, being hypothetical in nature, belong to the domain of possibility, and this domain is not finitized by the finitude of the actual' (1987, 48). The supernatural domain, in contrast, is a physically *im*possible world. At its simplest, then, our description of the fantastic rests on the opposition of physically possible and physically impossible. In other words, it is an *alethic* opposition, one that is 'subject to the restrictions of the "classical" modalities – possibility, impossibility and necessity' (Doležel 1978, 544).[11]

So far, it should be apparent that 'hesitation' is superfluous to this theory. If it had a place here at all, it would have to be grounded in the structural opposition of natural and supernatural. Indeed, even Todorov does not escape it, though he does sidestep it. He writes, 'the text must oblige the reader to consider the world of the characters as a world of living persons and to hesitate between a *natural and a supernatural explanation* of the events described' (1970, 37; 1975, 33; emphasis added). To speak of the 'implicit' reader's hesitation is only to observe the *consequence* of the oppositional dynamism that characterizes the structure of fantastic fictional worlds. As to speaking about the real reader, as many critics before and after Todorov have done, other problems are created. If the real reader hesitates, we have three choices: we can assume that he or she believes the supernatural domain actually exists; we can say that the reader is simply guided by and responding to the work's narrative strategies; or we can subscribe to the more interesting notion of mock participation, where the reader plays the literary communication game of permitting him/herself to be caught up in the narrative strategies. However one looks at it, 'reader hesitation' begs the question of just what those narrative strategies are and how they function; it is a by-product of those strategies. Circumventing the question by throwing the author's intentions in our teeth, as some critics feel compelled to do, is of no help whatsoever. We are neither more nor less likely to hesitate just because Horace Walpole hoped to terrify us out of 'too much sense' or because Clara Reeve was bent on scaring us into moral rectitude. Whatever the author had in mind, the reader may ignore or never chance to learn; but narrative strategies can be avoided only if we sacrifice the text.

Up to this point, we have a model of the fantastic based on a global semantic feature: a work is fantastic if the fictional world is made up of the two alethically contrastive domains, the natural and the supernatural. As a theoretical model it may suffice, but it is too abstract and static to be entirely satisfactory. There are other factors of equal importance at work, which serve to animate the opposition, to make it dynamic. Throughout literary history, authors have treated these modal opposites in diverse ways; they have 'configured' the fantastic fictional world in ways that we can set out in a typology of modes. The term 'mode,' incidentally, is neither mysterious nor technical. It means roughly what it did to Frye in *The Anatomy of Criticism* (1957), but is considerably narrower in its scope. It refers, quite simply, to a *kind*, or *type*, of fantastic fictional world. In Frye's broader usage, his criterion ('the hero's power of action, which may be greater than ours, less, or roughly the same') led to a general classification of fictional modes (myth, romance, high mimetic, low mimetic, ironic).

My use of the term *mode* allows us to view the fantastic across genres and across time, and to see how one fantastic narrative is like, or unlike, another. In this sense, too, the term is particularly to be distinguished from Rosemary Jackson's usage. She takes the fantastic (and fantasy) overall to be a 'literary mode,' a 'basic model,' which seems to me akin to the term 'genre,' even though she claims that 'there is no abstract entity called "fantasy"' (1981, 7–8).

The fantastic does not transcend history, though, even if we begin by speaking about it as an abstraction. All the modes described below are linked to changing intellectual, cultural, ideological, and aesthetic contexts. The point is that their relationship is not deterministic. We meet the modes over and over again, finding them more or less repeated in various period styles; they are clearly not to be derived from extraliterary factors. But studying extraliterary factors, as we shall do in chapter 2, has a secondary, descriptive, purpose. It shows us how the fantastic evolved and helps us to mark its course and its transformations.

The historicity of the fantastic can be studied, then, both synchronically and diachronically. The synchronic view reveals the artistic treatment of the supernatural and natural at a particular point in history – the stylistic and narrative devices brought to bear on the opposition in order to configure the fictional world. The diachronic shows the genesis and subsequent transformations of the modes. It is a method that discloses the preference for one mode over another at certain moments of history. For instance, the pre-Romantics had a taste for the antirationality of the disjunctive mode. The Romantics could not, in the philosophical uncertainty of their time, embrace such ontological certainties; their inclination was for the indeterminacy of the ambiguous mode, for the play of 'as if.' The Realists had harder heads, but not narrow minds, and devised the paranormal mode, with its integration of the supernatural into the natural domain. The artistic treatment of the fantastic changed as science gradually modified its conception of reality. The structure of the paranormal mode, especially – and the fact that it came into being at all – reflects this altered perception of reality in the nineteenth century.

A TYPOLOGY OF THE FANTASTIC

In the abstract, the possible-worlds model offered here is a static, logical model. But the many devices authors use for introducing the supernatural and natural domains ensure that the opposition is, in fact, dynamic and varied. The most important facet of this dynamism is the way the fictional status of the supernatural is constructed: how it is made to confront and engage with its counterpart, the natural domain.

This is not an *ad hoc* strategy. The status of the supernatural domain's fictional existence is determined by the degree of narrative authentication. A narrator's power to authenticate rests largely on whether it is a third-person omniscient narrator (the *Er*-form) or a first-person, subjective (*Ich*-form) narrator. By convention, the first is invested with the greatest authority; the second has the least and must 'earn' it.[12]

The Disjunctive Mode

In the world of the disjunctive mode, the two domains have the status of uncontested, unambiguous fictional 'facts.' With their exceptional powers, supernatural entities may enter the natural domain and interfere, for better or worse, in human affairs. They may take any of a number of suprahuman forms – whether demons, gods, gnomes, or revenants makes little difference for purposes of the model, the important point being that they violate natural laws. They may be humanlike, or entities which have metamorphosed from inanimate objects (such as the chair in Dickens's 'The Bagman's Story,' analysed in chapter 4). Or they may be events. The characters of both domains are able to coexist and interact, but each recognizes that the other is alien. The androgynous angel of Balzac's *Séraphîta* (1835) enters the natural domain where Minna and Wilfrid fall in love with him/her. And yet both are aware that the angel is exceptional. *Séraphîta* works a particular philosophical theme; but its world structure – its division into separate semantic domains – exemplifies the disjunctive mode. The same split can be seen in Nikolai Gogol's 'Viy' (1834–42) and 'A Terrible

Vengeance' [Strashnaya mest'] (1831), in Alain René Le Sage's *Le Diable boiteux* (1707) and in its seventeenth-century Spanish counterpart, Luis Vélez de Guevara's *El Diablo cojuelo*. In all four, supernatural and natural beings interact. Their interaction, like the very entry of supernatural characters into the natural domain, does not require any special narrative device to motivate it. A good example would be Ambrosio's fatal alliance with Matilda in Matthew Gregory Lewis's *The Monk* (1796). He owes his entanglement with her to nothing stranger than the lust of a deprived monk. Matilda is a fully authenticated supernatural being whose function it is to destroy Ambrosio by unleashing his repressed desires.

It need hardly be said, then, that in this mode, supernatural beings and events cannot be explained away (i.e., disauthenticated) as a dream, hallucination, madness, or any other aberration. The two domains coexist to the end.

The Fantasy Mode

In a subtype of the disjunctive mode, the supernatural domain fills the fictional world. Either the natural domain is altogether absent or it is a framing device, a domain constructed in the prologue, epilogue, or both, with a very limited function. In William Beckford's *Vathek* (1786) the entire fictional world is composed of the supernatural domain; only implicitly is a contrast established with the natural domain. Todorov suggests that the supernatural in *Vathek* is generated by figurative language: the Indian is described metaphorically as 'huddled into a ball,' an expression leading to the man's transformation into a ball rolled from room to room (1970, 83; 1975, 78). I would add, though, that metaphorical expressions can become fictional events when such transformations occur in the supernatural domain, where it is possible for characters literally to undergo this kind of alteration.

Jonathan Swift's *Gulliver's Travels* (1726) offers a specimen of the framing device. When Gulliver sets sail from Bristol he is in the natural domain of a fictional England; upon being shipwrecked, he enters the supernatural domain. Each new voyage, framed with the briefly sketched natural domain, lands Gulliver in a supernatural domain. Independently of any symbolic or ideological meaning one may attach to them, the Lilliputians, Brobdingnagians, Laputans, and Houyhnhnms are, in alethic terms, physically impossible – that is, supernatural – beings. In the epilogue, we find the reverse, with Gulliver leaving behind the supernatural to return to the natural domain of England. Each time, the frame has the rather narrow function of provoking Gulliver's wanderlust and causing him to set off again. It would be pointless to deny that the final chapters, 11 and 12, are more complex. The frame becomes polyfunctional; it not only closes Gulliver's voyages and has the rhetorical function of summarizing his experiences, but also offers more psychological detail than the earlier chapters, inviting, perhaps demanding, multiple interpretations.

I have used *Gulliver's Travels* to describe the structure of a subtype, the fantasy mode, but I would not argue if anyone insisted that it more appropriately exemplifies the disjunctive mode. The final frame, and therefore the natural domain, is *functionally* more developed (it is not a matter of quantity, or 'size'). That the question can be raised at all shows that the modes are not rigid slots, and at the same time indicates the close structural affinity of the fantasy and disjunctive modes.

The Ambiguous Mode

As we have seen, many critics and theorists disagree with Todorov's statement that ambiguity alone determines whether a work is fantastic. We can join them in this criticism, but also add that ambiguity makes for one kind of fantastic, and add that its particular handling of the alethic opposition can be described in our model.

The supernatural domain is constructed as a potentiality, as a shifting 'as if' or 'may be.' The narrator, or protagonist-narrator, does not fully authenticate it. In that most frequently cited of fantastic stories, Henry James's *The Turn of the Screw* (1898), the governess never hesitates, and we find clues to the events in both her discourse and in Mrs Grose's. For Brooke-Rose, the ambiguity-creating device is the fragmenting and distorting mirror, after Jacques Lacan's notion of 'le corps morcelé' (1981, 161ff.). She observes the analogy between the 'axes of variation' (far/near, up/down, whole/cut) created by the mirror structure and by the governess's state of mind. The formal structure modulates the narrative 'both psychoanalytically and poetically,' so that 'the whole system of repetition and reversal is the very language of the unconscious' (165). Like a mirror, with its artificial, distorted perspective, the structure of *The Turn of The Screw*, for Brooke-Rose, reflects the governess's state of mind. Her perspective is 'distorted' by her desire for her employer. The 'distorting mirror,' by affecting the governess's communication with others, makes her an unreliable narrator and makes the narrative ambiguous. In non-psychoanalytic terms, though, we could claim that the phenomenon Brooke-Rose calls fragmentation ('le corps morcelé') is itself a by-product of the story's complex chain of narrative transmission; the narrating act is filtered, and so distanced, from the narrated event, resulting in ambiguity.[13]

Todorov calls *The Turn of the Screw*, Prosper Mérimée's 'La Vénus d'Ille' (1837), and Gérard de Nerval's *Aurélia* (1855) perfect instances of the fantastic, of unresolved ambiguity. It is a small list, but one that can be augmented: Rosemary Jackson includes James Hogg's *The Private Memoirs and Confessions of a Justified Sinner* (1824), whose tension lies in the confusion of the editor's and sinner's voices, the mingling of the pronouns 'he' and 'I' (1981, 29). I would add that Aleksandr Pushkin's *The Queen of Spades* [*Pikovaya dama*, 1834] also remains indeterminate, because the supernatural domain is both authenticated and disauthenticated. Against the supernatural is Germann's obsession with winning at cards; his unaccustomed drinking on the night of the ghost's appearance; the fact that he was asleep (dreaming), or perhaps awake, but groggy with sleep and drink; and the fact that he was laden with guilt for having frightened the countess to death. For the supernatural is the allusion to Mephistopheles, and the narrator's remark, 'sleep had left him' (and Germann does quite a bit of reasoning before the ghost says a word). Most impressive of all is the ace: the 'magic' combination revealed by the countess *would* have won had Germann played the ace. When they opt for a natural explanation, critics usually point a little smugly to Germann's final confinement in a madhouse. But there is no *textual* evidence for Germann's going mad until well after the countess's ghost appears. Germann loses his life's savings either through the natural error of mistaking a card in his excitement or in being *made* to mistake the card by supernatural intervention. Whichever is the reason for his loss, it drives him mad. In 'The Conclusion' the narrator observes nonchalantly: 'Germann went out of his mind,' and the status of the supernatural remains indeterminate.

To take up an example analysed by Todorov, Gogol's 'The Nose' in its two printed versions (1835, 1842) is fantastic for the very reason Todorov gives for rejecting it. We may agree with him that the allegorical readings which some critics so predictably impose on the tale flout the narrator's Borgesian assertions of its meaninglessness.[14] Quite rightly, Todorov states that we are returned to the literal meaning. 'On this level,' he writes, '"The Nose" becomes a pure incarnation of the absurd, of the impossible.' Here it seems to me that in equating the terms 'absurd' and 'impossible' he is confusing them. 'The Nose' owes its absurdity largely to a feature of Gogol's style: the discrepancy between a 'form' that is serious and a 'content' that is, in Ivan Yakovlevich's words, 'ridiculous.' It is Michel Riffaterre's opinion that humour can be defined as a kind of 'catachresis' that establishes a 'discrepancy between a form that is funny and a content that is not' (1983, 163). By reversing these terms we have a good definition of the absurd, which may or may not be humorous. The deadpan *skaz* narrator who creates this discrepancy is one of Gogol's most celebrated stylistic markers.[15]

As to the impossible, we do indeed have that: Kovalëv's nose disappears from his face, appears in his barber's freshly baked loaf of bread, assumes a life of its own, and finally reappears on his face for no particular reason. In other words, a physically impossible (i.e., supernatural) event occurs in the natural domain – a fictional St Petersburg which is subject, we have no reason to doubt, to the same laws that govern the real world. Todorov's problem with the text is precisely that the event *does* occur in the natural domain and elicits, he claims, no reaction. This is not quite accurate, though. Ivan Yakovlevich is horrified and struck dumb, his wife indignant and enraged; Kovalëv is astonished and takes fright. What is troubling, in terms of Todorov's genre theory, is simply that beyond their reactions the characters *accept* that the event *has happened.* This acceptance should make the work marvellous in Todorov's terms, because it 'does not observe the first condition of the fantastic, that hesitation between the real and the illusory or imaginary be present ...' But then, calling it marvellous conflicts with the event's taking place in what Todorov concedes is the natural domain – 'St Petersburg down to its most mundane details' (1970, 77; 1975, 72). Once again, genre theory is wanting in ways to account for a fantastic tale. On examining the macrostructure, we find a physically impossible (supernatural) event occurring in the natural domain, and a *skaz* narrator who makes the story indeterminate: 'And such a thing happened in the northern capital of our vast country! Only now, when we ponder the entire story, do we see that it contains much that is highly implausible ...' The narrator goes on to enumerate the implausibilities, but concludes: 'All the same ... we probably can concede this and that, and the odd thing here and there ... I mean, strange things happen all the time, do they not?' It is quite in keeping with the features of the ambiguous mode, and indeed with Todorov's own definition of the fantastic, that the characters regard the supernatural event as fictional fact while the narrator questions it.

To repeat what was said earlier, reader hesitation is nothing other than a response to textual indeterminacy, the absence of total authentication. The fictional status of the supernatural domain is unstable to the end of the story. Of course, natural explanations are tried out; but when they are, they are made doubtful or unlikely.

The Supernatural Naturalized

The 'supernatural naturalized' mode corresponds, more or less, to Todorov's 'supernatural explained,' but I have chosen to avoid his term because I wish to draw attention to the dynamism of the fictional world structure, not just to the presence of an explanation.

The supernatural domain is constructed here as it is in the disjunctive mode but is, in the end, disauthenticated when the narrator imparts a natural explanation for the strange events: it was all a dream, a hallucination, a drug-induced illusion, or the effect of fear, madness, hysteria. Such is the fictional world of Emile Zola's 'Angéline or the Haunted House' (1898), where the narrator ponders, and is unnerved by, all the evidence for a ghostly little girl. Moments after he is sure she has appeared, it is made clear to him that the child he has seen is a real being. Still, there is no reason to say, with Todorov, that texts of this sort are not fantastic. For one thing, the explanations themselves are at times suspect, as Todorov himself concedes with respect to Jean Potocki's *Manuscrit trouvé à Saragosse* (1847) and Charles Nodier's *Inès de la Sierras* (1837): 'Indeed, the realistic solutions [given in these texts] ... are altogether improbable; supernatural solutions would have been, on the contrary, quite probable' (1970, 51; 1975, 46). But most important of all, how can we justify our suddenly rejecting the narrative strategies that have served throughout to authenticate the supernatural? It is this manoeuvre that would force us to regroup entire works on the slimmest of evidence, doing, in other words, just what Todorov would not have us do to Homer, Shakespeare, Cervantes, and Goethe. A work does not cease to be fantastic with the meagre statement that so and so woke up any more than it can be called fantastic because of a single supernatural incident (*Hamlet*, *Jane Eyre*, etc.) or an embedded tale (*Pickwick Papers*). With the exception of *Gaston de Blondeville* (1826), Ann Radcliffe's novels – one thinks especially of her best, *The Mysteries of Udolpho* (1794) and *The Italian* (1797) – are the classics of this mode, with human machination or misunderstanding invariably turning out to be behind the 'supernatural.' It runs altogether against intuition to exclude Radcliffe from the roster of the fantastic.

In Lewis Carroll's *Alice's Adventures in Wonderland* (1865) the supernatural is disauthenticated when Alice is wakened by her sister and exclaims: 'Oh, I've had such a curious dream!' Throughout the tale, the supernatural domain is constructed, and the fantastic generated, by metaphors and other poetic devices being literalized into events or creatures. The crazy March Hare, for instance, embodies the simile 'mad as a March hare.' Alice also must adapt physically (in ways impossible in the natural domain) to alien conditions, and she gains different perspectives by eating or drinking substances that make her shrink or grow. In *Through the Looking Glass* (1872), language is arbitrary. Space and time do not obey the laws and logic of the natural domain (implicit in Alice's reference to '*our* country'). For instance, running ahead means never passing the starting point; remembering is an anticipation of the future. Once again, the supernatural is disauthenticated only at the very end by Alice's waking from a dream.

So far, the modes – disjunctive, fantasy, ambiguous, and disauthenticated – all treat the supernatural as 'otherworldly,' as distinct from the natural domain. These can justifiably be called 'traditional' forms of the fantastic with a long history, though they still endure.[16] But the last mode of the fantastic offers another narrative treatment of the supernatural, one which dates only to the middle of the nineteenth century.

The Paranormal Mode

In a radical transformation, supernatural and natural are no longer mutually exclusive. The opposition loses its force because we find that the word 'supernatural' is merely a label for strange phenomena latent *within* the natural domain. Clairvoyance, telepathy, and precognition, for instance, are taken to be as *physically possible* as any commonplace human ability. In the other modes, such extraordinary faculties would be properties only of supernatural entities; where humans possess such abilities, they are usually the gift of deities or demons. In the paranormal mode, a structural change occurs: the natural domain is enlarged and encompasses a special region accessible to those with extraordinary perceptual capacities. Supernatural phenomena are reinterpreted and brought within the paradigm of the natural. They are latent in nature or innate in humans and other animals. The laws of the physically possible natural domain are not violated, but they are reassessed, and their range is extended to include the scientifically unproved. One of Maupassant's characters in 'Le Horla' expresses it well: 'While [human] intelligence remained in a rudimentary state this obsession with invisible phenomena took forms which were frightening in the commonplace way. That is the explanation of the popular notions of the supernatural, the legends of wandering spirits, fairies, gnomes, ghosts ...' (1887; 1979, 2: 922).

The fictional world is no longer split into natural and supernatural domains. A seemingly supernatural incident, such as a character's foreknowledge of an event, occurs within the natural domain and is part of the natural experience. Those who do not share the experience may reason that the character has been deluded, is insane, has had a hallucination, or that the whole thing is coincidence. Others may say that it is supernatural, a divine or demoniac gift of prophecy, a sign from God, a message from a dead relative. However, the precognitive experience cannot be attributed to deviant mental states or the intervention of supernatural entities. Indeed, some fundamental assumptions are challenged in such provocative suggestions as that insanity may be heightened perception, the mind's path into the unknown. One analogy, popular in the nineteenth century, would be the microscope, which gives the observer visual access into nature's otherwise hidden micro-world.

Such a state of affairs is not so far-fetched logically as to be shunned by contemporary philosophers. In *Analytical Philosophy of Action* (1973), Arthur Danto sets up a similar scenario. He introduces a 'repertoire R of basic powers' which defines formally the natural capacity of 'normal agents' to perform basic actions. (Basic actions must be distinguished from miracles – 'gods doing as basic actions what mere mortals must do as mediated ones'; 125.) A person with the power to foresee events – an ability outside the norm-defining R – would, in Danto's words, 'almost certainly strike us as having *uncanny* cognitive powers' (129). The paranormal mode posits just such a modal enhancement by assuming that these powers are included in the repertoire R of some exceptional 'mortals.'

Describing the various ways in which the supernatural and the natural are configured within the fictional world of a literary text is only half

Fictional Worlds of the Fantastic 19

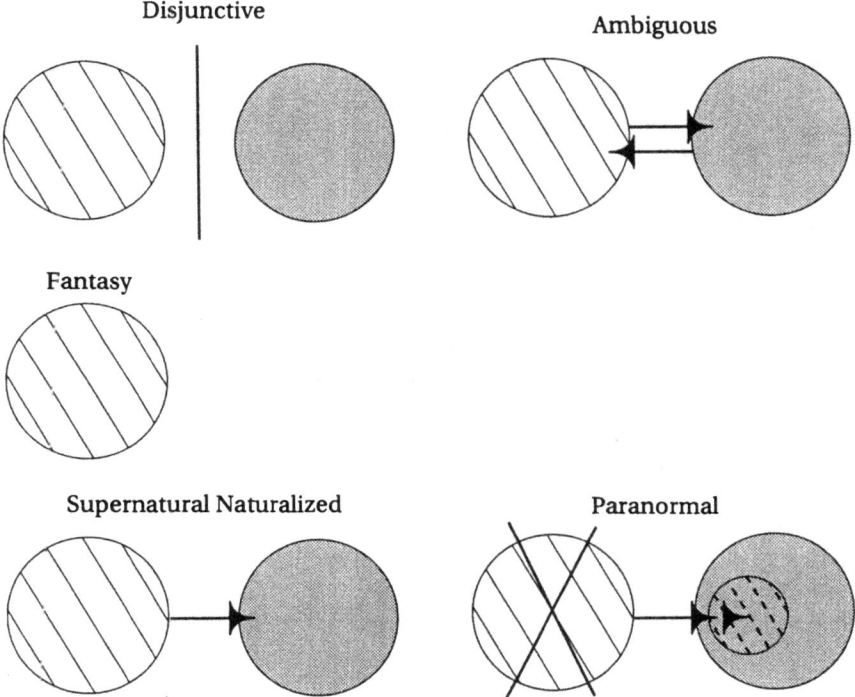

Figure 1

the task. It remains to analyse whole works – tales or novels – in order to test the theory. The last three chapters will be devoted to exemplifying the modes through an extensive analysis of stories by three well-known writers. Figure 1 is a visual summary of the opposition natural/supernatural which constitute the modes; it may be helpful to keep this figure in mind for the analyses. Hatched circles represent the supernatural domain; shaded circles, the natural. The arrows indicate *dynamic changes* in the existential status of the supernatural. The double arrowhead of the paranormal mode, in addition to suggesting dynamic change, denotes integration; the natural domain is enlarged and contains a marked area in which the 'supernatural,' under the new paradigm, is encompassed by the natural.

It cannot be repeated too often that these modes are not pigeonholes. They are *models*, and only models, exemplified by particular texts. As such, their purpose is purely theoretical. Many narratives, happily, blend features of more than one mode and so resist attempts to slot them neatly into a category. For the same reason, the modes do not prevent anyone from offering *interpretations* of a work. I assume that two or more readings of a work are possible (but are not necessarily equally valid); the typology assumes only that description precedes interpretation.

As I have already indicated, each mode's genesis is related to a moment in literary history. It is not tied to that moment, but transcends it. This is a general property of literature, but one that mitigates our surprise at the popularity of, say, the disjunctive mode today. Its origins may be prehistoric and the psychological and social determinants different, yet mischievous poltergeists and minatory demons remain a potent resource for literature, cinema, and television.[17] A host of writers and film-makers in the twentieth century have successfully plied the 'twilight zone' of the 'traditional' modes. In the same way, the paranormal mode created by Dickens, Turgenev, and Maupassant was novel in the second half of the nineteenth century. But far from being the last stage in the history of the fantastic, it led to newer transformations in the twentieth century. The typology, in short, is an open system.

2

Context and Intertext of the Paranormal Mode

In the second half of the nineteenth century, the natural sciences leapt ahead, prompting researchers to look anew at human cognitive abilities, often assailing, in the process, cherished conceptions of reality. Paradoxically, it was largely Darwin's explanation for the origin of species that led to a revival of interest in spiritualism as a solution to the conflict between scientific progress and Christian tradition.[1] Spiritualism filled a void by apparently proving that there was life after death, since communication with the spirits implies a repository of some sort for the souls of the dead. So those of a religious bent found in spiritualism a confirmation of their beliefs. But many of the scientists who troubled to study spiritualism found that it raised questions worth investigating and offered a testing ground for hypotheses. For instance, if there is communication between the living and the dead, by what means is it effected? How does the medium process the information? And what does such a capacity say about the human mind? Within a short time, an offshoot of spiritualism appeared that was concerned not with mystical or religious experiences, but with the implications of spiritualism for science, for what it could reveal about the mind and makeup of the human creature. Spiritualism was reshaped by the very scientific discoveries that had sparked its resurgence, 'naturalizing' phenomena once attributed only to supernatural agency. Within this new paradigm, such phenomena were described as 'paranormal,' and, therefore, natural.

Ancient mythologies and tribal practices are the pedigree of spiritualism.[2] Yet in spite of the universality and timelessness of some of its phenomena, spiritualism entered the nineteenth century in a distinctly modern form. By consensus, its revival is dated to 1848, when the Fox sisters of Hydesville, New York, were supposedly contacted by the spirit of a pedlar who claimed he had been murdered and buried in the cellar of their house.[3] By the 1850s, the booming American spiritualist movement had worked its way to England through such people as the Haydens and Mrs Hardinge-Britten, a mesmerist turned medium. From England, spiritualism spread to the continent. Spiritualism in France was more sharply split between the scientific and the mystical, the latter trend under the domination of Hyppolyte Rivail. Under the name 'Allan Kardec' he founded his own movement and a new 'gospel' based on the doctrine of reincarnation.[4] But perhaps the most famous export was the medium Daniel Dunglas Home, the American-born Scot who would come to preoccupy Dickens. Home became the darling of royalty, in England and abroad. Home was especially popular in Russia, where spiritualism often took the form, as in England, of a parlour game known as 'table turning' or 'table-tipping.'[5] M.M. Petrovo-Solovovo, a reporter on spiritualism in the late nineteenth and early twentieth centuries, mentions in his 1900 monograph on spiritualist experiments in the nineteenth century a few Russians of standing who were involved with spiritualism and its outgrowth, psychical research: the well-known chemist A.M. Butlerov; the zoologist N.P. Vagner; and Aleksey Nikolaevich Aksakov, the founder of the periodical *Psychische Studien* in 1874, who also wrote extensively on Swedenborg and mesmerism. Aleksandr II (1818–81; Emperor 1855–81) was well known for his enthusiasm and for his favours to visiting mediums like Home, Mrs Marshall, and Bredive. By the 1870s, spiritualism in Russia, as in England and America, had taken on epidemic proportions.[6] Petrovo-Solovovo tells us that Petersburg University established a commission under the noted chemist Professor D.I. Mendeleev for the study of mediumistic phenomena. He claims, though, that its results were coloured by prejudice against the very phenomena the commission was supposed to investigate; several mediums who had been invited were declared frauds in the published findings (1900, 90).

Interest in spiritualism, of the cruder sort as well as the more 'scientifically' founded, was not confined to charlatans, scientists, and royalty in Russia any more than it was in England. Some Russian writers participated in séances to gratify their curiosity. In a long letter to his wife, Aleksey Konstantinovich Tolstoy describes what he witnessed in London at a Home séance, which he attended in 1860 with Botkin, a friend of Turgenev's. Tolstoy was impressed: the medium levitated (Home's trademark), furniture moved, a piano mysteriously played itself, and messages were written on paper. The one phenomenon that convinced him (if, as he expressed it, he had needed convincing) was a hand gripping his own.[7]

Dostoevsky also declared that he 'decidedly cannot be indifferent about spiritualism.' In 1876 he wrote two tongue-in-cheek entries on spiritualism in his 'Diary of a Writer' [Dnevnik Pisatelya]; during the same period, he was in correspondence with N.P. Vagner and attended séances at Aksakov's home (1981, 22: 32–7, 126–32).

Among those who gave serious thought to spiritualism, whatever their nationality, we find two explanatory trends which, for want of better terms, can simply be called 'the popular' and 'the scientific.' It was a rare student of spiritualism, though, who could keep the two entirely separate.

The popular approach relied for its explanations on mesmerism and the many vulgarized accounts of scientific discoveries. In Mesmer's theory, a force analogous to, but distinct from, magnetism influences the body through an invisible fluid that connects people to the cosmos. Illness might arise from the improper distribution of the fluid, which Mesmer believed could be dispersed throughout the body of a sick patient by activating the body's magnetic poles. Initially he used magnets, but these alone were not responsible for the cures. He theorized that a force, 'animal magnetism,' which was accumulated in the mesmerist's own body, could be transmitted to the patient and would act upon his or her mysterious 'fluid' towards a cure (Hilgard 1980, xiii). 'Magnetized' patients undergoing the cure exhibited symptoms of trance accompanied at times by agitation or hysterical crisis. Mesmer's system disturbed some authorities in what was, after all, the period of Enlightenment, and Louis XVI set up a royal commission to investigate Mesmer's claims. This group of men, which included Lavoisier, Bailly, Jussieu, and Franklin, granted in 1784 that while mesmerism had benefits, the patient's expectations and imagination played a role as well. Paulet's 1784 monograph *L'Antimagnétisme* ascribed Mesmer's cures to a wave of irrationality accompanying the Enlightenment and linked his doctrines to the whole tradition of 'occult medicine' – Jean Baptiste van Helmont, Robert Fludd, and Paracelsus. In much the same vein as Mesmer's animal magnetism, Paracelsus had contended that people possess a force like that of the lodestone or electrified amber. According to Hilgard, though, Mesmer had more in common with Richard Mead, the famous physician of royalty who also tended Newton. He argued that tides and phases of the moon affect human periodicities

(Hilgard 1980, xvii). 'I asserted,' Mesmer wrote, 'according to the familiar principles of universal attraction, verified by observations which teach us how the planets mutually affect one another in their orbits, how the sun and moon cause and control the ocean tides on our globe and in the atmosphere. I asserted that these spheres also exert a direct action on all the parts that constitute animate bodies, particularly the nervous system, by means of an all-penetrating fluid' (quoted in Bloch 1980, 46).

In his early writings, at least, Mesmer was careful to avoid references to the metaphysical, insisting that 'all the phenomena of magnetism offer little difficulty in their explanation. It is no longer considered to be the action of an incomprehensible attraction completely similar to the occult faculties of Aristotle; it is a natural force, received equally by the senses and by reason' (quoted in Bloch 1980, 36). But, as Azouvi points out in his introduction to Paulet's monograph, Mesmer's crucial terms 'fluid' and 'attraction,' borrowed though they are from science, lost their rigour in popular interpretations and acquired meanings that had nothing to do with the original concepts (1980, iv). And in any case, Mesmer himself was less rigorously naturalistic in his later work. He remained entirely opposed to superstition and the tendency to blame natural symptoms ('madness, epilepsy and most convulsions') on supernatural causes (the 'marvellous'), but managed to accommodate clairvoyance: 'In this state of *crisis* these persons are able to foresee the future and bring the most remote past into the present. Their senses can extend to any distance and in all directions, without being checked by any obstacles' (quoted in Bloch 1980, 112).[8]

Most readily associated with spiritualism are the methods of one of Mesmer's disciples – the Marquis de Puységur, the eldest of three Puységur brothers. No less an authority than Charles Richet considered him, Ellenberger tells us, the 'true founder of magnetism' (1970, 70). Puységur alleged that he witnessed a trance state which did not result in hysteria, but in a condition – 'lucid somnambulism' – where the subject's mind was open to 'higher phenomena'; supposedly one could perceive objects not exposed to view and produce specific information about them, such as page numbers in a concealed book. The problem that remained to be solved was whether the mesmerized subject was clairvoyant (sensing the object's presence directly) or telepathic (perceiving it through another's consciousness).[9]

By mid century, the general public had confused Mesmer's pseudo-scientific theories with the new theories of physics – understandably,

Oppenheim suggests, considering the long-standing popular analogies between electromagnetism and mesmerism (1985, 211). The theories of physics were invoked to explain the workings of the mesmeric fluid at séances. Scientists, by contrast, insisted that the random phenomena of séances could hardly turn physical laws on their heads; it was essential to gather data from repeated and controlled experiments. Some, like Michael Faraday, just dismissed spiritualism and mesmerism out of hand and attributed 'table-tipping' phenomena to the sitters' involuntary muscular exertions (Nelson 1969, 90).

Other practising scientists discarded Mesmer's pseudoscientific explanations while retaining his technique. From the late 1830s, Dickens's renowned friend Dr John Elliotson used it to cure common ailments, though his persistence in calling it 'animal magnetism' discredited him in the eyes of his colleagues.[10] Further advances in the field came from James Braid in the 1840s and, two decades later, Jean Charcot. Braid was the first physician working in clinical hypnosis, which he called 'neurypnology,' to try to dispose of the transcendent overtones of 'higher phenomena' associated with magnetism. He claimed that the trance state of hypnosis was partly physiological, partly psychological, rather than 'psychic' – the result of what he called a 'bio-physiological rapport' between subject and hypnotist. Even so, he trod on thin ice by allowing for what he called 'hyperacuity,' or the peculiar sensitivity of the subject's senses of sight and hearing. Charcot accepted Braid's theories, but incorrectly concluded that hypnosis was 'an induced state of hystero-epilepsy' (Inglis 1986, 284–5; see also Ellenberger 1970, 143–5). None the less, their work placed what became known as hypnosis within the domain of clinical psychology and neurology.

The majority of spiritualists, regardless of their other convictions, relied on popular explanations for séance manifestations. They did not necessarily claim that these were signs of God's or Satan's intervention, unlike the Catholic Church, whose position was unambiguous: if supernatural phenomena were not divine in origin, they were demoniac. The Church in France, indeed, placed a ban on spiritualism for that reason, marking it as distinct from religion. In contrast, many spiritualists who were also theists found a middle ground in the belief that the souls of the dead were somehow able to communicate with the living through mediums, people highly sensitive to whatever channels the dead used, be they magnetic, electric, or fluid. The assumption that human personality survives after death was compatible with both nineteenth-century Christian theology and the oldest of myths and superstitions.

Theories about the age of the earth had also been digested in popular form by mid century, though they remained contentious. Popularizations of geological and paleontological discoveries had at least convinced the lay public of the grandness and importance of science. Most importantly, the sciences were making it increasingly difficult for people to hold irrational beliefs. After all, positivism existed for just that purpose – to make science respectable, to rid it of metaphor, metaphysics, superstition, and untenable hypotheses.

Those who were positivist in the extreme saw nature as a mass of uniformly evolving atoms and energy; if no supernatural creatures existed in these, then an experiential, materialist view of nature was justified. Underlying positivist philosophy is the assumption that all phenomena are firmly grounded in fact, not in immaterial causes. In the nineteenth century, it was thought to be the business of science to disclose the links between observable phenomena, not to seek the primary cause.[11] Comte's conception of philosophy was in the Newtonian tradition of the 'sum of all knowledge,' of which the sciences are particular branches. Positivist philosophy did not concern itself with the details of scientific research and discovery, but with how knowledge was obtained (Andreski 1974, 11). In his *Cours de philosophie positive* (1830–42), Comte writes that the human intellect passes through three theoretical stages. The *theological* is concerned with absolutes, with primary and final causes [*causes premières et finales*], and with the nature of the supernatural agents responsible for all phenomena; in the *metaphysical* stage, supernatural agents give way to abstract forces; the *positive* stage leaves aside all question of absolutes, essence, and primary causes and concentrates on discovering, by means of reasoning and observation, laws and relations (Comte 1892, 1: 3–4). In Comte's system, spiritualism would belong to the theological stage, and any positivist worth his salt would shun it. And yet not everyone who opposed spiritualism was a positivist. Those who rejected Comtism, or any form of it, usually condemned spiritualism on purely rational grounds. The campaign was not between spiritualism and positivism, but between spiritualism and rationalism.

In this context, the more enlightened spiritualists were not, and could not be, opposed to science, and many were themselves outstanding in its fields – Augustus de Morgan, William Crookes, Sir Oliver Lodge, Alfred Russell Wallace, Charles Richet, and Marie Curie are only a few.

The desire for scientific evaluation led spiritualists, as Pierssens observes, 'to the point where they adopted their language, their methods and their conception of truth, fact, experiment and proof' (1986, 1002). Reverend C.M. Davies expressed the view of this 'enlightened' body of spiritualists. Spiritualism rested 'on the demonstrations of science – a science, however, which does not illogically stop short at the physical or intellectual, ignoring the spiritual portion of man's being, but applies its rigorous analysis to the domain of revelation hitherto disposed of in the wide category of the supernatural. Spiritualism has no such word as Supernatural. It substitutes the certainly less objectionable term supra-sensual – for who shall presume to define the limits of nature?' (quoted in Oppenheim 1985, 201).[12] The 'scientific' version of spiritualism, then, offered ground to stand on with its synthesis of 'modern scientific knowledge and time-honoured religious traditions' (Oppenheim 1985, 59; see also Turner 1976). Physicist William Crookes, although at times accused of making his conclusions fit his expectations, was probably the first to monitor séance phenomena with gadgets meant to provide physical data.

T.H. Huxley, a biologist quite critical of spiritualism, refused to acknowledge phenomena that could not be subsumed under natural laws. He was by no means a positivist in Comte's sense of the word; indeed, he disparaged what he called 'Catholicism *minus* Christianity.' Comte, Huxley wrote, 'knew nothing about physical science'; the 'Law of the Three States' derived mainly 'from his [Comte's] own consciousness' (1913, 1: 432, 434).[13] In his 1891 article 'Possibilities and Impossibilities,' Huxley quotes the philosopher David Hume to the effect that 'whatever is intelligible and can be distinctly conceived implies no contradiction, and can never be proved false by any demonstrative argument or abstract reasoning *a priori*' (1913, 3: 187). Although Huxley's position on the supernatural was typical of many of his contemporaries, he also declared in the same article: 'we are *not* justified in the *a priori* assertion that the order of nature, as experience has revealed it to us, cannot change' (1913, 1: 188). As his remarks testify, not all nineteenth-century scientists laid claim to absolute truth; but they would accept only hypotheses that preserved the 'logical structure of any scientific argument' (Ellegård 1958, 146). In any case, Huxley was explicit about spiritualism. On being invited in 1871 to join a committee to investigate séance manifestations, he replied:

But supposing the phenomena to be genuine – they do not interest me. If anybody would endow me with the faculty of listening to the chatter of old women and curates in the nearest provincial town, I should decline the privilege, having better things to do. And if the folk in the spiritual world do not talk more wisely and sensibly than their friends report them to do, I put them in the same category. The only good that I can see in the demonstration of the Truth of 'Spiritualism' is to furnish an additional argument against suicide. Better live a crossing-sweeper, than die and be made to talk twaddle by a 'medium' hired at a guinea a *séance*. (1913, 2: 144)

Huxley spoke from first-hand experience. He had been exposed to such experiments at his brother's house with the medium Mrs Hayden, and in 1874 attended a séance at Darwin's prodding, sending him afterwards a lengthy and condemnatory report (1913, 1: 144–8).

Firm believer in scientific method that he was, Huxley in effect exposed the paradox of the positivist epistemology: it represents the 'closed' material world of secondary causes and natural laws, yet new scientific instruments and discoveries had 'opened' the world and were continuing to do so. Psychical researchers like psychologist/poet Frederic Myers reacted to the narrowness of the positivist canon by urging, in the 1880s, flexibility in the natural sciences. The history of science, he argued, continually proved that nature's rules are more accommodating than suspected. It was a challenge to science to stop dismissing and begin evaluating the unexplained, using its own rigorous methods.[14]

It was Myers who coined the word 'telepathy' for the ability to reproduce information about someone else's thoughts or life without knowing the facts beforehand. With his concept of telepathy, Myers posited a natural channel of communication, with no allusion to supernatural powers. But his hypothesis suffered from its inability to define the *nature* of the phenomenon, its characteristics beyond those necessitated by their role in the hypothesis. In Podmore's words, the question was not 'what new agencies may be inferred from the facts, but whether the facts justify the inference of any new agency at all' (1902, 2: 360).

One of the most interesting thinkers of the period whose influence spread from England to the continent was the social philosopher Herbert Spencer. He had tried to systematize knowledge within the framework of modern science, especially evolutionism, and formulated an epistemology based on his conviction that human perceptions are limited, that people are imprisoned in an imperfect organism which renders knowledge relative (1862, 96). Spencer's was a relativist philosophy, formulated at least in part as a rebuttal to the Comtian axiom of an absolute, objective and fully describable reality. 'Positive knowledge,' he declared, 'does not, and never can, fill the whole region of possible thought. At the uttermost reach of discovery there arises, and must ever arise, the question – What lies beyond?' (1862, 16). Spencer reinforced, then, the idea of science as an open process of cognition.

None the less, this focus on the cognitive and psychological aspects of phenomena now seen as paranormal rather than supernatural marked a shift away from crude, unscientific explanations. In France, the psychophysiologist and psychical researcher Charles Richet best typified this open-minded scientific approach. By the 1880s, he had introduced into psychical research the concepts of probability and statistical inference. He refused to believe that all the forces of nature were known and concluded, after decades of investigating the paranormal, that 'all scientific progress is an entrance into the unfathomable' (1923, vi). At the same time, Richet recognized that the phenomena he was studying eluded an essential criterion of science – repeatability – and that they manifested themselves spontaneously, usually in 'rapid and almost imperceptible flashes' ([1926?], 17). Without the data from repeated experiments, a rational explanation was urgently needed if the larger scientific community were ever to pay attention. The suggestion that the disincarnate had anything to do with it he found naïve, citing as illustration an incident connected with Dickens's unfinished novel *The Mystery of Edwin Drood* (1870). An uneducated American by the name of James claimed to have finished the novel in 1872 under the dead author's spiritual dictation; the results impressed some Dickensian scholars, but Richet was sceptical. Even if James's allegation was made in good faith, he claimed, 'any supposition would seem preferable to this naïve and simple, but terribly unlikely and for me, inadmissible, hypothesis, that Charles Dickens came back from the other world in order to move James's brachial muscles' (1923, 93).

Using the methods of physiology, Richet argued that the phenomena he subsumed under 'mental metapsychics' [métapsychique mentale] operate by means of 'vibratory forces,' or hypothetical waves undetected by our physical senses and instruments ([1926?], 209). Such a connection between natural forces and paranormal phenomena had already been proposed in the 1860s by the French astronomer, popularizer, and novelist Camille Flammarion. He was fond of using the analogies of meteorites and of lightning. Once rejected as superstition, they had turned out to be natural, though both still had unexplained quirks.

Towards the twentieth century, greater emphasis was placed on the possible connections between the human mind and paranormal phenomena. Henri Bergson, who was passively involved in psychical research, offered at least one idea which became important in psychological interpretations of the paranormal: the brain admits to the consciousness only perceptions of immediate usefulness, usually those gathered by the five senses. Fringe perceptions now and then surface as 'contraband,' a hypothesis that explains at least 'why extrasensory communications only rarely break through' (Inglis 1986, 277, 302). Bergson had conducted his own experiments in hypnosis and telepathy in 1886, and he decided that the subject in a state of trance experiences 'hyperesthesia,' or a sharpened capacity to discern minute, but normal, sensory data (Bergson 1886, 336).

The question of the mind's hidden potentialities was also influenced by theories of evolution, Darwinism in particular. By the middle of the century, biblical cosmogonists had faced, if not accepted, the implications of geological data. And, as they had bowed to Copernican heliocentrism, so they were compelled to rethink, on the basis of the geological studies, the biblical account of earth's creation. But they concentrated their attacks on the issue of human creation. If they sometimes conceded that the earth had not been created in six days, they still considered the geologists' dating exaggerated. However, they found nothing in the geological records to contradict the special place of humankind in natural history. Why doubt the biblical explanation if no trace of a human had been found below the most recent strata (Ellegård 1958, 97)? Darwin's theory subsumed all organic life under science and natural laws. The biblical view held that each species had been created separately, and humans, as a specially created, immutable species, differed from all others by their unique mental endowments. Darwin's yoking of human to simian did violence to that distinction, even though, as Morton notes, he was himself struck by the paradox that his theories were 'undercut by being the dubious product of an upstart monkey's brain' (1984, 8).

There was nothing novel about proposing a theory of evolution: Darwin had predecessors, including his grandfather Erasmus, who anticipated some of the work of a better-known evolutionist, Lamarck.[15] The general public was receptive, to a degree, before Darwin. Robert Chambers, editor of the popularizing science journal *Chambers's Journal*, had published his *Vestiges of the Natural History of Creation* in 1844. The book sparked people's imaginations and put Lamarckian evolution 'onto the table of many middle-class drawing-rooms,' as Chadwick puts it (1975, 165). Scientists remained unimpressed, though. Chambers lacked method, and had said nothing new, but had packaged evolution in creationism. The package, however, was immensely popular with the public. Lamarck himself, incidentally, had dodged the creation question, thus giving people the freedom to interpret his theories optimistically. There was allowance for progress and for the rewards, genetic and other, of effort (which indeed could be, and was, used to justify class distinctions). On the whole, the human species, with its discoveries and its technology, had not done so very badly.

What distinguished Darwin's theory of evolution, and caused a century of uproar, was natural selection. He proposed that by means of natural selection the environment eliminates poorly adapted organisms. One of the implications of his theory is that some organisms may be unable to survive in a changing environment, whereas other organisms may flourish and supersede it. The environment thus 'selects' for survival (or enables to survive) those organisms best equipped to meet its challenges. The more astute, like the co-discoverer of evolution, Alfred Russell Wallace, recognized the potentially negative impact of natural selection on conceptions of the human mind. If humans, like all other animal species, had evolved from earlier organisms, then they were not qualitatively different from them (Oppenheim 1985, 271). They had simply gone farther faster, for reasons Darwin did not venture to explain.

Darwin's theory assumes that evolution occurred over vast periods. His position corresponded to the geological views which, in their turn, refuted biblical catastrophism. In postulating such a slow course of development, Darwin found himself under attack for not having offered the material evidence needed to support his theory of natural selection. What he had brought into play were unobservables. Ironically, he was charged, too, with not having touched upon *primary* causes when his work was about *origins*. Perhaps much the same objection can be levelled at the spiritualists: laying spiritualist phenomena at the door of the dead pushes the question endlessly backwards. In any case, psychical researchers were inspired by Darwin's theory. Podmore speculated that if such faculties as precognition and clairvoyance were real, 'they must testify to a world of higher uses, and an evolution not conditioned by our material environment. In a word, such faculties must be regarded not as vestigial, but as rudimentary; a promise for the future, not an idle inheritance from the past' (1902, 2: 359).

Imaginations were fired, and popularizers were quick to exploit the implications, negative and otherwise, of Darwin's theory. For instance, if humans are not qualitatively different from other animals, then the privileged position we have assigned ourselves is not rightfully ours. It was a frightening prospect for human egocentricity, the idea that some animal species might enjoy perceptual abilities developed to a degree that makes them much the superior of man in those areas. Humans came to be seen as disadvantaged; once such limits are admitted, there unfolds before us a world of phenomena inaccessible to the five senses. Moreover, if humans occupy but a single slot in the continuity of species, we may not represent the end of the evolutionary process. Open-ended evolution could therefore lead to beings with more potent sensory and mental faculties, beings which may even be imperceptible. The powers that appear paranormal to humans might be standard for such higher-order beings. Humans, in other words, may be confined by their senses, their perceptions hampered by what Arthur Danto calls 'modal incapacity': 'It is a haunting thought that there might in fact be fields and modes we know nothing of, faces of the world which lie undetected and undetectable to such as ourselves, as are the colours of stone to the blindworm who responds only to their heat' (1973, 132). If other species were to evolve further and faster, humans must, under one interpretation of Darwin's theory of natural selection, lose their edge and be weeded out or enslaved by higher-order species. A recidivist interpretation of evolution pushes fancy still further: in such an environment, the very faculties that mark humans as such would gradually erode as they come to serve less and less in the struggle for survival; we would become unrecognizable, cease to exist. Such were the implications of Darwinism widely exploited in late nineteenth-century fiction.[16]

What Thomas Kuhn suggests about scientific evolution – that anomalous scientific discoveries are not theoretically explained until they are of sufficient intensity to make the existing paradigm obsolete – is fully applicable to the advances made in the sciences during the nineteenth century.[17] New discoveries offered the rational possibility of bringing in a new, positivist paradigm. This in part explains why spiritualism, and its outgrowth psychical research, was frowned upon by the scientific establishment. Despite the efforts of such scientists as Crookes, Myers, Richet, and Flammarion, it neither presented itself in a consistently rational form nor offered explanations that could be brought within the positivist paradigm. From a scientific point of view, if the supernatural is admitted, a violation of natural laws occurs which must be accounted for; and, if it is proved that supernatural phenomena fall within the natural order, then either they are not supernatural under any accepted definition of the term, or else everything is supernatural. Logically, any absurdity might be inferred from the premiss that everything is supernatural; but it is the first premiss that inspired the writers we will examine in the following chapters.

The closing years of the nineteenth century brought a gentler view of the capacities of science. It had provided, and was capable of providing, only a partial description and interpretation of reality. Even Huxley had cautioned against circumscribing nature, and psychologists increasingly came to acknowledge the subjective reality of the human mind, the irreducibility of mental processes to neurological or physiological factors. Theorists of the mind like George Romanes, James Ward, and William James recognized that cognitive processes are as real as anything physical.[18]

In this new intellectual atmosphere, paranormal phenomena attracted the attention of some scientists of the highest calibre – Lord Rayleigh (and his son, also a physicist), J.J. Thomson, and Pierre and Marie Curie. Their involvement in the Society for Psychical Research is well documented and needs no rehearsing here.[19] More relevant is that each brought to bear on psychical research a critical scientism balanced by the willingness to contemplate new proofs if they were well founded. After the turn of the century, these developments led to parapsychology.

3

The Realists: Experience and Inspiration

Under the onslaught of positive science, belief in the supernatural as a separate, superhuman territory was increasingly difficult to sustain. It was superseded by scientific or pseudo-scientific theories of the paranormal. As one might expect, writers of fiction were among the first to be inspired by these theories, which ranged from ridiculous to rigorously scientific, adopting and developing them in their works. In this way, they contributed both to the intellectual context and to the intertext of the paranormal. Charles Dickens, Edward Bulwer-Lytton, Laurence Oliphant, and Henry James in England were each in their own way involved, as were Villiers de l'Isle-Adam, Jules Claretie, J-K Huysmans, and Guy de Maupassant in France; Fyodor Mikhailovich Dostoevsky, Aleksey Konstantinovich Tolstoy, and Ivan Sergeevich Turgenev were among the Russians inclined to speculation. All of them dismissed the supernatural and explored the implications of expanding the concepts natural and real, of extending the scope of reality to encompass paranormal phenomena. The result of their literary experiments was the transformation of the fantastic into what I called in chapter 1 *the paranormal mode*, where phenomena such as clairvoyance, telepathy, and precognition are treated as compatible and coexistent with natural human abilities. Stories of the paranormal mode suggest that the term 'supernatural' is empty, a label misapplied by the ignorant to the unexplained potentialities of the human mind. Under the new paradigm, strange, unexplained phenomena are not caused by supernatural beings; they are the natural endowment of some humans.

    The paranormal mode became the fantastic for the realists. This is not to suggest that all realists were interested in the fantastic, or in paranormal phenomena. In *The Duke's Children*, for instance, Anthony Trollope's narrator dismisses the matter ironically: 'When you see a young woman read a closed book placed on her dorsal vertebrae – if you do believe that she so reads it, you think that she is endowed with a wonderful faculty! And should you also be made to believe that the same young woman had direct communication with Abraham, by means of some invisible wire, you would be apt to do a great many things as that young woman might tell you. Conjuring, when not known to be conjuring, is very effective' (1880, 166). Those realists who were interested in the fantastic usually transformed its fictional world in order to subsume unexplained phenomena under natural laws. Among those who most contributed to the transformation were Charles Dickens, Ivan Sergeevich Turgenev, and Guy de Maupassant. Each had had some contact with spiritualism, psychical research, and paranormal phenomena and occasionally commented on them in their non-fictional writings. On the whole, they rejected the supernatural in its traditional, mythological form, but were open to other possibilities, to cognitive experiences that science could not explain, to dimensions of reality that transcend the standard, narrow, positivistic conception. Their non-fictional writings on the subject of the paranormal form the extra-literary intertext of their fantastic fiction and, as such, are presented at some length.

Dickens's letters and articles in *Household Words* and *All the Year Round* reveal that his attitude towards spiritualism was consistent throughout his life. He nurtured a lively, if sceptical, curiosity about strange phenomena. He often attacked spiritualists for their commercialism and irrationality in reviews of such books as Catherine Crowe's *The Night Side of Nature: or, Ghosts and Ghost Seers*, where the author claims that the quantity of testimony handed down through the ages is reason enough to credit the existence of ghosts.[1] Their alleged appearances, Dickens rejoins, 'have been, in all ages, marvellous, exceptional, and resting on imperfect grounds of proof' (1848, 7). In some cases, apparitions can be put down to psychological factors, for instance, a fear of death: 'Very few men perhaps, placed in the dead of night in circumstances particularly lonely, terrifying and mysterious, would be able to shake off this vague alarm of something not belonging to the world in which we live. But all this is no evidence of there being any other ground for the misgiving, than the universal mystery surrounding universal death.' Other such manifestations, he says, may result from 'excited imaginations' (1848, 8, 9). Dickens also admits the possibility of coincidence between real effects and imaginary causes, which may be psychosomatic in origin. He cites the case of a lady who was beaten upon the arm by the 'phantoms' haunting her, and who experienced a very real soreness afterwards. 'But, experience had taught her that the approaching real effect suggested the imaginary cause' (1848, 11).[2]

Dickens dismisses the idea of communication with the dead in his review of William Howitt's *The History of the Supernatural* (1863).[3] He accuses the author of irrationality, and ridicules him for dredging up the 'Cock Lane Ghost,' a phenomenon reported in 1759 and pronounced a fraud by investigators that included Samuel Johnson and Oliver Goldsmith. By the nineteenth century, the 'Cock Lane Ghost' was generally thought to be the classic hoax.[4] Howitt's readers, Dickens writes, are asked to 'disbelieve all rational explanations of thoroughly proved experiences ... which appear supernatural.' He is pointing out, in other words, that to agree with Howitt is to prefer a supernatural interpretation of natural phenomena over empirically established evidence. He especially objects to the man's arrogant proselytizing against the 'stereotyped class of minds' who refuse to accept spiritualist claims. To the later reader, Dickens's review and Howitt's views on spiritualism place both men in the context of their time, albeit at opposite ends of the spectrum: Dickens accepted the empirical view, Howitt reacted against it, or 'militated against the fierce materialism of the age' (Reed 1981, 103). One cannot help but be reminded of Mesmer's attempts to reconcile material and non-material, and of Paulet's observation about the wave of irrationality that swept through the Enlightenment.

Dickens's real *bête noire* was the celebrated medium Daniel Dunglas Home, whose first book, *Incidents in My Life* (1863), he treated to a scathing review, thanks largely to Home's 'maudlin complaint' that scientists were hard on spiritualists.[5] Home had grumbled that physicist Sir David Brewster[6] was 'disloyal to scientific observation' for refusing to accept the evidence of séance materializations. Dickens was especially incensed by Home's saying that Brewster and Faraday 'have had ample time to regret that they should have so foolishly pledged themselves' (1863, 135). For Dickens, Home embodied the worst of the spiritualists: his rather theatrical performances, though usually conducted in daylight, were an imposition on the intelligence of the witnesses. Invited to a Home séance, Dickens replied in terms that bring to mind T.H. Huxley: 'I have not the least belief in the awful unseen world being available for evening parties at so much per night; and although I should be ready to receive enlightenment from any source, I must say I have little hope of it from the spirits who express themselves through mediums, as I have never yet observed them to talk anything but nonsense' (Dexter, ed. 1938, 2: 673).[7]

Dickens ruled out personal inquiry into séances because he found investigations into their phenomena lacking in scientific rigour.[8] In a letter to a friend, he explains his hesitation: '[f]irstly, because the conditions under which such inquiries take place – as I know in the recent case of two friends of mine, with whom I discussed them – are preposterously wanting in the common securities against deceit or mistake. Secondly, because the people lie so very hard, both concerning what did take place and what impression it made at the time on the inquirer.'[9] It is hardly surprising that Dickens would denounce spiritualists as a 'combination of addle-headed persons, Toadies, and Humbugs' (Dexter, ed. 1938, 3: 172).[10]

One anonymous contribution to *All the Year Round*, significantly entitled 'Is It Possible?,'[11] discusses the well-known story of Lady Beresford, whose shrivelled wrist forever bore witness to her contact with a dead friend. According to the article, Lady Beresford and her life-long friend Lord Tyrone had made a pact that whichever should die first would appear to the survivor. Lord Tyrone died and appeared before her, but Lady Beresford, doubting her senses, required proof. First the apparition caused the bed-curtain to pass over the tester; then he wrote in her notebook. Lady Beresford suggested that perhaps she could do these things herself, in a state of somnambulism. She required further proof. After a warning, he touched her wrist, whereupon 'the sinews instantly shrank up, the nerves seeming to wither, yet not so as to disable the hand' (1867, 620).

The writer of the article tackles the question of the dead reappearing and asks what science can do to disclose the truth; spiritualism is dead because of 'its own innate worthlessness.' Another explanation is offered for experiences like Lady Beresford's: 'Is it not *possible* that, in that convulsive moment which separates soul and body, there may be evolved a transient condition of being, which, neither body nor spirit – semi-material – possesses some attributes of both? It may be regarded as the veil of the disembodied spirit ...' (1867, 615). The writer attempts to remain within the bounds of the possible, but obviously still holds an *a priori* belief in life after death. Dickens first mentions the Lady Beresford story in the review of Catherine Crowe noted above, where he proposes two interpretations. He compares Lady Beresford's shrivelled wrist to the stigmata occasionally experienced by the devout. Where fraud would seem to be ruled out, Dickens suggests, 'the force of a strongly excited and concentrated imagination, in some ecstatic cases, has actually produced these marks upon the patient's body.' Dickens finds it significant that the subjects are usually women, 'as if the operating influence were some fantastic and distorted perversion of the power a mother has, of marking the body of her unborn child, with the visible stamp of any image strongly impressed on her imagination' (1848, 10). His second interpretation of Lady Beresford's experience is that she dreamt the entire episode: 'Is it greatly straining a point to suppose, that when she suggested the possibility of her doing these other acts in her sleep, she not only knew that she could do them, but was, then and there, actually doing them, with that disturbed, imperfect consciousness of doing them which is not uncommon in cases of somnambulism, or even in common dreams ...' (quoted in Collins 1963, 10).

Lady Beresford's wrist is thus analogous to the soreness experienced by Mrs de la Rue, whose phantom beat her upon the arm. Dickens's second reference to the Beresford tale is in the 'Note by the Conductor' appended to the anonymous article 'Is It Possible?' (1867, 620). Without denying possibility, Dickens advances three natural explanations: 'We offered the suggestion, some years ago, that this is very expressive of a state of sleep-walking or half-consciousness ... she being, either way, in an exceptional condition presently culminating in a stroke of local paralysis.' His second proposal is that Lady Beresford was ill with an infection that resulted in the paralysis of her wrist; the 'ghost' and the two acts he performed would be 'a diseased impression accompanying the paralysis.' His third point amounts to a confession: 'a broad margin of allowance, ... must always be left for coincidence in these cases.' The word 'coincidence,' rich with implications, interested Dickens and would be explored further in 'The Signal-Man.' His openness may stem from a personal incident, which he recounts in his 'Note': Dickens dreamed of attending a large assembly where he was introduced to a stranger, a Miss N***, who wore a bright red wrapper. The following day he was in fact introduced by a friend to a woman, a stranger, whose name and appearance were those of the woman in his dream. Dickens confessed himself unable to account for the episode, but insisted that he had not known the woman or her name from any previous source. He labelled the incident 'coincidence' (though his use of the term characteristically lacks the dismissiveness often associated with it); Richet, never one to mince words, would later cite the experience as an instance of premonition (1923, 501).

While not a scientist and far from having a committed interest in spiritualism, Dickens had something in common with the scientists – he was sceptical of the unproved, but open to possibility. And although it cannot be claimed that he was such an avid follower of discoveries in the sciences as Maupassant would prove to be, he was interested nevertheless, admiring in particular Michael Faraday (Levine 1986 and 1988, Wilkinson 1967). Ghosts were, for Dickens, an implausible explanation for séance phenomena, yet he did not deny that strange things may happen, as we see from one of his comments in *All the Year Round*: 'My own mind is perfectly unprejudiced and impressible on the subject. I do not in the least pretend that such things are not. ... I have always had a strong interest in the subject, and never knowingly lose an opportunity of pursuing it. But I think the testimony which I cannot cross-examine, sufficiently loose, to justify me in requiring to see and hear the modern witnesses with my own senses and then be reasonably sure that they were not suffering under a disordered condition of the nerves or senses ...' (quoted in Peyrouton 1959, 75).[12] For Dickens, then, the existence of paranormal phenomena was an *epistemic* issue, a problem of interpretation and the reliability of evidence.

Maupassant's attraction to unexplained phenomena was more closely allied to Dickens's than was Turgenev's, so he will be discussed first. True to his time as a writer, Maupassant considered himself a realist and emphasized the need for believability, as did both Dickens and Turgenev. None of them considered their interest in the arcane to be at variance with their principles as writers, and nor should we.

Maupassant's was the interest of the intellectual; he had little practical involvement with spiritualism. As Bancquart writes, he was 'content to breathe the particular atmosphere of his time' (1976a, 22). For a realist of his open-mindedness, it was as legitimate to draw upon the unexplained as upon science, to make use of both fancy and fact as resources for his fiction; but he had no patience with the mystical practices of French spiritualists. Though explicit remarks about spiritualism are rare in his non-fictional writings, it is clear that communication with the dead was for him irrational nonsense.

In 'Letter from a Madman' ['Lettre d'un Fou'] (1885) and the two versions of 'Le Horla' (1886, 1887), Maupassant made use of both

Darwin's and Lamarck's theories of evolution. In 'The Man from Mars' ['L'Homme de Mars'] (1887) he explored the possibility of life on other planets, Flammarion's topic as well in his speculative semi-fictions *La Pluralité des mondes habités* (1862) and *Les Terres du ciel* (1877). Maupassant was especially fascinated by hypnosis, and made use of the popular beliefs about mesmerism in 'Magnetism' ['Magnétisme'] (1882) and 'A Madman' ['Un Fou'] (1884). Charcot's work at Salpêtrière and Bernheim's at Nancy intrigued him, to the degree that he attended the lectures of both during the 1880s. Vial (1954, 227) and Steegmuller (1972, 254) report that Maupassant was even responsible for introducing the Belgian hypnotist (or, as some said, the charlatan) Donato to Paris in 1886.

He was, in Cogny's words, 'a man without a God' who was repelled by the mythological world, whether it was peopled with the deities and demons of religion or the disincarnate souls of spiritualism. In the *Chronicle* entitled 'The Fantastic' ['Le Fantastique'] (1883) he wrote: 'twenty years ago, the supernatural left our souls. It evaporated the way perfume does when you take the stopper out of the bottle' (1980, 2: 256). The readiness of people to accept the supernatural was, for Maupassant, their way of coping with phenomena they did not understand.

In the social philosopher Herbert Spencer, Maupassant found his greatest inspiration. It was Spencer who wrote that all the knowledge gathered by means of science, itself a tradition defined by humans, simply brings us 'into wider contact with surrounding nescience' (1862, 17). The idea would be echoed time and again in Maupassant's best works. In the *Chronicle* entitled 'An Emperor' ['Un Empereur'] (1890), Maupassant speaks about the potentialities of scientific knowledge for the art of fiction: 'A novelist should read nothing but science, because, if he is capable of understanding, he will perceive through it how people will be, think, feel in a hundred years. The studies of Herbert Spencer, of Mr. Pasteur and others are better preparation for all the observations than reading the greatest poets, since they cast our minds towards hypotheses about a clear and unexpected reality which tomorrow will be beliefs, replaced later by others' (1980, 3: 396).

Maupassant understood the limitations of scientific explanation and rejected positivist absolutes. Scientific progress, human knowledge, are necessarily circumscribed by the limitations of those who formulate and regulate the domain of inquiry: 'Our whole mental effort consists in recording insignificant facts by means of ridiculously imperfect instruments which none the less supplement a little the incapacity of our organs ...' ('Beyond' ['Par-delà'] 1884; 1980, 2: 402–3). There is room, then, in Maupassant's episteme for the unexplained and even for the inexplicable, best expressed perhaps in the words of his mentor: 'the deepest truths we can reach, are simply statements of the widest uniformities in our experience of the relations of Matter, Motion, and Force; and Matter, Motion, and Force are but symbols of the Unknown Reality' (Spencer 1862, 501).

Turgenev was not an active séance-goer either; at least, the evidence for his participation is sketchy, and a reading of his several volumes of letters reveals little interest on his part in spiritualism. It ought to be remembered, too, that he spent most of his adult life in France, where spiritualism was more closely allied with mysticism, and more sharply separated from the scientific approach to the paranormal that we find with investigators like Richet. Still, he was not oblivious to these matters and his work, in Kleman's words, 'sprang up in the atmosphere of spiritualism' (1936, 171). Waddington claims that in March 1857 Turgenev attended a Home séance in Paris with Tolstoy. He leaves us to guess which Tolstoy – Lev (the author of *War and Peace*) or the poet Aleksey Konstantinovich – but the reference is most likely to Lev, who did make his first trip to the West in that year (Waddington 1980, 108–9).[13] Whoever his companion was, Turgenev was apparently honest enough to admit that he could not decide whether Home was a charlatan; he was puzzled by three taps 'beneath the sole of his right foot' (108). In one of his few non-fictional references to spiritualism, Turgenev wrote rather cynically to his friend Polonsky about the medium Bredive, who had taken Paris by storm and was repeating the success in Petersburg: 'Bredive – in our present deaf and empty time would naturally cause a lot of disturbance in Petersburg – it's the natural order of things. Even here, mediums and somnambulists are supported by the Russians' (1966b, 11: 80).[14]

After the appearance of some of Turgenev's fantastic stories, notably 'Phantasms' [Prizraki] (1864) and 'The Dream' [Son] (1877), Turgenev felt called upon to defend his fictional treatment of unexplained phenomena. But he was vehement in denying his belief in them. To Avdeev, Turgenev wrote about 'Phantasms': 'I can assure you that without exception I am interested in one thing only: the physiognomy of life, and its faithful representation, and to mysticism in all its forms I am positively indifferent, and that in the story "Phantasms" I saw only the possibility of constructing a series of scenes' (quoted in Kleman

1936, 170). His disclaimer about the story is odd, since the events of 'Phantasms,' if not supernatural, are certainly not natural under any standard interpretation. But perhaps his response is directed at those who make no distinction between an author's personal convictions and the events and characters of his fictional worlds, his creations. In a letter to Miliutina, where he attempts briefly to characterize his approach to art, Turgenev repeats that he is 'indifferent to everything supernatural' (1966b, 11: 31).[15] But the worlds he created in some of his tales are structured around phenomena which lie on the fringe of reality, especially clairvoyance and precognitive dreams. If these are his way of faithfully representing life, then his conception of the natural world was broad enough to accommodate the unexplained. At any rate, though spiritualism may have bored him and science held less fascination for him than for Dickens and Maupassant, his comments on the supernatural certainly parallel those of the other two writers.

Like the psychical researchers and scientists who tried to understand paranormal phenomena, Dickens, Maupassant, and Turgenev were curious about the mind's untapped resources. Unlike the spiritualists, many of whom abused scientific theories to give weight to their irrational beliefs, they scorned supernatural explanations for phenomena which they deemed natural. Theories of evolution and the nascent field of hypnosis offered rich resources. These three realists, fully aware that scientific advances would continue to enlarge reality, ventured to explore this open-endedness in their works of the fantastic.

Their common attitude towards the supernatural and their development of the paranormal mode of fantastic literature is more than merely compatible with their approach to art. It is an outgrowth of their beliefs about the writer's task. The traditional modes of the fantastic were suspect because they did not allow the opposition of natural and supernatural to be recast. There is no need to rehearse the already well-documented poetics of Dickens, Maupassant, and Turgenev. It is enough for us to understand that the paranormal mode was linked to Realism as closely as physical research was to science. To ignore this apparently obvious point makes the fantastic narratives of these realists anomalous, anti-realistic, and even frivolous – having no place in their corpus. It was a mistake many of their contemporaries made. Turgenev's fantastic stories (especially his most important, 'The Dream') were dismissed as 'literary dessert' and 'trifles,' while Maupassant was presumed mad several years before he really did go insane. Dickens's traditional fantastic tales, so popular with the general readership, were explained by his having romantic leanings, but his innovative paranormal stories have hardly been noticed.

Both then and now, much of the problem of reconciling the fantastic tales of these writers with the rest of their works stems from confusion about just what 'Realism' means. Two approaches are relevant to our study. The first, which in large part is responsible for making the fantastic incompatible with the realist program, views fictional representation as the truthful depiction of reality. The concept itself is ahistorical – it takes no account of style or period, and applies equally to the Bible and to contemporary literature. But it does tie representation to mimesis, to the actual world, and this has led to attempts, all too often ridiculous, at matching fictional characters, events, or settings with actual (real world) places and people. (Who did Dickens have in mind when he created Fagan?[16]) Auerbach's term is 'serious realism,' or the representation of 'the most everyday phenomena of reality in a serious and significant context' (1953, 555). Obviously, fantastic literature cannot be accommodated in a program so tightly bound up with everyday phenomena, and a realist who produces it must be seen as making forays into an alien realm. The incompatibility is expressed clearly in a statement by the French theorist Hamon: 'In the realist programme, the world is describable, susceptible of naming. Thus, it is in opposition to the world of fantastic discourse (the unnameable, the indescribable, the monster ...)' (in Barthes et al. 1982, 162).

Just how *do* we reconcile these definitions with the fantastic works of Dickens, Maupassant, and Turgenev, without denying them their historical status as realists or being forced to label them dabblers or madmen? Quite simply, we review the term Realism. In contrast to the ahistorical concept, it is also used to designate an historically delimited artistic movement, or period style. Jakobson, whose 1921 essay 'On Realism in Art' is, remarkably, one of the few attempts to analyse the term conceptually, defined it as 'the sum total of the features characteristic of one specific artistic current of the nineteenth century' (rpt. 1987, 20).[17] These are the very features by which we identify Dickens, Turgenev, and Maupassant as realists. The confusion, then, has lain in equating the historical movement (period style) with the ahistorical requirement (mimesis).

None of the three writers I have chosen for analysis judged it desirable, or even possible, to copy reality. Like other realists of their time, they stress consistency, believability, coherence, the importance of observation, and so on. Yet, they did not consider the fantastic incompatible with such principles. Each emphasized the role of the imagination in transforming life into art. Dickens's comment in the preface to *Bleak House* (1853) about dwelling on 'the romantic side of familiar things' is quoted often enough to be almost proverbial. He referred to the 'little fanciful photographs' of real life that he would tuck away in his mind for the future when they would be 'artistically transformed by imagination,' all of which is nicely described by Fanger as Dickens's '"fantastic fidelity"' (1967, 94).

In a similar vein Turgenev, in his 1844 article on Goethe's *Faust*, quoted Goethe on the writer's task: 'to raise the real to a beautiful illusion' [die Wirklichkeit zum schönen Schein erheben]. In other words, reality alone is not sufficient for art (1962c, 10: 209). Turgenev denied in his *Literary Reminiscences* that he was 'just a photographer' (1959, 80). On the Russian literary scene, he was to find himself in the position of mediator between the two artistic trends which, according to Belinsky, dominated nineteenth-century Russia: the art for art's sake of Pushkin and the social realism of Gogol. It is essential to recognize this syncretic role of Turgenev's before the evolution of his fantastic tales can be understood.[18]

Similar ideas were expressed by Maupassant, though his statements about art in general sound much like his remarks about the fantastic. Reality, he argued in 1887, is relative, illusory, because it is filtered through imperfect organs of perception: 'What childishness to believe in reality, since we each carry our own, in thought and in our organs' ('Le Roman' 12). The best the artist can do is to reproduce as faithfully as possible his subjective *illusion* of reality.

While none of these three writers thought any subject was taboo (in Dickens's case, it would depend on *how* it was presented), only Maupassant discussed, very briefly, the differences between two fantastic fictional worlds: when people believed in the supernatural without reservation, writers of fantastic stories 'entered, right from the start, into the impossible and stayed there.' As knowledge made people more sophisticated, such a straightforward supernatural world was less acceptable; the modern writer would rather just 'rub shoulders with the fantastic.' The most poignant terror could be created by the merest hints, he believed; by the presence of 'natural facts where resides none the less something unexplained and almost impossible' ('The Fantastic' ['Le Fantastique'] 1883; 1980, 2: 257).

These few remarks indicate that for Dickens, Maupassant, and Turgenev the aim of realism was not to transpose reality into literature. The imagination, they believed, is not re-creative, but discovers and interprets a reality which is neither closed nor reducible to empirical knowledge. It was this aspect of their poetics, coupled with their interest in the unexplained, that led them to create new fictional worlds which transcend the limits of reality set by conventional beliefs. In this way, they challenged not only the crudely mimetic concept of realism in art, but also the narrow positivistic conception of reality itself. They were alive to the complex and provocative intellectual and scientific context of their time. As realists, their task was to fictionalize the possibilities that science suggested without adulterating their literary convictions. And, as men of imagination, they did so by ushering in the paranormal mode.

4
Charles Dickens: Tradition and Transition

Throughout his life, Dickens was interested in the fantastic; we find incidental ghost tales even in such novels as *Pickwick Papers* (1837), *Nicholas Nickleby* (1839), *Bleak House* (1853), and *Little Dorrit* (1857). Through the years, we find that he moved away from traditional to modern forms of the fantastic, no doubt because he was maturing as a writer but perhaps also because of his interest in spiritualism and paranormal phenomena. As a result, the transition is reflected in the chronology of his tales. Until we meet 'The Signal-Man,' Dickens's special offering to the body of paranormal fiction, several of his tales exemplify more than one mode. For this reason, it is the logic of the transformation, and not chronology, which has dictated my arrangement of the tales analysed below. In the first and second parts of this chapter, the traditional and the transitional, are the tales of the disjunctive and the ambiguous modes, while the third part is devoted to 'The Signal-Man,' Dickens's only tale of the paranormal mode.

THE TRADITIONAL FANTASTIC

Most of Dickens's traditional fantastic tales are constructed around a character's encounter with a supernatural being – a treatment shared with fairy-tales, Gothic novels, and some of the fantastic narratives of the Romantics. The better-developed works turn from action alone (What happened?) to perception and perceptibility (How or why do certain things happen?); from questions of *being* to questions of *knowing*. The same distinction separates the adventure story from the mystery or detective story, which highlights the mental process of gathering, evaluating, and interpreting clues. We will find this analogy useful as we move through the stories themselves.

The incidental tales embedded within the main story of *Pickwick Papers* are a good starting point for analysing the development of Dickens's fantastic. In one of the four tales told by the old man Jack Bamber (298–303),[1] a self-proclaimed spirit emerges from the clothes press addressed by the narrator in a soliloquy. There is a parallel with Aladdin's rubbing of the lamp, but animistic beliefs in the transmigration of souls to objects or other animals also come to mind. The clothes press is transformed from an inanimate and tangible object into a mythical being, an object with the soul of the person who owned it. It stands for the absent person, and the whole event plays on the word *spirit* in its sense of *essence of a person*. Such metonymic transpositions are found in the fantastic tales of the Romantics, Théophile Gautier's 'The Mummy's Foot' [Le Pied de Momie] (1840) being a classic example. From an ancient relic, a segment of a body, the narrator manages to reconstruct the 'owner' in the form of a beautiful female.

'The Bagman's Story' (*Pickwick Papers*, 193–206) is especially typical of Dickens's traditional fantastic. In this tale of a chair that comes alive one night to give the protagonist, Tom Smart, vital information, the supernatural being is never designated as such. One stormy night Tom takes refuge at 'a strange old place,' an inn where he finds a roguish-looking man flirting with the pretty, widowed innkeeper. Eventually Tom will expose him, with a letter from the man's abandoned wife. Preparing for bed, Tom notices in his room a grim-looking, fantastically carved chair, which impresses him as more than just odd: 'There was something about this particular chair, and yet he couldn't tell what it was, so odd and so unlike any other piece of furniture he had ever seen, that it seemed to fascinate him' (198). With this remark, the narrator creates the expectation that something strange will happen.

Half an hour after falling asleep, Tom wakes up with a start, and the transformation begins. The chair metamorphoses on the surface into an ugly, old gentleman from another century. The metamorphosed chair is flexible (it can 'cock up its legs' and point with its 'arms'), but its limbs still retain chair-features. The attributes that the old gentleman/chair ('whichever you like to call him,' as the narrator says, 199) claims for himself are purely metaphorical. His waistcoat and shoes are, respectively, the chair's damask cushion and the cloth mufflers on the chair-legs. The old gentleman/chair speaks of having been a 'great favourite' with women, many of whom sat in his 'lap.' These are of course innocent, purely rhetorical allusions. The human metaphor is extended when Tom addresses the chair as 'old nut-cracker face' and 'sir' (199), and the narrator dubs it 'old rascal' and 'profligate old debauchee' (200). Still, the old gentleman/chair alludes to certain of his chair-features: 'that's no way to address solid Spanish Mahogany. Dam'me, you couldn't treat me with less respect if I was veneered' (199). The blending of human and object is strongly marked when he is seized with a 'violent fit of creaking' (200). This play on the expression 'fit of coughing' is a fine metaphor, which is no mere personification of a chair; a hybrid is created that is *both* chair and man, with the attributes of the two in equal balance. As a supernatural entity, the old gentleman/chair is omniscient and able to interfere in human affairs. Although stationary, he can act indirectly through selected human agents, in this case Tom.

The same trope – metaphor as a device of animism – is found in Gautier's first fantastic tale, 'The Coffee-Pot' [La Cafetière] (1831). The objects in the narrator's room (chairs, portraits, and the coffee-pot) become animate, hold conversations, and dance at midnight. The most important object, the coffee-pot, metamorphoses not into an ugly old man, but into a beautiful girl with whom the narrator falls in love. As in Dickens's story, where the chair is and is not a man, in Gautier's version the coffee-pot is and is not Angéla. Both tales can be taken as ambiguous, for the characters may have dreamt their experiences. Tom Smart was tipsy after five tumblers of hot punch (even the old gentleman/chair remarks that Tom is 'much too fond of punch,' 199); and both Tom and Gautier's narrator in 'The Coffee-Pot' go to sleep and are woken up. Dickens's narrator, moreover, modalizes the event: 'a most extraordinary change *seemed* to come over it [the chair]' (198; emphasis added). Yet the narrator also adds that Tom was awake before the metamorphosis: 'the first object that presented itself to his *waking* imagination was the queer chair' (198; emphasis added). In both stories, the characters wake up the following morning with at least some material evidence of their experiences having happened, and these circumstances tend to authenticate the supernatural events. In Gautier, the narrator-protagonist is dressed in old-fashioned clothes, much to his friends' astonishment when they come to his room; and when he attempts to sketch the coffee-pot, he instead renders what the landlord declares is a remarkable likeness of his dead sister, Angéla. Even so, we have only the *Ich*-narrator's word for the events themselves. In Dickens, Tom does find in the rogue's pocket the damning letter to which the old gentleman/chair had directed him. This circumstance might corroborate his experience, or it might, indeed, be coincidence.

'The Story of the Bagman's Uncle' is another tale embedded within *Pickwick Papers* (719–36). The uncle, wakened from a doze, finds himself waiting for a mail coach in the sixteenth century. It turns out to be a damsel-in-distress adventure, with the uncle engaging in a sword fight to protect the lady.[2] Although the uncle finds himself in the natural world of the sixteenth century, it is peopled with supernatural beings. The tale is in some degree ambiguous (the uncle may or may not have fallen asleep), but we are inclined to take up the narrator's hint that his uncle dreamt the event.

The adventure of the clothes-press spirit took place forty years before Jack Bamber narrates it to Mr Pickwick. It is a second-hand narrative, though the narrator tries to boost its authenticity by placing himself in proximity to the tale. He uses direct discourse to convey the tenant's dialogue with the spirit and insists on the truth of the tale. But we cannot forget that the story is filtered through still another narrator by being embedded in *Pickwick Papers,* and therefore loses some authenticity. 'The Bagman's Story,' we are told, recounts an occurrence some eighty years old. It is a third-hand narrative, originally told by Tom Smart to the Bagman's uncle, who in turn related it to others. Both Tom Smart and the uncle are long dead, as we learn in the bagman's last tale. 'The Bagman's Story,' then, is an example of oral storytelling in which the tale is duly embellished with each repetition. In the narrator's words, 'he *used* to tell it, *something* in this way' (193; emphasis added). His comment reveals that the story is not first-hand and that it is not being related verbatim.[3] In such a complex chain of narrative transmission, the authentication of the events is weakened.[4]

The conventions of oral storytelling are highlighted when speakers imitate the formulas used in folk-tales. The events of these embedded tales are placed within a vague temporal and spatial framework, signalled by such a phrase as 'One winter's evening.' 'The story of the Bagman's Uncle' is similar, but makes use of one more convention: the narrator offsets the vagueness of 'one night' by piling up temporal markers intended to authenticate his tale.

The *multiple tale* is yet another device taken from the folk narrative. In many folk-tale cycles, the narrator is a professional with a stock of tales that he (or she) uses to fill in the main narrative. In the European tradition, the technique is most readily associated with Russian literature, Gogol' in particular, and with his narrator Rudi Pan'ko in 'Evenings on a Farm Near Dikan'ka' [Vechera na khutore bliz Dikan'ki].[5] Undoubtedly, though, Scheherazade, the narrator of *A Thousand and One Nights*, is the most widely known of the tellers with a stock of tales. To illustrate from the cycle which concerns us, the bagman tells one story about Tom Smart and a second about his uncle, prefaced by digressive mini-tales about his uncle's fondness for pickled walnuts and his ability to outdrink the inhabitants of Dundee. Jack Bamber begins with an irreverent sketch of a man who was struck with apoplexy and died with his head in his letter box, and ends with a fourth, the 'Tale about the Queer Client.' Each story, in other words, forms part of a longer and more varied storytelling performance.

Dickens's early fantastic stories are significant for their intertextual links to Gothic narratives. Both Jack Bamber's tale and the bagman's stories take place in inns, which in Gothic novels are a conventional setting for the unexpected and mysterious. There, protagonists are waylaid, and vicious attempts are made on life or virtue; occasionally the inn is a place of refuge and protection. Inns are also places where one is likely to hear a good tale, just as Mr Pickwick hears all of those just discussed.[6] They are a fitting background for romantic tales of lonely young men who wither away under the burden of their studies (298) or commit suicide over their unhappy lot (299). Bamber even salutes the Gothic explicitly: 'Talk of your German universities ... there's romance enough at home without going half a mile for it' (299). Exotic settings, usually Germany, Italy, or Spain, were standard fare in English Gothic narratives.[7] Dickens's own 'The Baron of Grogzwig' (1839) is set in a German castle. The device of pathetic fallacy, where the state of nature is in harmony with the event, creates yet another affinity with the Gothic novel. The adventure of the bagman's uncle occurs on a wild and gusty night, with the moon appearing and disappearing between fast-drifting clouds; the Gothic chapel and palace of Holyrood stand in the distance. Tom Smart takes refuge at the widow's inn on a gloomy winter's evening; a hard wind is blowing, the rain pelting, and the road miry and sloppy.[8]

A Christmas Carol (1843) offers a good Gothic description by linking the house with the weather: 'It [Marley's house] was old enough now, and dreary enough, for nobody lived in it but Scrooge ... The fog and frost so hung about the black old gateway of the house, that it seemed as if the Genius of the Weather sat in mournful meditation on the threshold' (18). *A Christmas Carol* is perhaps the richest of Dickens's traditional fantastic texts. Davis (1963) and Stone (1979) have remarked on its indebtedness to the fairy-tale and chapbook tradition, its adaptation of 'fairy-tale effects and fairy-tale techniques' (Stone 1979, 120).[9] But the features of this long tale which might lead one to point to the Gothic or the fairy-tale were not Dickens's sole means, or even the most important, for generating the fantastic.

The story is told by a narrator who shifts from third person undramatized narrator, impersonal and seemingly omniscient, to the role of a rhetorical narrator. The first term, commonly (if imprecisely) called the omniscient narrator, refers to a narrator who remains in the background and whose personality does not obtrude on the reader. The second term is more specialized, and ought perhaps to be clarified. According to Doležel, the rhetorical narrator is created when the interpretive function is activated: the narrator becomes 'an exposed creator and judge of the narrated events and of the depicted characters, making explicitly known his attitudes, value judgements and feelings' (1973, 104–5). The keywords here are 'exposed' and 'judge'; in other words, the narrator puts himself (or herself) forward as a personality and shapes an identity of sorts by filtering the characters and events explicitly through his own subjective viewpoint. It is important to remember, though, that the narrator remains apart, distanced, from the world of the characters – he (or she) is not one of them and does not participate in the events of their world. The narrator reports them and, above all, remarks on and evaluates them.[10]

The narrator of *A Christmas Carol*, while in this rhetorical role, sometimes deviates from the course of the main narrative into a secondary discourse, which creates counterfactual (that is, hypothetical) situations. His devices are more typical of eighteenth-century fiction than of the fairy-tale, and he frequently makes ironic comments. After Scrooge's attempt to be witty about Marley's ghost ('There's more of gravy than of grave about you, whatever you are!'), the narrator interjects: 'Scrooge was not much in the habit of cracking jokes, nor did he feel, in his heart, by any means waggish then. The truth is, that he tried to be smart ...' (22). While Scrooge awaits the 'Ghost of Christmas Present,' pondering the strange light coming from another room, the narrator remarks: 'At last, however, he began to think – as you or I would have thought at first ...' (46–7). Not infrequently, the narrator insists on the certainty of his information. The effect of this strategy is to make the narrator seem reliable. For instance, 'Marley was dead: to begin with. There is no doubt whatever about that' (11). A few lines further, he reinforces his words with the inversion 'There is no doubt that Marley was dead,' and 'Marley's voice, no doubt about it' (11). When the 'Ghost of Christmas Past' arrives, the narrator proclaims: 'the curtains of his bed were drawn aside, I tell you, by a hand' (29). He makes use here of the passive voice characteristic of the third-person, undramatized narrator; but, by contrast, the phrase 'I tell you' marks his privileged knowledge, as well as his autonomy as narrator (the rhetorical, or writing, 'I'). Indeed, his frequent repetitions of entire sentences, sometimes inverted, underscore his status as the writing 'I' very much in control of the narrative. On occasion, he draws attention to his personhood by projecting himself into the events with hypothetical reactions. At these moments, he appropriates the narrative: 'What would I not have given to be one of them! Though I never could have been so rude, no, no! I wouldn't for the wealth of all the world have crushed that braided hair, and torn it down; and for the precious little shoe, I wouldn't have plucked it off, God bless my soul! to save my life' (43). The narrator, it would seem, is reliable not only because his information is accurate, but because he is a good-natured, agreeable, kind-hearted fellow. At the same time, his assessment of Scrooge is unsparing. Scrooge's obsession, motives, and errors are laid bare, but it is never suggested that he is beyond reclamation.

Scrooge is as hard of belief as he is hard fisted. With the first intrusion of the supernatural (the metamorphosis of the door-knocker into Marley's head), the narrator tells us that Scrooge 'had as little of what is called fancy about him as any man in the City of London' (18). When Marley's ghost appears, Scrooge refuses to believe his senses and blames the apparition on a bout of indigestion. Only its terrifying display of wrath and indignation convinces him. All the props of the stereotypical ghost are brought into play, from its 'frightful cry' to its rattling of chains 'with such a dismal and appalling noise, that Scrooge held on tight to his chair, to save himself from falling in a swoon' (24). And the ghost's features are typical: Marley's body is transparent (and fully clothed, incidentally, as ghosts in and out of fiction tend to be), its eyes are fixed, glazed, not looking at Scrooge, but able to see him; its hair, skirts, and tassels are 'agitated as by the hot vapour from an oven' (22). The stereotype is momentarily neutralized in the first incident, where the face materializes in the door-knocker. It is not angry or ferocious, but merely 'looked at Scrooge as Marley used to look' (19).[11]

Three 'Ghosts of Christmas,' whose mission it is to redeem

Scrooge, confront him with disturbing glimpses of the past, present, and future. Each spirit has attributes which contravene the logic of the fictional world as it has been established before their entrance. The 'Ghost of Christmas Past' is a conjunction of opposites. It has the appearance of being at once young and old, frail and strong, large and small; parts of the Ghost twinkle, so that at any given moment it is both light and dark. It holds a branch of fresh holly in its hand but, 'in singular contradiction of that wintry emblem, had its dress trimmed in summer flowers' (30). It has human attributes (melancholy, compassionate, smiling) and is not human, as the consistent use of the neuter pronoun 'it' indicates. The 'Ghost of Christmas Yet to Come' is the most strongly marked as a depersonalized entity, with few, if any, human qualities. It is unfriendly, relentlessly cold, and conceals its gender under a heavy shroud: 'The cover was so carelessly adjusted that the slightest raising of it, the motion of a finger upon Scrooge's part, would have disclosed the face. He thought of it, felt how easy it would be to do, and longed to do it; but had no more power to withdraw the veil than to dismiss the spectre at his side' (74). Although the neuter pronoun is sometimes used, this spirit is most often designated by the related words 'Phantom,' 'Ghost,' 'Spirit,' 'Unseen Eyes,' and 'Spectre.'

The jolly and dignified 'Ghost of Christmas Present' is always referred to in the masculine. He is the most human-like of the three spirits, yet his traits are far from natural. He is enormous, but 'could accommodate himself to any place with ease,' standing in doorways or 'beneath a low roof quite as gracefully and like a supernatural creature, as it was possible he could have done in any lofty hall' (52).

Time and space signify differently for the spirits and for the mortal Scrooge. In their limited time with Scrooge, they span years, reconstructing the past and constructing the future almost instantly. The 'Ghost of Christmas Present' describes himself as young (49), but has grown 'clearly older' by the time he leaves Scrooge (66). Distance is irrelevant, and the spirits whisk Scrooge about England at the mere touch of a robe. The last spirit, the 'Ghost of Christmas Yet to Come,' approaches him 'like a mist along the ground' (67). As Scrooge trails behind, he feels the phantom's shadow bearing him up and carrying him along (69). In the absence of any object around them, the city 'springs up' and 'encompasses' them. This spontaneous generation of something from a misty void, the creation of vast, filled space from minimal, empty space, and the spilling over of the past into the present are a most remarkable violation of the logic of the natural within the fictional world.

Marley's ghost has warned Scrooge to expect visits from the spirits on three consecutive nights. However, when he wakens in the dark before the visit of the first spirit, the clock tolls rapidly from four to twelve, where it stops. In order to account for the impossibility of its being twelve midnight (he had gone to bed after two in the morning Christmas day), Scrooge presents and then rejects three rational explanations. The first is that he has slept through a night and a day, a hypothesis he decides is impossible. The second is that it is in fact noon, and that something has happened to the sun. To verify this conjecture, he goes to the window to check the streets; finding no stir 'as there unquestionably would have been if night had beaten off bright day' (28), he must reject this idea as well. Third, he asks himself whether it was 'all a dream.' Satisfied with none of these hypotheses, Scrooge finds that there is no accounting rationally (that is, in natural terms) for the temporal paradox of his experience (28). At the end of his adventures, he learns that it is Christmas day and understands that 'the spirits have done it all in one night. They can do anything they like. Of course they can' (83). It is typical of the disjunctive mode, defined in chapter 1, that spirits, as supernatural beings, are not confined by physical laws any more than they are constrained by distance or means of conveyance.

Critics often assert that Scrooge's experiences are either dream or hallucination. Several markers in the text, though, work against these explanations. Just before Scrooge's first two adventures, we are told that he woke up. On both occasions, he got out of bed, once to go to the window, the second time to trace the source of the strange light. Of course, we are not prohibited from claiming that Scrooge dreamt even these actions, but this interpretation throws doubt upon the narrator's reliability when it has already been well established, and we would in effect arbitrarily be imposing an interpretation on the fictional world. There are other clues if we look for them. When the clock chimes twelve forty-five, he 'resolved to lie awake until the hour was passed; and, *considering that he could no more go to sleep than go to Heaven,* this was perhaps the wisest resolution in his power' (29; emphasis added). Although he momentarily thinks he has missed the hour by sinking into a doze, the sound finally reaches his 'listening ear.' After the 'Ghost of Christmas Past' departs, Scrooge is returned to his bed where, 'conscious of being exhausted, and overcome by an irresistible drowsiness,' he falls into a heavy sleep (45). When the 'Ghost of Christmas Present' disappears, Scrooge does not fall asleep; he is left standing in the street, where the third spirit meets him. It is perhaps the final episode of his experience with this phantom that has suggested to some critics that Scrooge dreamt the events. Scrooge had been clutching the robe and hand of the 'Ghost of Christmas Yet to Come,' when he sees 'an alteration in the Phantom's hood and dress. It shrunk, collapsed, and dwindled down into a bedpost' (80). The celebrated 1952 film version seems to opt for the dream explanation, as Scrooge (Alastair Sim) seems to *come to* or revive at the bedpost. But one should take care to distinguish the film from the written story, in which the figure *becomes* the bedpost, or dissolves into it. This transformation is not sufficient to disauthenticate Scrooge's supernatural experiences. He has struggled with the spirit and been repulsed; at the moment of the ghost's transformation, Scrooge is not touching it, but supplicating. The transfiguration occurs before his eyes, which are open – a metamorphosis inverse to that of the door-knocker, since here it is the supernatural being that apparently metamorphoses into a commonplace object.

Humour is a special, idiosyncratic feature of Dickens's early fantastic stories which ties them to the rest of his oeuvre. He uses three vehicles to create it: (1) Types, or 'humours' (Frye 1968), usually involving the overdetermination of a certain trait. (2) Linguistic tags, or keywords, which identify particular characters.[12] (3) Incongruity between discourse and situation, as defined by Riffaterre – a 'discrepancy between a form that is funny and a content that is not' (1983, 163; see chapter 1, p. 15).

The first device places the character in a certain universal context, makes him or her readily identifiable to the reader as part of a category. Often the character's name expresses this category, such as Gradgrind, the hard-fisted purveyor of 'Hard Facts,' in *Hard Times*; or Miss Flite, the eccentric little old lady in *Bleak House* who keeps birds. The typecasting is reinforced by rhetorical devices. Before we see in Stave I how miserly and disagreeable Scrooge is in action – in conversations with his nephew, his clerk, and the visiting philanthropists – the narrator describes him as 'a squeezing, wrenching, grasping, scraping, clutching, covetous old sinner! Hard and sharp as flint, from which no steel had ever struck out generous fire ... The cold within him froze his old features, nipped his pointed nose, shrivelled his cheek, stiffened his gait ...' (12). The description is pleonastic, for all the terms converge to signify miser. The present participles, even though adjectivized, make the description dynamic: Scrooge is an active, or practising, miser. A complex metaphor is generated, whose constituents – hardness, sharpness, stiffness, tightness – turn Scrooge into a symbol of miserly hard-heartedness. Dickens may sometimes belabour the rhetoric used for a character and his physiognomy, but his stories are humorous (for some of us at least) precisely because of this verbal overplay.

The second device, the linguistic tag, may be a word or a set phrase that marks a particular character within a general category. For example, the word 'humbug' is readily associated with Scrooge, the miser type, whereas the locution 'discipline must be maintained' directs us to Major Bagnet, the military type in *Our Mutual Friend* (1865). Less commonly, the tag might be gestural, such as Mr Podsnap's flourish with his hand when he prefers not to know something, or Mr Venus's incessant tea-drinking when nervous (*Our Mutual Friend*).

The third device, incongruity between discourse and situation, is also found throughout Dickens's works. One example would be an uneducated (and sometimes pretentious) character attempting to show off his epistolary skills, as in the illiterate, ill-considered letter Tony Weller in *Pickwick Papers* writes to his son (770–1). The style may be amusing, but the subject (death) is not.

In the fantastic tales embedded in *Pickwick Papers*, the first two vehicles for creating humour, types and linguistic tags, are suppressed. But we do find incongruity between situation and language. In 'The Story of the Bagman's Uncle,' the events are rendered either in the uncle's words, in direct discourse, or indirectly through the narrator's own interpositions in that discourse. In the first case, the uncle demonstrates an impressive contempt for danger. In order to keep close to the abducted woman, he adopts a waggish, bluffing tone to her villainous abductors: 'Well ... A mail travelling at the rate of six miles and a half an hour, and stopping for an indefinite time at such a hole as this, is rather an irregular sort of proceeding, I fancy. This shall be made known. I shall write to the papers' (731). In using direct discourse, the narrator aims at being believed, at authenticating the events; he in effect *decreases* the incongruity of discourse and situation. So, if his uncle really is as cool and sharp as his own words suggest, then there's nothing remarkable about his handling an unaccustomed sword. Even so, the events strike us as absurd, because the narrator subtly plants in our minds the strong suspicion that exaggeration is the rule: '"why, my dear, there's nobody else to kill, is there?" My uncle was rather disappointed, gentlemen, for he thought a little quiet bit of love-making would be agreeable after the slaughtering, if it were only to change the subject' (733). In a similar way, the clothes-press spectre in Jack Bamber's story is ultimately made out to be a figure of farce. Initially rather fierce, he ends by agreeing to try a change of air in some exotic clime away from the bugs in the clothes-press (302).

In 'The Baron of Grogzwig' (*Nicholas Nickleby* (71–80; ch. 6), an embedded story related to Nickleby and Squeers at a roadside inn, humour becomes a vehicle for debunking the supernatural. Tongue in cheek, the narrator calls attention to the tale's Gothic conventions, clearly suggesting that it is a parodic transcription: 'I needn't say that he lived in a castle, because that's of course; neither need I say that he lived in an old castle; for what German baron ever lived in a new one?' (71). The characters are also stereotyped – the baron is bluff and hard-drinking, a man who threatens a neighbouring baron with death if his daughter is not handed over in marriage. The parody is evident when the narrator ironically abuses the conventions of the Gothic: 'If the daughter of the Baron Von Swillenhausen had pleaded a preoccupied heart, or fallen at her father's feet and corned them in salt tears, or only fainted away ... the odds are a hundred to one but Swillenhausen castle would have been turned out of window, or rather the baron turned out of window, and the castle demolished' (73).

It is a common motif in Gothic narratives, often the one on which the plot hinges, that the woman courted by an unappealing, unromantic character is in love with a young, handsome man. She cannot declare it because her lover lacks property, rank, or power, and her rejection of the repulsive suitor invariably lands her in a dungeon or other prison.[13] But in 'The Baron of Grogzwig,' as the narrator observes, 'she was no sooner assured that the horseman with the large moustachios was her proffered husband, than she hastened to her father's presence, and expressed her readiness to sacrifice herself to secure his peace' (73). Gothic conventions are reversed in the dénouement, too. Far from being shut up in a castle while her husband carouses, the baroness of Grogzwig is the despot. The baron was 'slily unhorsed' from his favourite hobbies, and rapidly became the father of twelve. The supernatural, introduced when the baron contemplates suicide, is motivated primarily by the setting; Gothic convention, after all, requires a spectre of some sort. But there is nothing horrific about this one. It calls itself the 'Genius of Despair and Suicide,' and flaunts the stake run through its body, pulling it out 'as composedly as if it had been a walking-stick' (77). The lively banter of the baron and the spectre continues the parody of Gothic conventions. The spirit orders the baron to 'look sharp' if he means to commit suicide, while the baron dawdles over his pipe and retorts that the spirit seems in rather a hurry. The spectre's rejoinder is a dig at the splenetic English and French Werthers who were busily doing away with themselves in and out of literature: 'Why, yes, I am; they're doing a pretty brisk business in my way, over in England and France just now, and my time is a good deal taken up' (77). Parody is generated by the semantic and pragmatic discrepancy between Dickens's tale and its intertext; the rules of dialogue between man and spectre – which the Gothic canonized and the reader expects – are violated.

Three strains, then, make these stories of Dickens's traditional: the folkloristic, the Gothic, and the parodic or humorous, the last of which weakens or destroys the authentication of the supernatural. Interestingly, in his next set of tales these strains, most noticeably humour, are virtually absent. I am tempted to suggest that Dickens did not take the traditional fantastic seriously, but perhaps found it a springboard to transformation.

TRANSITIONAL FANTASTIC STORIES

Dickens's fantastic and non-fantastic narratives follow a similar course of development. Gradually, he retired the oral storytelling devices, Gothic conventions, and parodic humour of his earlier tales. His last major novels (*Great Expectations, Our Mutual Friend, The Mystery of Edwin Drood*) exhibit marked structural and stylistic departures. The narrator's language is terse, sometimes sarcastic, and the point of view detached, especially in *Our Mutual Friend*. In harmony with this shift, Dickens moved steadily towards a 'modern' fantastic, with a soberer style and a simpler rhetoric. Several stories which may be called transitional fall in between the traditional and modern Dickensian fantastic. Here, we see the paranormal mode emerging as the natural/supernatural opposition is reinterpreted.

Three of these transitional stories will be analysed in detail: 'To Be Read at Dusk' (1852), 'Mr H.'s Own Narrative' (1861), and 'To Be Taken with a Grain of Salt' (1865).

'To Be Read at Dusk'[14] is an early instance of the transition, but is relevant because its explanations are, in a tentative way, those of the paranormal mode. Yet it retains many of the structural and stylistic features typical of the traditional stories.

The story is composed of the first-person narratives of two couriers, a Genoese and a German, who relate their strange experiences to two other couriers, a Swiss and a Neapolitan. The anonymous narrator who overhears them frames their tales with a prologue and an epilogue. To describe the setting where he overhears the couriers, the narrator makes use of Gothic conventions, thereby generating an aura of mystery and a sense of expectation. The couriers are seated in a Swiss convent on the summit of St Bernard, which is 'stained by the setting sun, as if a mighty quantity of red wine had been broached' on it (661). 'Red wine' shares with 'blood' the seme of red, but the blood metaphor is actualized only retrospectively; in the following paragraph, the narrator looks at the 'reddened' snow and at the hut where some snowed-in travellers had died. We come across this metaphor again in the Neapolitan courier's ironic remark about the 'blood of San Gennaro' liquefying at the request of the clergy (662). Both the blood metaphor and the nearby bodies of the dead travellers reinforce a Gothic topos and at the same time prepare the reader for the unexpected. The narrative of one courier is set in England, that of the other in an Italian palazzo. From the Swiss and German couriers' exchange, we surmise that the topic of conversation was strange phenomena, before the anonymous narrator tuned in.

Wilhelm, the German courier, begins by sketching an episode of clairvoyance. The Neapolitan's ironic words about San Gennaro are meant to force him to confess his belief in miracula. But Wilhelm, true to his name, is the stereotypical German – rational, philosophical, and not easily duped. When asked just what he is talking about, he states categorically that it is not ghosts (of which he is contemptuous), but that he would know a good deal more if he were able to answer that question (662). Gothic convention is undone with Wilhelm's rationality. He quotes his employer's assessment of his character to underscore the point: 'You come from a sensible country, where mysterious things are inquired into ...' (670). We ought not to forget that Mr James's ability to recognize Wilhelm's rationality speaks also to his own.

In Wilhelm's story, he and Mr James are about to leave England for Germany. John, Mr James's twin brother, pays a visit and complains of not feeling well; the two agree to meet again before Mr James's departure. One night, when Mr James is retiring, John's phantom appears before him, dressed in white. Within minutes of his telling Wilhelm what he has seen, Mr James is summoned to John's deathbed. Wilhelm, who functions as a witness, accompanies his employer and observes that the dying man is wearing a white nightdress (671).

In the story of Baptista, the Genoese courier, the bride of his English employer is haunted by the nightmare of a man she has never met. When she encounters the stranger in Italy, she knows her fate is sealed: he abducts her, and all trace of her is lost. Even though the incident is ten years removed from its telling, it is not hearsay; the courier was a witness. Before they arrived in Italy, he had heard about his mistress's dream from her maid and had observed her nervousness; he was also present when the mysterious stranger was eventually introduced at Genoa. Such precognitive dreams may be more common in the modern fantastic, but Baptista's account is rife with the pathetic fallacy typical of traditional modes of the fantastic: 'it was a stormy dismal evening when we, at last, approached that part of the Riviera. It thundered; and the thunder of my city and its environs, rolling among the high hills, is very loud. The lizards ran in and out of the chinks in the broken stone wall of the garden, as if they were frightened; the frogs bubbled and croaked their loudest; the sea-wind moaned, and the wet trees dripped; and the lightning – body of San Lorenzo, how it lightened!' (665). To describe the palazzo, Baptista draws upon Gothic conventions, and he relies on his audience's knowledge of them: 'We all know what an old palace in or near Genoa is ... Our palazzo was one of the true kind ... It had an earthy smell, like a tomb' (665). The stranger's name, 'Dellombra,' also strikes Baptista as odd. But the fact that Baptista was a witness, and relates the story without embellishment (he merely stages them), helps to authenticate the events.

Baptista does not attempt to explain or interpret what he has seen. Implicitly, however, the figure of Dellombra is demoniac, betokening the conventional Gothic or Romantic nasty, the villain with the power to mesmerize his victims. He is a 'dark remarkable-looking man,' with black hair and a grey moustache. He dresses in black and has a 'reserved and secret air' (667). Baptista notes that his mistress 'would look at him with a terrified and fascinated glance, as if his presence had some evil influence or power upon her' (668). There is no shortage of such characters in the nineteenth century, two of the most memorable in English fiction being Count Fosco in Wilkie Collins's *The Woman in White* (1860) and Du Maurier's Svengali in *Trilby* (1894).

In Wilhelm's narrative, the experiencing character, Mr James, offers

Charles Dickens: Tradition and Transition 61

a natural explanation, as might be expected of a sensible Englishman: 'Now, I am not in the least mad, and am not in the least disposed to invest that phantom with any external existence out of myself. I think it is a warning to me that I am ill; and I think I had better be bled' (671). His interpretation is impeccably logical: the onset of illness could bring about an hallucination. The hallucination might take any form – his brother's, for instance – so that the phantom is a symptom. But this rational explanation collapses when Mr James (and the reader with him) learns that John is dying, and that the phantom therefore represents not his own illness, but his brother's. Mr James has experienced clairvoyance, or the ability to know of events at a distance.

'To Be Taken with a Grain of Salt'[15] is a story in two parts: an enigma in the first part, and its resolution in the second. It is not in the strict sense of the term a mystery story as Shklovsky defines it – the manipulation of true and false solutions and the avoidance of fantastic solutions (1929, 149–76). False solutions are conspicuously absent, and the second part consists of the aftermath of the events without actually explaining them. But there are some common features.

In the first part, the narrator has three separate visions:

1 While reading the newspaper account of a murder, he 'seemed to see that bedroom' where the victim's body was discovered.
2 Immediately afterwards, looking out of his window into Piccadilly below, he sees one man in pursuit of another; both men stare up at him.
3 Later, in his own bedroom, he sees, beckoning from the dressing-room, the Piccadilly pursuer.

In the second part of the story, these mysterious and seemingly gratuitous visions of two men make sense when the narrator is summoned to serve on a jury. In the accused, he recognizes the man who was *being* chased along Piccadilly.

We have already been prepared for a strange event, and specifically for a paranormal occurrence, at the beginning of the narrative before the visions occur. In a kind of prologue, the narrator reflects on how difficult it is to recount subjective, psychological experiences, such as 'some singular presentiment, impulse, vagary of thought, vision (so-called), dream, or other remarkable mental impression' (474). Once he is in court and recognizes who the accused is, the narrator understands that the man in pursuit in Piccadilly (and who also beckoned from the narrator's dressing-room) was the victim. He, too, is present at the trial, but the narrator is certain that he is unperceived by anyone but himself. The mystery of *why* the apparition has appeared is resolved early. As the narrator explains: 'I came to the conclusion that on the first occasion [in Piccadilly] it had sought to fasten itself upon my memory, and that on the second occasion [in the dressing-room] it had made sure of being immediately remembered' (477). This interpretation is given weight when we later learn that the murdered man seemed satisfied when the narrator was about to deliver a verdict of guilty (484). Obviously, we are confronted with the stereotyped plot schema often encountered in tales of the disjunctive mode: the restless spirit who works to see justice done.

Even so, 'To Be Taken with a Grain of Salt' is an important stage before the paranormal mode. The narrative strategies are geared towards resolving the dilemma introduced at the start: how do you make subjective psychological experiences – presentiments, visions, or other 'remarkable mental impressions' – credible? The narrator solves this dilemma by strengthening the force of his authentication: that is, he mitigates his subjectivity by adopting a legalistic style reminiscent of a brief: 'It is essential that this fact be remembered' (475); 'Of that I am as strictly sure as of every other statement that I make here' (478); 'I do not theorise upon it; I accurately state it, and there leave it' (482); 'I must not omit, as a matter of fact ...' (483). He quotes his doctor as to his mental balance and rationality: 'I am assured by my renowned doctor that my real state of health at that time justifies no stronger description [than dyspepsia], and I quote his own from his written answer to my request for it' (476).

The narrator is equally pleased to point to his lack of imagination, showing that he is not given to flights of fancy: 'It was in no romantic place that I had this curious sensation, but in Chambers in Piccadilly.' And although his strange visions are preceded by a shiver that causes his chair to move slightly, he is quick to add that 'the chair ran easily on castors' (475). In these remarks he indicates not only that he is rational, but also that he is no believer in spiritualism. The answer is not to be looked for in those quarters, he seems to say, and clearly he knows what he is talking about. He is well acquainted with spiritualist theories, having studied particular cases, which he mentions. He lets drop the term 'spectral illusion' and the name 'Sir David Brewster' (474) to make his point.[16] His use of an actual (historical) name, by the way, is a metonymic transfer: Brewster's name stands for all those engaged in

Charles Dickens: Tradition and Transition 63

investigating and debunking spiritualism, and becomes part of the same code to which 'spectral illusion' belongs.

Occasionally, the narrator remembers imperfectly an important detail, a lapse which might be thought to weigh against his objectivity. But when that happens, he points frankly to the omission. Since it is difficult, after all, to credit too flawless a memory, his frankness only reinforces our sense that he is objective, or is doing his best to be: 'But this must not be received as a positive assertion, for I am not completely satisfied in my mind on either point' (478).

The narrator discovers that in representing the experiences of others, he has yet another means of objectifying his account: some of them were shared. The vision in his dressing-room was shared by his valet; in the jury room, his touch momentarily conveys to the night guard the ability to perceive the murdered man, so that the experience is, again, a common one; it is true that only the narrator claims to be able to see the apparition, but he carefully notes that its proximity to witnesses, spectators, the judge, and so on, causes trepidation, that it can 'invisibly, dumbly, and darkly overshadow their minds' (482). And, after the narrator sees the apparition making the rounds of the jurors' beds, as though communicating with them telepathically, each one confesses to having dreamt of the murdered man. Lastly, the murderer, found guilty, is heard to describe a similar experience: he declares that the narrator (who is the jury foreman) visited him during the night to put a rope around his neck.

True to form, the narrator never ventures to explain the mechanisms of his odd experience. He remarks simply that 'the Appearance,' as he calls it, seemed to be 'prevented, by laws to which I was not amenable, from fully revealing itself to others' (482). He does not theorize, he does not doubt his senses, and he presents the apparition as any other fact.

Where does the fictional world of 'To Be Taken with a Grain of Salt' stand with respect to the modes? It has most in common with the disjunctive and the paranormal modes – as we recall, a narrative can exemplify two or even more modes. On the one hand, the narrator's speculations and clairvoyant experience have prepared us for the possible expansion of the natural domain. Knowledge in the form of a 'veridical hallucination,' as Richet called such visions as the narrator's, might be an impression picked up through uncharted channels. On the other hand, the vehicle of the knowledge is the murdered man, who behaves like the stereotypical ghost rather than an extrasensory impression. 'To Be Taken with a Grain of Salt' might accurately be called a prototype of the paranormal mode. It is primitive (prototypical) in that the epistemic questions of the first part are not answered on epistemic grounds in the second. The narrator's speculations about paranormal occurrences, the psychological problems he raises, and his own experience dissolve, in the end, in a supernatural interpretation. His visions, it seems, are not the mind's translation of knowledge gained paranormally, but the visitations of a supernatural being. Such a spiritualist resolution for a paranormal experience is inconsistent with the epistemic questions the narrator has raised. The ghost, in effect, pre-empts any analysis of the phenomenon originally described. Most notable in this respect are the dead man's bizarre courtroom antics: from the hands of a court officer, he snatches a miniature (destined for the jury anyway), and personally conveys it to the narrator, miraculously without being detected (481). He acts within the natural domain for a set purpose, and is capable of influencing its inhabitants. The narrator he manipulates by virtue of the man's ability to 'see' the crime re-enacted; the others he acts upon by giving them 'the creeps.'

The murdered man brings spiritualism to mind in many ways, all stereotypical: he moves seemingly without touching the ground (475) and appears and disappears in otherwise inaccessible or impenetrable rooms, especially at night (476–7; 480); he speaks (to the narrator only) in a 'low and hollow tone' (481), and has a face 'drained of blood' (481), 'the colour of impure wax' (476). Most dramatic is his departure: when the verdict of guilty is pronounced, he disappears wonderfully into a 'great grey veil.' The courtroom itself, a gloomy Gothic setting, is heavy with the 'cloud of fog and breath' (478) that has penetrated from without, with 'black vapour hanging like a murky curtain outside the great windows' (478).

All the same, 'To Be Taken with a Grain of Salt' is quite different from *A Christmas Carol* and the stories embedded in *Pickwick* Papers. As we have seen, it is replete with traditional elements, but its style is sober and humourless. Perhaps most revealing is the title, with its hint of scepticism, incompatible with the narrator's attempts to authenticate his first-hand experience. The paranormal mode is incipient.

In 1861, Dickens published 'Four Stories' in *All the Year Round*. The first purports to be a true account of the strange experience of Mr H., a well-known London portrait painter. On October 5, Dickens published a revision (*AYR*, 36–43) where he claims that the real Mr H. had sent to the 'conductor of the journal' a corrected account of his adventure;

Charles Dickens: Tradition and Transition   65

this tale he calls 'Mr H.'s Own Narrative.' The device of introducing a narrative as someone else's true story, though not novel, functions as a means of authentication. The conductor insists that the story is firsthand and untampered with, and that Mr H. has himself corrected the proofs. In this way the conductor avoids acting as a filter for the narrative that follows; so far does he place himself from the narrated events, that he even refuses to enter upon a 'theory of our own towards the explanation of any part of this remarkable narrative' (36).

The narrative is structured as a mystery story with two planes which we will simply call *the vertical* and *the horizontal*. Along the vertical plane are the questions which must be solved: who is the mysterious girl in black, what is her significance to the artist, who is Mr Lute? The question of prime importance, when all the others have been answered, will be how or by what means the events occur. (It is on this plane, incidentally, that 'To Be Taken with a Grain of Salt' failed us, by offering a second vertical plane which itself begged further explanations.) On the horizontal axis of 'Mr H.'s Own Narrative,' solutions and false solutions are offered as the plot unfolds.

Mr H. is commissioned to paint the portrait of Mr and Mrs Kirkbeck. An oversight results in a delay of some months before he acquires their address by chance. In September, on his way to the Kirkbecks, he meets on the train a pretty young girl dressed in black. They converse, and he finds himself intrigued. Two mysteries subsequently present themselves for solution, each consisting of two apparently inexplicable circumstances.

The first mystery takes shape when the girl in black arrives at the Kirkbecks before Mr H., a seemingly impossible feat since the artist had left her on a train bound for London. During their conversation before dinner, in private, she shows him an engraving of Lady M.A., whom she considers like her, and asks if he could paint her from memory. She does not reveal her identity; when Mr H. questions both a servant and the Kirkbecks, he learns that there is no such girl at their house. The same young woman then visits the artist in London towards Christmas, again carrying the engraving of Lady M.A., and this time presses him to paint her portrait. Because she enters his studio unannounced, Mr H. cannot understand how she came to be in his house. A plausible and natural solution is put forward, although it ultimately proves to be false: the girl may have walked in through the front door, which the maid left open when she went across the street. The first mystery, then, is the identity of the strange young woman, a girl no one else has seen and who, for some reason, goes to some trouble to commission Mr H. As she tells him, much depends on his painting her portrait (40).

A mix-up in train schedules gets the second mystery under way; Mr H., on his way to another commission, is forced to spend the night in the town of Lichfield. To pass the time, he decides to write to an acquaintance living there; unaccountably he mistakes his friend's name (Clyne) and instead summons to the station a stranger, Mr Lute. To Mr H.'s surprise, Mr Lute claims to have been hoping to see him, and invites him home to paint his daughter's portrait. Through the artist's conversations with Mr Lute's teenaged daughter, Maria, the identity of the girl in black is brought to light, and so the first mystery is unravelled. But before this, a piece of seemingly unrelated information provides a false lead: Mr Lute is thought to be insane, suffering from 'fearful delusions' since the death of his elder daughter, Caroline. A portrait of the girl might be an antidote to his obsession. Mr H.'s arrival in Lichfield therefore appears to be a happy coincidence, independent of the first mystery. Only when Maria mentions that Caroline was very like an engraving of Lady M.A. does the artist recall the girl in black and bring out the two sketches made on the occasion of her visit to his studio. By identifying the subject of the sketches as her sister, Maria establishes a connection between the girl in black and the dead Caroline. Both the sketches and the engraving of Lady M.A. confirm this. Maria finds that the engraving has mysteriously disappeared – no doubt into the hands of Caroline, who had produced it ostentatiously for the artist at the Kirkbecks. Clearly, then, Mr H. has met Caroline's ghost. Mr Lute's story corroborates this as well, and ties up the last loose thread of the mystery: he has seen his daughter in a series of visions – first with a stranger in a railway carriage, next at dinner with several people, and finally standing by a man who was writing or drawing. The coincidences that brought Mr H. to Lichfield were orchestrated by the dead Caroline, who wished to cure her father. Caroline's spirit is thus able to act in the fictional world by bringing people together for her own purpose. It may also have been she who caused the mix-up with the train schedule that led to the painter's presence in Lichfield. Certainly she manipulated the artist's consciousness by planting in his mind her father's name, and perhaps prepared her father, through visions, to recognize Mr H. on his arrival.

Once again, Dickens has created a story of the disjunctive mode; but here, too, there is overlap. Mr H. seems to have some special perceptual abilities, though they may be purely the result of Caroline's intervention. But Mr Lute's visions, even if indirectly brought about by his dead daughter, are, in form, altogether paranormal. He does not see or encounter a ghost; he witnesses, in his mind, something taking place elsewhere; certainly Mr H., who is also in his visions, is no ghost. His experiences of 'seeing at a distance' seem to be simultaneous with the events themselves.

THE PARANORMAL MODE

In each of the transitional stories analysed above, the features of the paranormal mode remain incipient, undeveloped. The juryman, for all his logic and rationality towards his experience in 'To Be Taken with a Grain of Salt,' does not dismiss the paranormal, yet the tale falls into its own narrative trap. In 'Mr H's Own Narrative,' Mr Lute, it is true, experiences clairvoyance; but it is also true that Mr H. encounters a ghost. The epistemic questions that arise when the tale verges on the paranormal mode are ousted by the supernatural. In 'The Signal-Man,' just the opposite happens: when the supernatural is introduced, it is at once rejected. The narrative continually resists the supernatural/natural opposition in favour of the structure of the paranormal mode.

'The Signal-Man,' on the rare occasions when it is analysed, is generally studied as an independent short story. It in fact comprises chapter 4 of the set *Mugby Junction* (1866),[17] to which it is linked by the motif of trains. The protagonist of *Mugby Junction*, Mr Jackson – nicknamed 'The Gentleman for Nowhere' – arrives in Mugby Junction by one of its seven railway lines to escape his unhappy past. His interest in life is renewed by a chance friendship with a paralysed young woman, Phoebe. Settling in Mugby Junction, Jackson collects tales from and about passing railway travellers to relate to the confined Phoebe. Chapters 3 ('Main Line: The Boy at Mugby') and 4 ('No. 1 Branchline: The Signal-Man') are first-person narratives introduced by the statement: 'Here follows the substance of what was seen, heard or otherwise picked up, by the Gentleman for Nowhere in his careful study of the Junction' (533; ch. 2). The boy at Mugby tells his own story, which is not fantastic, while 'The Signal-Man' is related by an anonymous first-person narrator. It is impossible to determine whether this narrator is Mr Jackson himself, or an unidentified person whose story is reproduced by Mr Jackson, for no clue is given in the text.

The story poses a fundamental epistemological question: when a succession of mysterious events appears to be coincidence, is there not perhaps some other force at work and coincidence a mere label for what has not yet been identified?

The narrator of 'The Signal-Man' is only marginally involved in the narrated events. His main function is traditional; that is, he tells a story. He reports on the events he himself has witnessed and he mediates the accounts of the other characters. But he has a further, and more important, role. He becomes the focus for the authentication of all of the threads of the story, not just his own. He alone looks for and discovers links between the different characters' experiences, and he does so by collecting and interpreting a variety of clues. He forms, evaluates, and changes his hypothesis by comparing and synthesizing information from three independent sources:

1 From the signal-man, who tells him about a spectre gesticulating at the tunnel entrance;
2 From his own private experience of assigning words to the gestures described by the signal-man;
3 From the engine-driver, who accidentally runs down the signal-man, and whose words and gestures at that moment are of great significance.

While the narrator is putting together the clues, he uses a cognitive strategy that leads him progressively from irrational to rational interpretations, from the supernatural to the paranormal. We see this from the beginning, when he first arrives at the cutting where the signal-man looks after his stretch of tracks. The description of that uninviting habitat evokes mystery and strangeness, 'the perspective one way only a crooked prolongation of this great dungeon; the shorter perspective in the other direction terminating in a gloomy red light, and the gloomier entrance to a black tunnel, in whose massive architecture there was a barbarous, depressing, and forbidding air ...' (545). This is Gothic staging and more: it portends death. The phrase 'earthy, deadly smell' expresses semes readily associated with the lexemes 'dungeon' and 'tomb' – dankness, darkness, airlessness, death (546). Indeed, the signal-man's environs are both dungeon and tomb, for he rarely escapes his place of isolation and will die there.

Not surprisingly, the narrator feels 'as if I had left the natural world' (546). The supernatural is introduced into the fictional world by means of a counterfactual statement which expresses the narrator's reaction to the gloom of the cutting. Immediately afterwards, though, the narrator avoids referring explicitly to the supernatural. He tells the signal-man, 'You look at me as if you had a dread of me' (546), where we might expect the commonplace 'as if you had seen a ghost.'

The signal-man's story accounts for his bizarre behaviour on seeing the narrator. Three times he has seen at the tunnel's entrance a figure making warning gestures. The first time, it called out the very words the narrator used to greet the signal-man – 'Halloa! Below there!' (552). The second time, it stood silently before the red danger-light, making a mourning gesture (which the narrator, on being told, associates with the stone figures on tombs). After both incidents, there followed tragic train disasters. The seme of death is revived and linked here to the tunnel (553). On its third appearance, the figure makes a gesture to which the narrator assigns the words 'For God's sake, clear the way!' (554). The signal-man has observed similarities between the spectre and the narrator other than the words used by both. For instance, at the narrator's arrival, he is 'steeped in the glow of an angry sunset' (analogous to the red danger-light); he shades his eyes with his hand, a movement that, to the signal-man, corresponds to one of the figure's gestures. And, after each of the figure's appearances, a train disaster occurs. Compare this with the moment of the narrator's greeting, when a train roars out of the tunnel, and we can understand the signal-man's expectation of yet another disaster.[18]

The signal-man's terms for the figure are interesting, because they become more and more definite in meaning as suspense mounts. Opening the subject with the narrator, he explains: 'I took you for some one else yesterday evening' (551). The vague and neutral pronoun becomes emphatic, almost insistent, when the narrator capitalizes it: 'this Some one else standing by the red light near the tunnel' (552). As the signal-man continues his description, he substitutes the still vaguer 'figure,' a term he also uses to designate the distance-markers within the tunnel (552). In one instance he employs the non-committal word 'Appearance.' When he narrates the second incident, he calls the phenomenon 'spectre' (553), a word which may denote a haunting presentiment, or so the *OED* tells us. Thereafter the signal-man is uniform in his use of this word, except for one early instance where he calls the phenomenon 'ghost' (553). This word, sometimes used synonymously with 'spectre,' more frequently denotes the soul of a dead person. The signal-man therefore seems to be undecided about the creature's status (natural or supernatural) as well as its function.

Only briefly does the narrator find himself considering the supernatural, first when he encounters the signal-man and confesses, 'The monstrous thought came into my mind ... that this was a spirit, not a man.' His second allusion to it is subtle and oblique, and occurs on his final visit to the cutting, after the signal-man has been killed. Without knowing it, he is seeing the engine-driver re-enacting his part in the accident near the mouth of the tunnel; because the man fits the signal-man's description of the spectre, the narrator is for a moment 'seized upon' by a 'thrill' and 'oppressed' by a 'nameless horror' until 'I saw that this appearance of a man was a man indeed' (557). In the first instance, the narrator restores rationality by pursuing natural explanations. Has the signal-man's isolation taken its toll on his mind?[19] Have his senses merely been deceived by the wind and the light (552)? Though the narrator claims to 'put aside all question of reality or unreality,' it is telling that he resolves to accompany the signal-man to a doctor. His third natural explanation is 'coincidence': 'remarkable coincidences did continually occur,' and 'men of common sense did not allow much for coincidence in making the ordinary calculations of life' (553).[20] In the second instance, he compensates for his lapse into the supernatural by deciding that the signal-man has caused a train disaster through carelessness, without knowing, of course, that the man has just been killed.

Even so, just as he has rejected the supernatural explanation (after all, only the signal-man saw the spectre), the narrator is forced to abandon his rather standard, natural explanations after he comes to know the circumstances of the signal-man's death. If there had been only a single subjective experience – that of the signal-man – the explanations might have remained plausible. But the three separate events are linked in what can be described a *paranormal causal chain*, as follows:

1 In his mind, the narrator assigns words to the gestures of a spectre he has only heard about from the signal-man.
2 When the narrator arrives for the last time at the cutting, just after the signal-man is killed, he sees the engine-driver re-enacting his part in the accident, and mistakes him for the spectre.
3 The engine-driver's gesticulations exactly reproduce the spectre's, as originally demonstrated by the signal-man, while his words are those the narrator had privately assigned to the spectre.

The narrator's experience authenticates the signal-man's, while the engine-driver's authenticates both. Thus, the signal-man's encounters with the spectre logically acquire the status of a precognitive experience.[21] This has been skilfully constructed in the text: as the train comes through the tunnel, the engine-driver sees the signal-man 'like as if I saw him down a perspective glass' (558). From the point of view of the signal-man, the engine-driver is the image of the spectre at the tunnel entrance. The engine-driver, bearing down on the signal-man from within the tunnel, sees him from the spectre's perspective. This is the second time the signal-man has mistaken a person for the spectre, the first occasion being the narrator's arrival. With the details of this accident, the narrative forms a complete circle, for the narrator at the start sees the signal-man's figure foreshortened and in shadow – as though through a 'perspective glass' or, indeed, a tunnel.

For some unexplained reason, the signal-man is peculiarly sensitive to disasters about to happen, and it is he who poses the most trenchant questions about the elusiveness of paranormal phenomena. First, he wonders why the spectre is not more precise about when and where the disasters will occur, and why it does not appear to somebody with more 'power to act.' Second, he puts his finger on the precognitive paradox: backward causation. Do such forewarnings mean that the disasters can be averted? Can the course of an event be changed by knowing about it beforehand? (556).[22]

In this triple perspective, the spectre is decidedly not supernatural; nor is it natural in the limited, standard sense of the word, which would ascribe it to imagination, hallucination, and so on. It foretokens the engine-driver and is a metonymy of the signal-man's own death. The spectre is authenticated as a paranormal phenomenon, and it is significant that the authentication occurs by means of the other characters' *independent* experiences; individually those experiences are unremarkable, yet they are striking in conjunction with the signal-man's.

With 'The Signal-Man,' Dickens has woven together elements from the traditional fantastic and mystery narratives. From the traditional modes he has borrowed a motif, the spectre, which he then transforms by interpreting it as a phenomenon that belongs within an expanded natural domain. From mystery narratives he has borrowed the epistemic strategies which go into the solving of mysteries – gathering clues, synthesizing the various characters' accounts, collecting and comparing clues, and making deductions (hypotheses). In this way,

72 Possible Worlds of the Fantastic

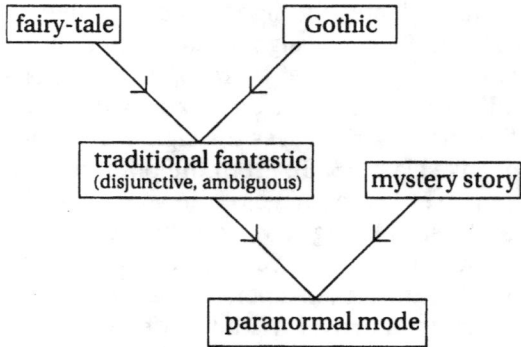

Figure 2

Dickens restructured a fictional world and fashioned his own brand of paranormal fiction.

Dickens's fantastic developed with remarkable consistency; figure 2 shows how the traditional narrative categories are interrelated in his work and how they lead to the paranormal mode.

Dickens's traditional fantastic tales utilize elements of the fairy-tale and the Gothic, as we have seen with *A Christmas Carol* and the tales embedded in *Pickwick Papers*. 'Mr H.'s Own Narrative' uses the mystery story structure to deal with a paranormal phenomenon, in such a way that the story would be situated on the line between *mystery story* and *paranormal*. Between *traditional fantastic* and *mystery story* is 'To Be Taken with a Grain of Salt,' a tale that attempts, with its speculations on paranormal phenomena, to confine the events to the natural domain, though it fails to do so; it, too, borrows from the *Gothic* and from the *mystery story* structure. In 'To Be Read at Dusk' we also find features of the paranormal mode, but it displays many devices more typical of the disjunctive mode. The mystery of the bride's disappearance in Baptista's narrative is of secondary significance, as a dénouement to the woman's precognitive dream, and goes unsolved. The structure of the paranormal mode is best developed in 'The Signal-Man,' though its play of questions and answers betrays its mystery story origins.

Since Dickens's death, it has been periodically fashionable to dismiss his work as an extravagant bow to the tastes of the general public. But the coherency and consistency of his development suggest that he was better than that; in spite of what some critics say, he had artistic principles and some sound practices. As to his exploration of spiritualism and paranormal phenomena in his fiction, it is just that: an *exploration* of the possible, of the potential, in a variety of forms. The other commonplace popular with critics is that Dickens neglected the psychology of his characters. Both criticisms seem to me cheap, empty, and dated, particularly if we look at 'The Signal-Man,' which has been perhaps the most neglected of Dickens's works. Both the signal-man's and the narrator's psychologies are subtly etched in the personal nature of their cognitive experiences and, indeed, through the very elusiveness of paranormal phenomena.

5

Ivan Sergeevich Turgenev: Tentative Beginnings

If the transformations in Dickens's fantastic tales correspond roughly to the order in which they were written, the same cannot be said of Turgenev's. Where Dickens moved fairly consistently towards the paranormal mode, Turgenev juggled with a variety of modes. For instance, in 'Knock! ... Knock! ... Knock! ...' [Stuk! ... stuk! ... stuk! ...] (1871), two rather primitive supernatural incidents are, respectively, disauthenticated and made ambiguous. Yet the story appeared after 'An Unhappy Girl' [Neschastnaya] (1869), where there is a suggestion of the paranormal in the dénouement. In 'Faust' (1856), a very early tale, the secondary plot exemplifies the paranormal mode; it is concerned with the nature of a special rapport, between lovers in the main plot (the narrator and Vera) and between the living and the dead in the subplot (Vera and her mother). But his traditional 'fantasy,' as he called 'Phantasms' [Prizraki] (1864), followed years afterwards.[1] 'The Dream' [Son] (1877) looks further, to the psychological and genetic bonds of heredity as the channels that permit paranormal communication.

Like both Dickens and Maupassant, Turgenev wrote fantastic tales along with his realistic novels in which, incidentally, we find scattered a few allusions to the fantastic. *Smoke* [*Dym*] (1867) has a celebrated medium fail dismally to mesmerize a crab (ch. 15). Critic Marina Ledkovsky mentions the character Irina in *Smoke,* and Mar'ya Polozova of *Spring Torrents* [*Veshnie vody*] (1872), two 'predatory women' who are 'subtly presented as endowed with demonic power.' Irina is disposed by heredity towards sorcery (her ancestors were accused of witchcraft) and uses it to 'bewitch' Litvinov. The sensual Mar'ya Polozova believes in love potions and plies her 'demonic charms' lavishly to 'possess'

Sanin (Ledkovsky 1973, 55, 56). The possession and bewitching are metaphorical, of course, but not less meaningful for that.

For the Russian critic Gruzinsky, Turgenev characteristically 'treads cautiously and deliberately along the edge of a precipice which separates the possible from the impossible' (1918, 212). His assessment is apt for the traditional tales 'Phantasms,' 'Father Aleksey's Tale,' and 'The Dog,' where the status of the supernatural is indeterminate. Like Dickens's traditional fantastic stories, they focus on the character's direct contact with the supposedly supernatural.

Seven of Turgenev's tales will be discussed in detail. There are three tales of the traditional modes, 'Phantasms,' 'Father Aleksey's Tale' [Rasskaz otsa Alekseya] (1877) and 'The Dog' [Sobaka] (1866). In the next three, 'A Strange Story' [Strannaya istoriya] (1870),[2] 'The Song of Triumphant Love' [Pesn' torzhestvuyushchey liubvi] (1881), and 'Klara Milich (After Death)' [Klara Milich (Posle smerti)] (1883), the paranormal mode is incipient, its fictional world structure not mature. We do see, though, the beginnings of stylistic and semantic devices characteristic of the paranormal mode. 'A Strange Story' shares with this group as a whole its treatment of the mysterious power of the will and, with 'The Dog,' its preoccupation with sectarianism. As Turgenev's most accomplished tale of the paranormal mode 'The Dream' will be analysed separately.

THE TRADITIONAL FANTASTIC

'Phantasms,' Turgenev insisted, is not an allegory, but a 'series of pictures' [ryad kartin], a 'series of spiritual *dissolving views*' [ryad kakikh-to dushevnykh *dissolving views*] (1963b, 5: 179).[3] The narrator is transported to distant lands at various moments in history by the mysterious, hazy woman, Ellis. She shows him nature at its most terrifying off the coast of the Isle of Wight. She takes him to the Black Forest, the 'vanity fair' of a decadent Paris, the Volga of Stenka Razin, and to Lago Maggiore, where he is charmed by a beautiful singer.[4] Chased by a menacing, evil yellow mist, they fall to the ground and Ellis vanishes.

'Phantasms' has something in common with Dickens's *A Christmas Carol*. Like Scrooge, Turgenev's narrator is buoyed along on the air by a creature for whom time and space are irrelevant; both characters are unsettled and altered by their visions.[5] Unlike *A Christmas Carol*, which is a third-person narrative, Turgenev's tale is told subjectively, in the first person.

Dessaix considers 'Phantasms' a throwback to Hoffmann, Gogol', and Poe; to *l'école frénétique*, with its 'Gothic and Romantic elements' (1979, xi). The story's structure is more complex than this, I believe. At three distinct stages, Turgenev constructs and dismantles the fictional worlds of three modes – the paranormal, the ambiguous, and the disjunctive, in that order, so that we might loosely call 'Phantasms' the evolution of the paranormal mode in reverse, or an inverted history of the fantastic. Keeping in mind his comment about the 'series of pictures,' I would even venture to call 'Phantasms' a *study* of the fantastic. The features of the various modes are flaunted rather obviously.

The fantastic is triggered by a remark that seems to set the stage for paranormal events of the sort we were led to expect from the narrator's speculations in Dickens's 'To Be Taken with a Grain of Salt.' Turgenev's narrator has clearly just come from a séance on the night of Ellis's appearance. Whatever he saw or failed to see is left unsaid: 'The devil take those table-tipping idiocies! They only upset the nerves' ((9: 77; ch. 1; A1).[6]

In this state of nervous sleeplessness he twice hears the sound of a chord in his room. He rationalizes the experience, without fear, by modalizing it: 'I *seemed* to hear, *as if* in the room ...' (9: 77; ch. 1; A2; my emphasis). The second time, he is slightly alarmed but reflects: 'just see what one can bring oneself to' (9: 77; ch. 1; A3). His scepticism, already apparent from his gibe at table-tipping, provides a rational reason for the sounds – the atmosphere of the séance has excited his imagination. Here, the paranormal functions as a purely literary device for motivating the succeeding events.

The ambiguous mode is signalled by the narrator's growing doubts. Is he sane? Did he have a 'remarkable dream'? The narrator's dream is, in fact, a continuation of what he has experienced in trying to fall asleep – it is a dream within a dream. When he first heard the sound of a chord, he personified the moon. It was 'hanging low in the sky, and staring me straight in the eye. White as chalk its light lay on the floor ...' (9: 77; ch. 1; A4). In the dream, the moonlight metaphor is literalized when the streak of light is transformed into a white, female figure who summons the narrator to join her.[7]

By acting on Ellis's request on her third visit, he in effect gives life to the phantom. He ceases to doubt and thereby brings the disjunctive mode into play, introducing the opposition between the natural and the supernatural and motivating his experience with Ellis. *Structurally*, though, neither his action nor his new-found certainty is motivated.

There is no authenticating force behind the narrator's acceptance of the creature's reality, nothing that compels him to believe in it; he simply does. In other words, only the fact of the narrator's acceptance, a purely subjective device, motivates the shift from the ambiguous to the disjunctive mode.

Immediately before the narrator's adventures, two devices are used which augur this shift. The first, pathetic fallacy, recalls the Gothic motifs Dickens was fond of: 'Not only did the sky grow red – the whole air suddenly became suffused with an almost unnatural crimson; the leaves and grass, as though covered with fresh lacquer, did not stir; in their stony immobility, in the sharp brilliancy of their outlines, in that commingling of a strong glow and death-like tranquillity, there was something strange, enigmatical' (9: 80; ch. 3; A5). The words 'unnatural,' 'death-like,' 'strange,' 'enigmatical,' are dramatic and create an appropriately ominous atmosphere. The second device brings Poe to mind. A large grey bird flies silently to the window, looks at the narrator, and flies off, an apparently ordinary incident which the narrator construes as an omen. 'I seemed to have got into a charmed circle' (9: 80; ch. 3; A6), he observes, signalling the end of ambiguity and a transition to the disjunctive mode, which will culminate in his meeting Ellis.

In the part of the tale which is ambiguous, the narrator is preoccupied with epistemic questions about Ellis: how is such a phenomenon possible? where does it come from? how can an immaterial being love, and be loved by, a material being? He fears the collision of irrationality and rationality. With the transition into the disjunctive mode, Ellis acquires fictional existence. The narrator's fear dissipates and the tenor of his questions changes. He is now concerned with Ellis's identity: 'What was Ellis, as a matter of fact? A vision, a wandering soul, an evil spirit, a sylph, a vampire? Sometimes it again seemed to me that Ellis was a woman whom I had formerly known ...' (9: 109; ch. 25; A7).

Ellis herself does not understand the narrator's questions; her only concrete answer is that she did not know him before (9: 85). As Muratov points out, Ellis's inability to reply – she herself may not know the answers – removes any possibility of solving the mystery of her identity. It is not merely undecided, but undecidable (1972, 12). None the less, Ellis's existence, and therefore the supernatural domain of the fictional world, is indirectly authenticated by the housekeeper's testimony. For the last time the narrator asks himself whether he is dreaming: 'But is it not in a dream that I am seeing all this?' ((9: 97; ch. 17; A8). His cautious phrasing and his use of particles (in the original) suggest that he doubts the validity of the question more than the visions themselves. But his housekeeper's confirmation of his nocturnal absences convinces him, finally, that his experiences are real (9: 97). Once the narrator becomes convinced that Ellis exists, he no longer feels the need to identify her.

More than one critic has called Ellis a vampire because the narrator closes his story with a complaint about anaemia.[8] Dostoevsky bemoaned this superfluous hint of vampirism in a letter to Turgenev: 'In your story, the creature that appears is explained as a vampire. In my opinion, this explanation is not necessary' (Turgenev 1967b, 12: 61; bk. 1; A9).[9] Whatever species of mythological creature Ellis might be doesn't really concern us. That is, her thematic category is of less relevance than the fact that her existence has been authenticated by the means available to the first-person narrator. She achieves full status as a supernatural entity in the fictional world, even without her precise nature or the cause of the narrator's anaemia being explained. At the same time, the narrator's speculation that Ellis may be a woman he once knew hints at a potential shift in the status of the supernatural. If this were so, Ellis might be a woman who, by some paranormal means, has managed to communicate with the narrator. Whether or not that woman is dead, the narrator's speculation brings the narrative full circle back to the séance and to the hint of the paranormal at the beginning of the story.

For Dessaix, 'Phantasms' is 'a fantastic view of things rather than a more rational view of fantastic things,' in contrast to Turgenev's later tales (1979, 106). And yet, is 'Phantasms' a way of looking at things, at the world? Is it not perhaps more interesting to read it, as I proposed above, as a survey, a panorama of the fantastic itself? Turgenev's own characterization seems to suggest it. Each segment of the narrative and each event, taken separately, is structurally and psychologically unmotivated. The story's coherence hinges on a purely literary motivation. Every new mode of this tale is generated from the previous one, successively laying bare the devices. Because the story begins (and, it would seem, ends) with an unelaborated paranormal episode, the paranormal mode is ranked with all the other modes. In other words, Turgenev links the paranormal to other modes of the fantastic, specifically the more traditional ambiguous and disjunctive modes. 'Phantasms' points to the fictionality of paranormal phenomena and sets them side by side with revenants and hauntings as well as realistic sketches of the natural domain. In this way, paranormal fictional events reveal their origins: they are a specific instance of the fantastic, of the imaginary phenomena which writers have never tired of cultivating.[10]

The title of the story is a significant expression of this literary motivation. The Russian word 'prizrak' refers to anything imaginary, fantastic; it connects the table-turning of the first part with the ambiguous apparition of the second part, and then with the supernatural of the last part. Death and destruction dominate the scenes shown to the narrator, though love and beauty are alluded to – at Lago Maggiore, in Ellis's declarations of love, and in the narrator's vague sense of having known her as a woman before. According to Dessaix, these antidotes to Schopenhauerian moral pessimism may be the narrator's last bulwark against dull tedium (1980, 108). Yet the narrator does not escape the void; Ellis, the spectre of death, and everything the narrator experiences before and after the encounter, are 'prizraki.' Love, beauty, and human existence are no less elusive, or transitory, or fictional than any other 'phantasm.'

A very different story is 'Father Aleksey's Tale,' which exemplifies the disjunctive mode. With that in mind, it will come as no surprise that it is linked intertextually to the fairy-tale and especially to Christian legend. It is a *skaz*[11] told by Father Aleksey to an anonymous enframing, mediating narrator. Many years elapse between the events and Aleksey's telling of them, and there is a further lapse of twenty years before the mediator puts Aleksey's oral story into writing. The events, then, are twice removed temporally from the version that we read, and are filtered through two narrators, neither of whom experienced them.

The tale originates *in* the act of storytelling. On one level, it is a tale about the fantastic experiences of Aleksey's son. On another, it is the self-portrait of the primary narrator, Aleksey, a holy man whose beliefs and whose very nature demand that he should tell a legend in the Christian tradition. Aleksey is 'father' in three senses: in the material sense of having a son, in the religious sense of being a priest, and, in the narrative sense, as the one who conceives the tale.

Aleksey's son, Yakov, is an intelligent and questioning man who undergoes a crisis of faith. As a clergyman, his father belonged to a special class, and Yakov was destined, as the sons of priests usually were, to become a priest himself. That is, except for his fatal inclination for the natural sciences, which leads him to abandon the seminary and take up medicine. As more than one critic has pointed out, he is one of the mid-century 'raznochintsy,' intellectuals who questioned the religious creed and adopted a rational, scientific world-view (Dessaix 1980, 116). Yakov trades Christianity for a religion of humanism.

The first allusion to the supernatural is Aleksey's report of his son having seen, as a youth, a little old green man in the forest. Yakov produced a strange nut which he said the man had given him. Later, as his religious crisis intensifies, he feels himself driven by a demon that tempts him away from faith and finally induces him to commit the sacrilegious act of spitting out the Communion bread.

Aleksey at first leans towards natural explanations for his son's transformation: drinking, gambling, and a weakness for women (11: 296). He dismisses these explanations when he finds no evidence for them, and considers instead whether his son has gone mad or is just deluded (11: 297, 298). But since ambiguity and indeterminacy are not in Father Aleksey's repertoire, he must yield to a supernatural explanation. He comes to accept the existence of the demon and opens his kit of Christian tools – prayer, incense, holy water, and a pilgrimage to Voronezh.

Nothing in Yakov's character disauthenticates the young man's claims. He was not a liar (11: 293), never worried his parents (11: 292), and was not mischievous (11: 293). He was a brilliant student, a loving son, and a humanitarian (11: 294). One of Aleksey's Christian 'tools' is Marfa Savishna, a devout and virtuous woman who Aleksey believes can help Yakov. The subplot of Yakov's relationship with her is not developed; we learn only that Marfa's piety and charity seem to have had a temporary or superficial effect on Yakov. But when Father Aleksey meets Marfa Savishna, he is shocked to see that the changes in Yakov's countenance have to some extent been transferred to hers. For him, it is proof of demoniac forces at work (11: 300).

The story of the strange nut, that first suggestion of the supernatural, establishes an intertextual link with the fairy-tale. Yakov brings the ostensibly magic object home and Aleksey examines it. He lays it aside to show the doctor, but the nut disappears and is not found again, a chance loss that is also a fairy-tale motif. This bit of objective evidence creates as well an intertext with other fantastic tales, such as the key in Villiers de l'Isle-Adam's 'Véra,' the strand of hair in Maupassant's 'The Apparition,' or the lock of hair in his 'The Hair.' The purpose of such physical (i.e., natural) objects being left behind is to authenticate the supernatural being to whom they belonged.

Christian legends about the Enemy of God are the other, and the most important, intertextual resource. On this level, the story is Father Aleksey's, not Yakov's. Aleksey's question about whether the demon appeared at the moment of his son's doubting is the first clue, implicitly, to the Enemy (11: 298), and Yakov's refusal to answer may be construed as confirmation. The tormentor's physical appearance also corresponds to legend: he is black and like a man, although the horns popularly associated with Satan are absent. And Yakov, who had once been 'a comely boy,' 'a pleasure to look at,' grows more and more devilish in his looks (11: 297). It is noteworthy, too, that the demon is usually designated (rather than named) by the pronouns 'he' [on], 'that one' [tot], and, in Aleksey's case, 'the evil power' [navazhdenie]. All of these are readily associated with taboo and the euphemisms of Russian folk speech.

In the demon's traditional, biblical function of seducer we find the connection with Christian legend made explicit: he addresses Yakov directly in the church at Voronezh and induces him to spit out the Communion bread. After Yakov's death, another feature of Father Aleksey's narration strengthens the bond with Christian legend as well as with folk legends about the possessed, or the 'undead.' His remark, 'but I do not want to believe that the Lord would judge him with his severe judgement ...' (11: 304; A10) is reminiscent of the parable of Jesus casting the devils out of the possessed into a herd of swine. Like Jesus, Aleksey is aware that the possessed person is a victim, and therefore not responsible in the eyes of God. Yakov's face after death gives Aleksey reason to believe that God will not judge harshly. Like the possessed man in the parable of the swine, who afterwards sat 'clothed and in his right mind' (Mark 5: 15), Yakov 'seemed to have grown young again and resembled the Yakov of days gone by. His face was so tranquil and pure, his hair curled in little rings, and there was a smile on his lips' (11: 304; A11).

The enframing narrator's prologue has already prepared us for the Christian legend by a metanarrative device. Aleksey's narrative performance, as it is revealed by the enframing narrator, is predetermined by his character. We are told that Aleksey is not like most of the priests the narrator has encountered, who are 'pretty much of one pattern, and made after one model' – corrupt, in other words (11: 291). He is a holy man in the best sense, asking nothing for himself and bearing physical traces of great suffering, of the Christian tried: 'I have never seen in any human face a more sorrowful, thoroughly listless expression – what is called "downcast"' (11: 291; A12).

These traits at once give Father Aleksey individuality as a fictional person and ordain the sort of narrative that a man of his cast must spin. More than anything else, his stylistic imprint suggests that the tale is *his* story, rather than Yakov's. The enframing narrator points to the absence of 'seminary and provincial mannerisms and turns of phrase' (11: 292; A13). Aleksey's *skaz* combines the colloquial speech [prostorechie] of the folk storyteller with the Church Slavonic phraseology of Christian legend.[12] Aleksey cannot *but* tell a story which is essentially a Christian legend. That it happens to be about his own son's fate is incidental. Transposed by the storyteller onto a higher level, Yakov's life story becomes yet another legend about the workings of the Enemy of God, of the unexpected and uncalled for meddling of evil creatures into the everyday lives of innocent mortals.

'The Dog,' even more clearly than the two preceding tales, illustrates how the *skaz* technique inherited from Gogol' produces a fantastic tale. At first blush, the story seems to make sense only as a literary joke. It was ill received by contemporary critics and many considered it a failure. Botkin, to whom Turgenev had read the tale before its publication, wrote that 'The Dog' was an unsuccessful mix of tragedy and comedy. 'In art, nothing is worse than something that is neither one thing nor the other' (Letter of 4 June (23 May) 1864; Brodsky, ed. 1930, 202–3).[13]

'The Dog' may be read as the storyteller's casual, even facetious, response to the philosophical question posed in the prologue: does the supernatural exist? Those hoping for a scientific or philosophical answer are bound to be disappointed, for the story offers a *literary* solution to the puzzle. The matter is introduced by a state councillor who asks, in the not very fitting role of philosopher, 'but if we admit the possibility of the supernatural, the possibility of its intervention in real life, then allow me to ask what role sound reason should play after this?' (9: 123; A14). This pose of the sceptical positivist is treated with irony in the enframing narrator's description of him: 'Anton Stepanych ... served in some sort of ingenious department and, since he spoke with great care, firmly, and in a bass voice, enjoyed universal esteem' (9: 123; A15).

The 'philosophical challenge' is taken up by Porfiry Kapitonych, who narrates the apparently straightforward, humorous tale about a faithful dog who saves his master from two disasters: an attack by a rabid dog and marriage to a moody, capricious woman. He purchases 'Treasure' [Trezorushka], the dog who will rescue him, after he is visited by a supernatural dog.[14] In this way, a tale about ordinary, natural incidents is cloaked in a variety of supernatural motifs, and these are borrowed from two sources: the Russian folk-tale and the culture of the Schismatics, whose persistent mythological thinking is an important subcontext.[15] Both sources converge in the figure of Sergey Prokhorych Pervushin, who is as much a folk character as he is an Old Believer. Prokhorych, as he is known to his followers, exerts over Porfiry Kapitonych some kind of 'magnetic' influence which links him to the mythological world of superstitious belief. From their first encounter, Porfiry comments on Prokhorych's extraordinarily penetrating eyes and his own feeling of being 'cowed' by the man (9: 130). That Porfiry finds himself under the influence of a special power is clear when he is leaving Prokhorych: 'I bowed down to the ground, and didn't even rise; I felt such a fear of that man, and such submissiveness that, it seems, whatever he might have ordered I would have done at once!' (9: 131; A16).[16] The enigmatic Prokhorych correctly, as it turns out, interprets the supernatural dog's visitation.[17] It is a sign that someone is praying for Porfiry Kapitonych. Significantly, both men use the word 'vision' [viden'e] for the supernatural experience.

Dessaix finds 'The Dog' interesting primarily as one of Turgenev's two stories (the other, in his opinion, being 'The Dream') where 'the supernatural intrudes *unequivocally* on an equal footing with the operation of natural law' (1980, 125). But let's look a little more closely at the status of the supernatural here. Three sources apparently authenticate it: Porfiry has experienced the event and witnessed its outcome; his servant Fil'ka, after suspecting his master of drunkenness (9: 125), also hears the dog; and Vasily Vasil'ich, Porfiry's neighbour, both sees and hears the dog. Three witnesses, then, provide the testimony of their senses. Yet all of their experiences are mediated by Porfiry; that is, the secondary authentications of Fil'ka and Vasiliy Vasil'ich depend upon the authenticity of Porfiry's own storytelling act. And there is every reason to doubt it.

The enframing narrator explains that Porfiry had been a hussar and a landowner who gambled away his property. He has no social standing, no influential connections, and no talent, we are told. He simply lives by his spectacularly good luck. The first Schismatic he speaks with tells him that 'with luck' the famed Prokhorych will see him, and indeed he does. The happy result of that visit is Porfiry's escape from the rabid dog. His greatest good fortune, we are told, is that 'he obtained the post of overseer of public warehouses, a profitable, even honourable position, which did not require extraordinary talents: the warehouses themselves existed only in supposition, and it was not even known exactly what they were filled with' (9: 124; A17).

Porfiry's being an overseer of fictional warehouses blends perfectly with his status as a teller of tales. He is a consummate fictionalist whose skills mitigate the narrative authentication of the eyewitness accounts since, in Porfiry's storytelling, anything is possible. The distinction between 'natural' and 'supernatural' is irrelevant, for the success of his story does not depend on philosophical argument, but on his style and on the power of his performance. His digressions into the supernatural make his tale less commonplace and give it the savour of the unexpected. All the *skaz* devices are used to embroider it; colloquialisms, popular phrases, and folk expressions are mixed with poetic language, as in his description of the moon – the ordinariness of the words (round, big, yellow, flat) is in contrast to the poetic syntax (9: 136). That the *skaz* is successful is clear from the way his listeners participate. They interrupt with questions or comments, and continually reassure the storyteller that they want him to go on. At all times the narrative monologue is potentially dialogic. The listeners move the story along, encouraging the storyteller to heap detail upon detail.

The story is, as well, a comic travesty of the fantastic. A supernatural dog is introduced to explain why the narrator buys a real dog. Typically for the *skaz*, seriousness is blended with ironic humour. For instance, Porfiry dilates upon Vasiliy Vasil'ich's losses at cards, but then digresses to characteristics which have nothing to do with the tale: 'that neighbour of mine had a vast mind! He manipulated his mother-in-law, by the way, something wonderful: he palmed off an IOU on her, which means he chose the most sensitive moment! ... Now, that's really something, pulling a fast one on a mother-in-law, eh?' (9: 127; A18). Such apparent trivialities draw attention to Porfiry as narrator and as a performer of an improvised storytelling act.

In the best tradition of Gogolian social satire, the rabid dog is killed by a soldier who has never fired a shot in his life; equally absurd is the medal the soldier received for service in the War of 1812. But the strongest index of the comic *skaz* is a metonymic transfer, an intertextual pun or literary joke that connects 'The Dog' with a story by Gogol': the name of the man who sells Porfiry the real dog is *Shinel'*, or *Overcoat*, which is the title of one of Gogol's most famous tales.

As a storyteller's reply to a philosopher's question, 'The Dog' offers an interesting perspective on the fantastic, and perhaps more generally, if somewhat obviously, on literature. It seems to suggest that literature can take up philosophical questions in narrative; it can develop them stylistically, making them samples of a colourful, expressive, and national style. But fiction is neither science nor philosophy; it is play. It's all about weaving tales, not solving philosophical problems. Porfiry has told a good tale but certainly has not provided an argument for or against the supernatural. The question posed in the prologue remains unanswered; Anton Stepanych repeats it in the epilogue, while the enframing narrator closes with the remark, 'None of us found any answer, and we remained, as before, perplexed' (9: 139; A19).

THE INCIPIENT PARANORMAL

The subjection of the human will to a mysterious external power was Maupassant's particular interest, as we shall see in the next chapter. 'A Strange Story' is Turgenev's first fantastic tale of this sort, the first too in which the narrator speculates about the conditions of domination. At the time, it would have been politically loaded, and is often read as Turgenev's response to the social and political conditions of Russia in the 1860s.

Several narrative features link it to other of Turgenev's fantastic stories. An authorial filtering voice is established in a single, brief note: 'Fifteen years ago – *began Mr "X"* ...' (emphasis added). The reference to a Mr X using direct discourse indicates that the writer is not the person who underwent the experiences described; he is transcribing a tale told to him by Mr X, who becomes our first-person (*Ich*-form) narrator. As the 'fifteen years' reveals, a good deal of time has elapsed between the events and their telling, as was the case with Father Aleksey's tale. Since the story-line is quite complicated, I will briefly summarize it.

Mr 'X' arrives in a provincial town, on government business, and meets there a former acquaintance of his father's. He is intrigued by the man's daughter, Sofya, a childlike seventeen-year-old who plays the role of mother and housekeeper in her widowed father's household. The narrator pities her, and finds her 'enigmatic,' 'sincere,' a creature with 'a particular stamp' (10: 162). He meets her later at a ball, where they discuss her beliefs and she reveals her desire to embrace a life of humiliation (10: 176). She longs for a preceptor who will show her by his own example how to sacrifice herself. Two years later the narrator learns that Sofya has run off to parts unknown, and in the autumn he unexpectedly meets her at an inn. She has indeed humbled herself; degraded herself, rather, in becoming the servant of a filthy holy fool, the magnetizer Vasiliy. The narrator does not fail to point out his certainty that she is still 'pure.' Vasiliy – or, more precisely, his powers and their effect – is the pivot around which the narrator's and Sofya's stories revolve and where they converge.

Magnetism appears in three graduated manifestations: first as a personal experience; second, as the force that motivates the characters' interaction; and lastly, as a form of ideology. Conceptually, the term is heavily loaded. It is not just a synonym for 'Mesmerism' ('animal magnetism') or 'hypnosis.'

The narrator crosses Vasiliy's path when a waiter suggests that he go to the magnetizer for fun. Mr X's curiosity is excited when he hears that he will 'see the dead.' The local people revere Vasiliy as a mystic and 'a man of great wisdom' (10: 173), 'strong in divine things' (10; 165). Vasiliy's tippling foster mother tells the narrator to hold in his mind the thought of a dead friend and not to utter a word when her son makes his appearance. The experience is truly extraordinary: from the moment Vasiliy enters the room, Mr X is terrified. He is riveted by Vasiliy's eyes, and suffers a torpidity that makes him feel like a hare caught in the fiery gaze of a borzoi. Vasiliy is obscured by a mist, and the figure Mr X has in his mind – a long-dead tutor of unmistakable appearance – rises in his place. Byalyy has pointed out that the narrator depersonalizes Vasiliy into a force by calling him '*that one*' [*tot*] (10: 172; Turgenev's emphasis). This euphemistic pronoun and the adjectives 'persistent' [upornyy], 'oppressive' [tyazhëlyy], 'menacing' [groznyy], and 'sinister' [zloveshchiy] applied to Vasiliy's gaze heighten the sense of terror (Byalyy 1962, 215). What seems to be a taboo on naming Vasiliy may link him, Ledkovsky writes, with evil forces in much the way that the devil is first implied by the pronoun 'tot' in 'Father Aleksey's Tale' (1973, 108).

Meditating on his experience, Mr X. rejects the supernatural folk interpretation and arrives at what he deems a scientific explanation: 'Without a doubt that man possessed a remarkable magnetic power; acting, of course, on my nerves in some way incomprehensible to me, he had so clearly, so certainly evoked within me the image of the old man I was thinking of, that it seemed to me at last that I saw him before my eyes' (10: 173–4; A20). What he describes is similar to the hypnotic state as scientists came to understand it later in the nineteenth century. His explanation (seeing what his own thoughts had predetermined that he should see) is far removed from the popular notions about electro-biology and magnetism that led people to believe one could be induced to commit all sorts of improprieties. All the same, he finds it incomprehensible that Vasiliy could will him to believe that his internal thoughts were projected outward in a visible image of his dead tutor. This phenomenon Mr X calls 'metastasis' or 'the transposition of sensation' [perestanovlenie oshchushcheniy], a phenomenon well known to science, he claims, though its source remains 'amazing and mysterious' (10: 174).[18]

He never admits any other hypothesis. His conversation with Sofya at the ball proves that he does not incline to her mystical view of Vasiliy as 'one beloved of God' [bogougodnyy] (10: 175). He mocks the absence of empirical evidence for her beliefs and tries to explain to her the 'scientific' fact of magnetism. But Sofya, steadfast in her own convictions, is unmoved. Her desire for a preceptor springs from the Church's inability to satisfy her spiritual needs; she longs for higher knowledge than institutional religion offers. Vasiliy represents this higher knowledge because his superior abilities are, for her, divine in origin. From Sofya's point of view, the narrator's experience with Vasiliy is unremarkable, since the immortal souls of the dead may wander among the living unseen until they are called (10: 176).

Even though Vasiliy has no status with the official church, he is bound up with Russian popular religion: the magnetizer becomes a holy fool [yurodivyy] (10: 182). In this, the story has something in common with 'The Dog,' where Turgenev explored the relation between superior powers and the sectarian beliefs of the Russian folk. In a mythological world, one encounters individuals with supernatural powers.

Magnetism is first presented as Mr X's private experience, in an episode which concerned him alone and took place, as it were, in his own mind. Its second appearance, as the motivation for interaction, has to do with Sofya. Only at the end of the story do we (along with Mr X) grasp just what was so enigmatic and otherworldly about Sofya. And only in retrospect is it clear why she reacts so strongly to the narrator's remarks about Vasiliy. Her conversation with him at the ball told us something of her creed and inclinations, yet obviously concealed a close relationship with Vasiliy. Her faith in his piety, her desire for a preceptor and for humiliation were all hints of a course decided upon, of an intention, already formed, to place herself under his influence. As the narrator himself comes to understand, Sofya did not divorce words from deeds (10: 185). She therefore allows herself to be acted upon and, by means of this submission, to be brought to degradation. An attractive, well-bred, wealthy girl leaves her family to wait on a dirty, demented magnetizer. The narrator recognizes in her actions what we now call cultism. Sofya is hypnotised not so much by Vasiliy, but by what she takes him to represent. She bears physical traces of her fanatical devotion: 'to her former meditatively wonder-stricken expression another had been added – a resolute, almost daring, concentrated ecstatic expression. In this face, no trace of childishness was left' (10: 183; A21).

Magnetism as a social, ideological force is the third manifestation and comes into play at this point. Sofya is stimulated to act by her acceptance of an ideology, her mystical-religious interpretation of Vasiliy's powers as divine. Although the narrator claims not to understand Sofya's behaviour or her motives for selecting Vasiliy, he does seem to grasp that her subjugation has a socio-ideological dimension: 'I did not condemn her, just as afterwards I did not condemn other young girls who also sacrificed everything to what *they* deemed right, in which *they* discerned their calling' (10: 185; A22).

By generalizing Sofya's experience to all such girls, Mr X makes a political statement and, perhaps more interestingly, examines the political and social 'magnetism' of ideology, the charismatic appeal by which it operates. Sofya is as good as mesmerized by an ideology and the man she has elected to represent it. The narrator's expansion of the concept of magnetism to the socio-political level and his allusion to other girls like Sofya grounds the story in the Russian social context of the 1860s, when the radical intelligentsia was drawing young people away from their homes with its revolutionary message (called populism [narodnichestvo] in the 1870s). Vasiliy is a holy fool, but his power also stands for other no less alluring ideologies.[19]

Quite strikingly, magnetism determines even the structure of 'A Strange Story,' especially its plot composition. The two strands of the plot are the narrator's and Sofya's experiences with the 'magnetizer,' and these alternate, switching back and forth suddenly. Mr X's mention of his visit to Sofya's father and his meeting the girl is a preface to the second plot strand. For a time, the two strands seem to have little in common and run along separately. The narrator's dialogue with Sofya at the ball establishes a tenuous connection. Only when her leaving home is explained do they converge. The plot structure, then, is iconic: the two strands for a period run parallel and *repel* one another like the opposite poles of a magnet; they are finally *attracted* and joined in the story's resolution. Certain problems are caused by

Ivan Sergeevich Turgenev: Tentative Beginnings 89

these compositional intricacies. To bring the threads of the narrative together, Turgenev is obliged to abuse the device of the chance encounter; in addition, he has recourse to two shop-worn plot devices. First, the friend who by coincidence knows Sofya's father is abruptly introduced for no other purpose than to supply the information that Sofya has run away, and he is just as quickly dispatched. The second rather trite device, information gathered by eavesdropping, gives us the reason for the girl's flight: Mr X stops at an inn and overhears Sofya and her preceptor Vasiliy, through a crack in the wall. In spite of these hackneyed strategies, the iconic representation of magnetic repulsion and attraction in the narrative structure itself make 'A Strange Story' a remarkable step in Turgenev's development of the paranormal mode.

'The Song of Triumphant Love,' as Brang observes, is Turgenev's only tale to be set outside Russia (1977, 176), although 'The Dream,' which has no geographical markers, may well be, too. Its intertextuality is explicitly established by the enframing narrator, who characterizes the text as an ancient Italian *manuscrit trouvé*. The manuscript is precisely dated 1542, and there are indirect datings as well, in the textual references to Ariosto, to the son of Lucrezia Borgia – the second Ercole, Duke of Ferrara – and to the Holy Roman Emperor Charles. Even the prominence of art in the text functions as an index, for sixteenth-century Ferrara was an important cultural centre. These markers are strong ties to Renaissance works and style. Gabel', in a brief but interesting comparison, finds that the plot structure and composition of 'The Song of Triumphant Love' have much in common with formulaic Renaissance Italian love novellas, especially in its theme of the romantic triangle. The love of two of the characters and the obstacles they must overcome generate the story and its specific incidents. Such narratives often end with the death of one member of the triangle or the separation of the lovers. The Renaissance novellas, like Turgenev's narrative, lack psychological analysis (usually vital for Turgenev), and in both much attention is given to reproducing historical colour (Gabel' 1923, 218; see also Brang 1977, 177, and Ledkovsky 1973, 100). In the Italian Renaissance novella an enframing narrator often introduces his story by offering a reason for having written it. It has been remarked that the highly stylized language of Turgenev's story gives a sense of the period, and Koni claims that the 'tempo of the language symbolises the course of the action' (quoted in Gabel' 1923, 218). Perhaps it is more important to observe that even if Turgenev wrote this subtle, complex, and texturally dense tale under the inspiration of the Renaissance novella, he also substantially transformed the model.

As Gabel' points out, some of Turgenev's motifs are not to be found in the Renaissance novella, and he resolves the traditional plot in an original way (1923, 216–19). In this respect the 'author's' epigraph taken from Schiller, 'Dare to err and to dream!' [*Wage Du zu irren und zu träumen!*] – again an explicit intertext – may be taken as an anachronistic directive for reading this 'sixteenth-century manuscript.' The story's departures from its models, its signals of difference, make the epigraph ironic, for the dreams in 'The Song of Triumphant Love' are nightmares, and daring leads the characters into the frightening labyrinth of the unknown.

Two friends, Fabio and Muzio, and the beautiful, sweet Valeria compose the love triangle. The story is structured in two parts. The first is a pastoral where the three ideal characters are introduced. Fabio, the painter, and Muzio, the musician are unlike in physique and temperament in spite of their friendship. There is nothing fantastic in this part of the story, yet their contrasting physiognomies come to symbolize the sinister events of the second part. Fabio is tall, fair, and blue-eyed, almost angelic in appearance and disposition. Muzio is shorter, dark-complexioned, less animated and cordial, and shares with Valeria a gift for music. Her decision to marry Fabio creates no animosity, and the love triangle is apparently resolved in an friendly way: Muzio heads for the Orient.

The second part is the core of the story. Muzio returns and strange events begin to happen soon afterwards. When Fabio encounters him by chance, his initial and brief reaction is an indefinite fear, a fear which will however take shape in Valeria. Physically Muzio is unchanged, although the Hoffmannesque cast of his features has become more pronounced: he is darker, and his eyes are more deeply set. It is primarily his expression and demeanour which are altered, his face concentrated and grave, his voice quieter. There is, as Valeria observes, 'something strange and unprecedented generally in all Muzio's ways, and in all his habits' (13: 58; A23). The completeness of his transformation is signalled even by the spicy fragrance of his garments, his hair, and his breath (13: 63). Muzio is accompanied by a devoted and keenly intelligent Malay whose tongue has been cut out. According to Muzio, this remarkable servant had 'made a great sacrifice, and in compensation now possessed great power' (13: 64; A24).

The strangeness of all of this is represented on the level of language.

Words belonging to the same lexical group continually recur, the first two more frequently than others: 'mysterious' [tainstvennyy], 'strange' [strannyy], 'enigmatic' [zagadochnyy], 'marvellous' [chudnyy], 'magical' [skazochnyy]. A second and related lexical category, 'incomprehensible' [neponyatnyy], serves as a key to the story. For instance, Muzio has chests filled with precious objects collected on his travels – fabrics, rugs, spices, jewels – 'objects, the very use of which seemed mysterious and incomprehensible' (13: 57; A25). The pearl necklace he gives to Valeria, obtained in return for some secret service rendered to the Shah of Persia, 'seemed to her heavy, and as though endowed with some sort of strange warmth' (13: 57; A26). Valeria and Fabio listen to Muzio's tales 'as though enchanted' [kak ocharovannye] (13: 57). He has travelled in many lands associated with mystery – Persia, Arabia, India, and China – and has learned strange conjuring tricks [fokusy] such as levitation (13: 57).[20] All these objects and skills function as indices of Muzio's transformation. They are negative indices not only because they are 'strange,' but also because Muzio uses them in a sinister way to gain ascendency over Valeria.[21]

Three incidents foreshadow Muzio's control over Valeria: the strange sensation Valeria associates with the necklace; the drinking of the Shiraz wine, over which Muzio seems to utter an incantation; and Muzio's passionate rendition of a Ceylonese melody on an odd, three-stringed violin. This song, which sends tremors through both Valeria and Fabio, is produced with a bow whose diamond tip 'scattered ray-like sparks in its flight, as though it too were kindled with the fire of that wondrous song' (13: 59; A27). Although Muzio describes it as a song of 'happy, satisfied love,' here it is an instrument for his passionate seduction of Valeria.

Muzio sets about conquering Valeria by exercising the powers he has acquired in the East. Her first dream (if in fact it was a dream) would seem to be part of Muzio's carefully orchestrated strategy, and functions as a prolepsis of later events. In her dream, she finds herself in a strange and exotic chamber where she succumbs to Muzio. The next morning, Muzio himself recounts an almost identical dream. He does not name Fabio's wife as the woman seduced, but substitutes 'a woman I once loved,' a hint Valeria does not mistake (13: 62). The coincidence of detail in the two dreams, as well as Muzio's gaze, fixed upon Valeria while he recounts his dream, suggests that he has implanted the dream in her mind. Yet there is some evidence that Valeria was not dreaming; she seems to be drugged when she goes to bed: 'her blood was surging softly and languidly, and there was a faint ringing in her head ...' (13: 60; A28). The chamber in which she is seduced corresponds, if not in detail, at least in style, to Muzio's room in the pavilion as we see it through Fabio's eyes much later (13: 70, 72–3). There are no precise time markers; Valeria falls asleep 'towards morning,' and the moonlight is bright when she awakens. Perhaps most telling is the face of her sleeping husband, 'pale as that of a corpse ... more melancholy than a dead face' (13: 61; A29). Fabio, too, had drunk the Shiraz wine and may have been drugged to the point of helplessness. Of particular significance is the inverse symmetry in the wording of the two paragraphs, and the switch to the present tense. At the moment Valeria yields to Muzio (in the dream) we read, 'his dry lips consumed her utterly ... She falls back on the cushions ...' (13: 60; A30). When she awakens, her action and sensations are opposite those experienced in the dream: 'she raises herself up in bed a little and gazes about her ... A shiver runs through her whole body ...' (13: 60–1; A31). These stylistic devices give prominence to the dream episode and set it in relief, as a unit, against the rest of the text. The following morning, Muzio seemed 'contented' [dovol'nyy] and 'merry' [vesëlyy] (13: 61). The implication that Muzio's passion has been gratified is supported by both words being repeated twice in a single paragraph.[22]

Muzio's most powerful bait is the Ceylonese song. Part of its allure and potency is of course its exotic unfamiliarity, its difference from the Italian music of the period. The song is so strongly associated with Muzio that it becomes an index. Whenever something occurs between Muzio and Valeria (in dream or in waking), the song is audible. When Valeria awakens from her dream she hears it (13: 61), and Fabio hears it when Valeria returns to bed after her encounter, later, with Muzio in the garden. In these contexts, the song becomes a metaphor for consummation, Muzio's unspoken expression of triumph over Valeria's will or repressed desire. This is especially apparent in the closing episode, which is also semantically the richest. Muzio has disappeared, dead or alive after a scuffle with Fabio, who stabs him; weeks have passed and Fabio and Valeria have regained their former peace. Seated at the organ, Valeria spontaneously, uncontrollably, finds herself playing Muzio's song of triumphant love. At that instant she feels a new life within her. That the symbol for Muzio's passion is juxtaposed with Valeria's pregnancy speaks for itself. The semantic indeterminacy is just a veil over an underlying, logically coherent meaning.

Music was an essential part of Valeria's contact with Muzio before his travels and her marriage to Fabio. When Muzio and Fabio were courting her, Valeria 'loved to sing ancient songs to the strains of a lute, which she played herself' (13: 54; A32). It is consistent with Muzio's alteration that he has developed a taste for the strange music of distant lands. All the melodies he plays for his hosts are 'strange and even wild to the Italian ear,' though Muzio claims they are popular songs (13: 59). Music for Valeria is an innocent and pleasant pastime. Her husband even tries to paint her as St Cecilia, the sweet patroness of musicians. But he soon observes that Valeria has lost the 'pure, holy expression' which had inspired him. One day, when he expects her in his studio, he finds her in a remote path of the garden; behind her 'a marble satyr with face distorted in a malicious smile, was applying his pointed lips to his reed-pipes' (13: 63; A33). The noble beauty of music evident in the first part of the story is replaced with the capacity of music to rouse the passions, the eroticism symbolized by the satyr and expressed in Muzio's new repertoire.

The moon is a recurring motif that connects the events. After her dream, Valeria sees her husband's corpse-like face by the light of the moon; when the last strains of Muzio's song die away, the moon disappears behind a cloud (13: 61). When Fabio sees Valeria returning after her first rendezvous in the garden, 'moonlight was flooding everything with a harsh light' (13: 65; A34). The moon's 'harshness' corresponds to Muzio's embrace in Valeria's dream: 'his harsh arms twine around her waist' (13: 60; A35). The verbs 'oblivat" and 'obvivat" are phonetically similar, as well as semantically related by the prefix 'ob,' expressive of taking over, or absorption. Through such linguistic affinities as these, the proleptic dream becomes virtually inseparable from its ostensible realization.

The moon acquires an added function with Fabio's suggestive remark about Valeria's actions. When he sees Muzio and Valeria moving irresistibly towards one another, again in the moonlight, he describes her as 'like a somnambulist' [kak lunatik], a word that, literally translated, means also 'moonstruck' (13: 68). Whatever the influence she is under, the allusion is never pushed beyond this subjective interpretation.

Other explanations for the events are just as equivocal. The expression on Muzio's face, in the passage just cited, is compared to the Malay's, and one cannot avoid taking the hint that Muzio may be acting under his servant's power. The Malay's uncommon abilities have already been attested, and it is conceivable that Muzio is his apprentice. Both Valeria and Fabio have called Muzio a 'sorcerer' [chernoknizhnik] (13: 68), but it may be that the Malay is master. Certainly his skill in animating Muzio's body after the stabbing testifies to an extraordinary knowledge of the so-called black arts.

The requisite Christian explanation is also offered. Valeria's confessor, Father Lorenzo, is of the opinion that witchcraft [koldovstvo] and diabolical spells [besovskie chary] lie behind everything. Muzio may have been infected with false doctrines in the unenlightened lands of his travels (13: 67). Fabio uses the expression 'diabolical incantations' [besovskie zaklinaniya] when he observes from his place of concealment the Malay's efforts to resuscitate Muzio (13: 73).

Each of these explanations is in fact merely a subjective, unauthenticated *interpretation* of the events. At a loss to understand their experiences, the characters simply annotate them by redescribing them within the narrow framework of their respective dogmas; for Fabio, Valeria, and Father Lorenzo, locked as they are in their beliefs, the events would otherwise remain incomprehensible. For the reader, the text's indeterminacy makes certain decisions impossible. We cannot know whether Valeria loves Muzio, whether Muzio died and was resurrected after being stabbed or was just barely alive. Nor, indeed, can we ever know whether Muzio is the father of Valeria's child. The mysteries remain unsolved. But Muzio has incontestably acquired a set of extraordinary skills. What Valeria observes as the change in Muzio, his being less Italian, is nothing more than a state compatible with, perhaps necessary for, the application of the knowledge he has gained.[23] Apart from the fact that 'The Song of Triumphant Love' is an intricate and highly readable tale, Turgenev's accomplishment lies in his successfully transforming a Renaissance narrative schema into a prototypical tale of the paranormal mode by blending a story of passion with an Oriental adventure tale.

The tale is not so much concerned with the process of solving the mysteries as it is with the possibility that occult skills may be acquired. However enigmatic they are, the story seems to suggest, strange abilities may exist. The story adds an interesting element to the fantastic by proposing that paranormal capacities may be *learned*. Fabio, Valeria, and the priest cannot acquire these skills without first embracing an episteme that would force them to repudiate their beliefs. The source of Muzio's power lies precisely in his having embraced and made use of a different episteme. In this respect, his skills and knowledge are not incomprehensible; they are simply beyond the comprehension of those who will not or cannot abandon the Western cultural tradition.

'Klara Milich (After Death)' is one of Turgenev's few fantastic tales narrated in the third person. It blends perfectly the fantastic and the realistic of everyday life. Shatalov considers 'Klara Milich' unique in Russian literature because of its 'astounding strength of psychological analysis' (1979, 289). It has been likened to Villiers de l'Isle-Adam's 'Véra' (1874), which makes a narrative out of the expression 'love is stronger than death.'[24] Dessaix and Ledkovsky both find in it affinities with Schopenhauer's views on the survival of the will after death (Dessaix 1979, xxiii; Ledkovsky 1973, 62), while others connect it with Calderón's play *Love after Death*, whose heroine is Doña Clara Malek.

Aratov encounters Klara at a literary matinée where she will read and sing. Though she is far from his ideal of a woman, he finds himself thinking about her constantly (13: 90). Aratov is an unremarkable young man, withdrawn, gentle, and virginal, who depends entirely for society on his doting aunt. Physically he is like his mother, but his character is that of his dead father, a naturalist and mystic who claimed descendance from the supposed sorcerer Jacob Bruce (13: 76–7).[25] Klara's note to Aratov asking for a private meeting causes him to spurn her as a disreputable woman. Three months afterwards, Klara commits suicide. Only from this point do the events become fantastic. Aratov dreams of Klara, hears her and sees her in his room, and finally dies uttering the words 'love is stronger than death.'

The story is structured as two layers superimposed one on the other. Realistic descriptions, predominant in the early chapters, are overlaid with fantastic events in the last chapters. The coexistence of these two layers makes it possible for Turgenev to shift repeatedly from the realistic to the fantastic.[26]

Even in Aratov's first encounter with Klara, there is a hint of the lurking fatality that will culminate in the fantastic events. At Klara's concert, Aratov notices how she stares at him, and recalls having seen her at an earlier soirée, where she looked at him 'several times with a peculiar insistence in her dark, intense eyes' (13: 86; A36). He is struck by the immobility of her face, and likens her to a somnambulist or someone under hypnosis (13: 88), an analogy which for Gruzinsky reflects Turgenev's interest in Charcot's experiments in hypnotism (1918, 218). And Klara's somnambulism is reminiscent of Valeria's in 'The Song of Triumphant Love.' But if Klara's physical movements are wooden, her songs and readings are not. They heighten the sense of impending tragedy with their powerful intertextual references. From Pushkin's *Evgeny Onegin* (1831), she reads Tatyana's letter with great emotion, exulting over the words 'My whole life has betokened my meeting you one day'; she herself then writes a similar letter to Aratov (13: 89). Her songs tell of suffering, and waiting, and fidelity. One of the audience connects Klara with the songs she sings by remarking on her tragic eyes (13: 86). Another intertextual reference connects her still more strongly to the tragedy she sings of, and functions as a leitmotif: Aratov finds himself haunted by the words of a poem by Krasov, based on Scott's *St. Ronan's Well* – 'Poor Clara! Mad Clara! Poor Clara Mowbray!' (13: 90). Her final, most dramatic action, her suicide, is the most powerful signifying gesture and her strongest message to Aratov. While acting in a play about a girl betrayed in love, she takes poison and dies after the first act. Aratov eventually realizes that she died for him (13: 121), but he does not learn the name of the play and the intertext thus remains a mystery (13: 125). All of these increasingly potent messages – songs, letter, and suicide – are the prelude for a series of messages after death that Aratov will finally grasp. Aratov's later musings on abiding love draw upon the Bible ('death, where is thy sting?'), Schiller ('And the dead also shall live'), Mickiewicz ('I shall love until life ends ... and after life ends'), and Villiers de l'Isle-Adam ('love is stronger than death') in order to explain and justify the strangeness of his dreams and his sense of Klara's power over him (13: 120). In combination, all of these intertextual strategies greatly help to generate the fantastic.

Klara's appearances after death follow a pattern of gradation, beginning with dreams. In the first, Aratov sees her wearing a wreath of roses, and hears her voice; he is conscious on waking that 'something had taken root in him ... something had taken possession of him' (13: 107; A37). Klara tells him, 'if you want to know who I am, go there!' On waking, he feels compelled to travel to her home in Kazan', where her sister Anna gives him a diary and a photograph. Klara's diary is a posthumous message to Aratov. It persuades him of her purity, and gives him the key to her power: 'She was chaste, I am chaste, and that's what has given her this power!' (13: 120; A38). Spiritual belonging born of shared innocence is his mystical explanation for their link across the grave. It has its counterpart in Aratov's description of himself as 'taken' [vzyat], not by physical love but by the power of a dead woman to possess him. The second dream becomes an audible presence in the room, with the word 'roses' repeated several times; Aratov recognizes Klara's voice, but then doubts his senses and compares his experience to a hallucination (13: 122). From his last dream he awakens to Klara herself in his room. He declares his passion for her, and they exchange a kiss that leaves him weak, but with the blissful expression of a man who has solved a universal mystery. He knows that he must die, and babbles deliriously about rapture and consummated marriage, always repeating that love is stronger than death. Klara's final manifestation is left implicit. Aratov's strongest physical experience, the consummation of their 'marriage,' is never described. The only clue to her having been there at all is the lock of black hair clutched in his hand. The narrator leaves the status of this crucial motif ambiguous, arguing both for and against a natural explanation: 'Where did it come from? Anna Semënovna had preserved such a lock of Klara's, but why would she give Aratov a thing so precious to her? Could she somehow have placed it between the pages of the diary and not noticed that she had given it to him?' (13: 133; A39). The narrator is unconvinced and unconvincing. His hypothesis is a mere query, after all, and the origin of the lock of hair is never made known.

In some ways, the structure of 'Klara Milich' seems to correspond to the ambiguous mode, especially if we privilege the narrator's final comments. Aratov, like other of Turgenev's heroes, has a psychological propensity that might explain his experiences naturally. We are told that he is 'given to the mysterious and the mystical,' like his father; he is sickly, reclusive, uncorrupted by the world, and fond of idle psychologizing. Above all, he feels guilty for having wronged Klara. His remarks belittling her talents reached her ears, as such remarks will, and he did not hide his disdain for her at their rendezvous.

The tale's ambiguity persists to the climax. The status of Klara's first brief manifestation in Aratov's room is indeterminate, much like Ellis's in 'Phantasms.' Ledkovsky draws our attention to the conventionality of the setting, the room either dark or lighted by candles, a faint glow coming from an unknown source (1973, 113).[27] In 'Phantasms,' Ellis takes shape from a streak of moonlight, becoming a white, misty woman; Klara, complete with the wreath of roses, materializes from the blurred door Aratov is looking at. In neither case can we decide whether the appearance is really a dream. As the narrator points out, Aratov 'once or twice closed his eyes in sleep ... He opened them wide at once, at any rate it seemed to him that he opened them' (13: 123; A40). There is a possibility that Aratov's vision is at least half oneiric, for his aunt enters the room in a white bedjacket and a nightcap with a large red bow.

At the same time, these events, precisely because they are ambiguous, allow us to conjecture that Aratov is controlled by an unknown force that has determined his fate, just as the narrator of 'The Dream' will find himself pushed irresistibly towards his fate. Aratov tries to account for his strange compulsion by a sort of transcendent magnetism: 'Isn't the soul immortal? Does it need an earthly organ in order to exercise its power? Has not magnetism proved to us that one living soul can influence another? Then why can't this influence continue after death as well if the soul lives on?' (13: 118; A41).

His hypothesis is plausible when applied to Klara's behaviour. Aratov's belated obsession and Klara's early obsession are indeed symmetrical. At both the matinée and the soirée, where she first sees Aratov, Klara stares insistently at him with her immobile face as though drawn to him by a force. This presumption is reinforced in a passage of her diary that refers to these episodes: '"Moscow. Tuesday ..th June. Sang and recited at a literary matinée. This is a day full of meaning for me. *He must decide my fate.* (This sentence was underlined twice). I again saw ..." Here followed several lines carefully blotted out' (13: 116; A42).[28] Klara's fatalism is comparable to Aratov's: they have both been sentenced, as he recognizes from her underlined words (13: 120). She is as much a prisoner of fate as he, and equally powerless to escape. They both seem to be in the grip of an identical power.

Is Klara in love with Aratov? Interestingly, there is no evidence that she is. In her songs and recitation, Klara never mentions love; each line quoted by the narrator refers only to the pain of single-minded waiting. Klara is as oddly obsessed with Aratov as he is adamant in his denials of love. Except in the few last moments of his emotionally charged meeting with her sister, Aratov is conscious of exhibiting none of the usual symptoms of a bereft lover. He feels himself always impelled by the external and incomprehensible force that he attributes to Klara's will. Klara's diary entries and Aratov's interpretations give the impression that their meeting was somehow foreordained. Both seem to be driven by an unknown, mysterious power that fastens them together. Klara's behaviour at their rendezvous is, in this respect, highly significant: she addresses Aratov as though they are already acquainted, and as though he must know her reason for wanting to meet him. She has staked everything on the conviction that Aratov is under the same spell as she (13: 96). When it becomes clear to her that Aratov has no inkling of their common destiny, Klara is first grieved, then angry at his misinterpretation of her actions. Klara's anticipation, along with her diary entry, suggests that she had seen Aratov before, or sees in him someone she knew. The revelation that Aratov does not share that vision prompts her abrupt change of attitude: the logic of fatality drives her to commit suicide.

In this reading, the ambiguity and indeterminacy of the text are explained from within its latent meaning, its allusions, fragments, and semantic connections. Perhaps Klara and Aratov knew each other in another life; more likely, just as Aratov had visions of her, so may Klara have had visions of Aratov that caused her passionate fixation on him.

Turgenev's tale transforms the realistic world of ordinary human experience into a fantastic domain governed by mysterious, transcendent bonds.[29] Klara is a step ahead of Aratov with her recognition of this bond, and with her obsession and death. In the end, it is the lack of synchronization that destroys the lives of Klara and Aratov. Because of his blindness, Aratov delays his passage from contingent actuality into the realm of fantastic necessity. Only in the timelessness of death are the two united.

THE PARANORMAL ACHIEVED

'The Dream' is Turgenev's most sophisticated fantastic narrative, published at the same time as *Virgin Soil*. Not unexpectedly, it was *Virgin Soil* that the critics took notice of, while those who paid any attention at all to 'The Dream' could not agree on its worth. Anonymous contributors to the moderate liberal newspaper *News* [Novosti] and the conservative *The Russian World* [Russkiy mir], called it, respectively, a 'mere trifle' [bezdelushka], and a 'half-fantastic bagatelle' and 'literary dessert' (Turgenev 1966a, 11: 528). Another critic, V. Pechkin, praised with a great deal more shrewdness Turgenev's masterly handling of language, with which he brings out 'in a few phrases the deepest psychological phenomena' (Turgenev 1966a, 11: 528–9). Among the twentieth-century critics, Garnett found 'The Dream' 'curiously Byronic in imagery and atmosphere, and artistically not convincing' (1917, 169). Brang considers it thematically similar to 'The Song of Triumphant Love' (1977, 179), and Byalyy sees in both stories the author's attempt to generalize or universalize the theme of 'the mysterious' (1962, 218).

Turgenev expressed his own view in a letter to his English translator Ralston. With 'The Dream,' he was trying 'to solve a physiological riddle' (1966b, 12: 1, 63).[30] He achieved his goal, and more, for 'The Dream' above all solves the problem of the fantastic for the realist writer. The fictional world structure of the paranormal mode is more thoroughly constructed in 'The Dream' than in any of his other fantastic tales. And, like 'Father Aleksey's Tale,' a Christian tale by a Christian priest, there is an almost perfect correspondence between the form and the content of the tale.

The story is triggered by a paranormal phenomenon: the narrator has a recurring dream in which he is searching for his father. Standing in the window of a house on a narrow, badly paved street is a stranger. The narrator hears the man's 'angry, almost bear-like muttering' before the scene vanishes in a fog (11: 271). He senses that the man in the dream is his father; but the person he was raised to believe was his father (and who died when the narrator was seven), in no way resembles this dream parent. The dream is precognitive, for the narrator will meet the stranger he has dreamt about and discover that the man is indeed his biological father. The device of a recurring dream that comes true generates a narrative in which the standard logic of reason is supplanted by oneiric logic.

From his childhood, the narrator has had a penchant for solitude and reverie [mechtanie].[31] It is reverie that first leads the narrator to feel himself surrounded by a transcendent reality. His musings are indefinite, filled with feelings and longings, 'as though I were standing before a half-closed door behind which lay mysterious secrets; standing and waiting, thrilling – yet not crossing the threshold' (11: 270; A43). His disposition leads him to think of becoming a poet or a monk, but he decides against both.

The door, half-open and inviting exploration, hides a dreamlike transcendence, a possible experience that is neither poetic nor religious. It is precisely the visionary, the dreamer [mechtatel'], who refuses to limit reality to empirical sensory experience and has access to such transcendence. 'The Dream' is therefore the story of a young man with a capacity for reverie who gains admittance through his dream into a world unlike that of his everyday experience. In itself, of course, dreaming is neither supernatural nor paranormal; but it may act as a channel, or so some claim, and it is this potentiality which Turgenev brings into play.

The narrator's relationship with his mother is a 'half-open door' as well. Some of his psychological traits (avoidance of boys his own age, nervousness, shyness, and fondness for solitude and meditation) can be ascribed to his secluded life with her, to the 'merging' of their lives, as he expresses it. His mother is beautiful but melancholy, 'as though some mysterious, incurable and undeserved sorrow were constantly sapping the root of her existence' (11: 269; A44). More significantly, the narrator is conscious of his mother's occasional aversion to him, fits that he puts down to her shattered health and to his own strange, incomprehensible outbursts of wicked and criminal feelings (11: 270).

Here we find two mysteries: just who is his father, and why is his mother sad? They begin to unravel when the narrator meets his 'dream' father by chance in a café, and engages him in conversation. The man, who calls himself a baron, learns the narrator's name and address, but then eludes him in the company of a Negro [Arap]. The narrator's mother eventually tells him a transparent story about a married friend who was raped by an officer and later gave birth to a son. The narrator sees through the story, of course, and recognizes it as his mother's own. After the rape, she saw the officer lying in the street dead, or so she thought, with his skull split open. For the narrator's mother, the return of the rapist is a waking dream, a 'daymare' that parallels the narrator's precognitive dream during sleep. The psychology of the rape victim, one of those realistic details which pervade even Turgenev's fantastic tales, is finely and subtly portrayed. The mother's sense of guilt and sorrow for having withheld her secret from her husband, her sense of involuntary complicity in a crime for which she was not responsible, and, chiefly, her mixed feelings for her son, the offspring of that crime, all express her great suffering. The secrets behind her sorrow and her moments of aversion are now explained by the psychological burden she has borne for so many years. And the criminal feelings the narrator occasionally experiences are accounted for by heredity. Turgenev's exploration of what Dessaix calls the 'metabiological relationship' (1980, 127) is most interesting, for it is the genetic tie that opens the channel between the narrator and his biological father.

The narrator is driven to meet his 'dream' father again. He feels himself led through the streets by a mysterious force, with an impression of something 'extraordinary' [neobyknovennyy] and 'impossible' [nevozmozhnyy] about to happen. Oneiric logic prevails and determines the events: ahead of him suddenly appears the Negro who had been with the baron. The narrator's own will and intentions are overpowered by a force that propels him onwards. He follows the Negro and is led to the very house of his dream, where the man ahead vanishes. These dream-like events take place in an appropriate setting: a narrow, misty, cobbled street, with the mysterious house in a yard full of debris and planks. The narrator wanders on until he finds himself on the beach, where he discovers the baron, his father, drowned and washed up on shore. His recurring dream had not had this dénouement: now, it would appear, the dream is unfolding simultaneously with the events, and the narrator living and acting it out as it progresses.

At the same time, the dream-like experience is supplemented and semantically transformed by a piece of physical evidence. The narrator wrenches off the corpse's hand a wedding ring, which his mother will identify as the one taken from her when she was raped. The precognitive dream, then, couples the narrator and the baron, while the ring functions, as Dessaix has pointed out (1980, 127), as the concrete, unifying object that brings together the narrator, his mother, and the baron. Thus the ring confirms empirically that the narrator's dream is truly precognitive and that his experience is paranormal. It is fully consistent with the nature of this fictional world that the narrator, in running away from the corpse, feels himself pursued by something unnameable, something that 'rushes after me, and overtakes me and catches me' (11: 287; A45). The same holds true about another fleeting motif, which connects the narrator's mother to the ring and the baron: after showing the ring to his mother, the narrator observes that for an instant her eyes opened unusually wide 'and took on a dead look, like *his*' (11: 287; A46).

It is not surprising that a story of the paranormal mode should be open-ended, as 'The Dream' is. When the narrator first discovered the body, he studied it to be sure the man was dead. When he returns to the beach with his mother, the corpse has vanished, leaving only traces of its having lain there. Fleetingly, a supernatural explanation is offered: 'Can he have got up of himself and gone away?' (11: 288; A47). The narration of this episode suddenly shifts into the present tense. The narrating act is made simultaneous with the event being narrated.

The original dream does not recur. But in keeping with the indeterminacy of the last episode, there is an opening out onto another recurring dream, undeveloped and fragmentary. The narrator hears screams, groans, and mutterings that seem to emanate at once from a man and from the sea.[32] These sounds identify the new dream with the old one, but now the dreamer is aware that he is no longer searching for his father. Instead, all the sounds associated with his biological father at different stages return in the form of a new mystery surrounding that man's fate. The dead baron – the narrator's father – if indeed he is dead, continues to haunt him.

In 'The Dream' there is no trace either of the *skaz* or of any storytelling situation such as we find in 'The Dog' and 'Father Aleksey's Tale.' This is the text of a poet with a gift for representing complex situations like the psychology of rape, the probing of the state of reverie, and the dramatic sequence of dream-like events. The narrator is particularly skilful in manipulating the three temporal levels which are essential to the story: (1) the past, which consists of the events that took place when the narrator was seventeen. This level is signalled by the word 'then' [togda]; (2) the present, or the time of narrating, which is marked by the word 'now' [teper']; and (3) the narrative's prehistory, in which the narrator recalls the time when he was seven and his presumptive father was dying. The narrator's recognition of his 'dream' father as his biological father (the baron) depends on his remembering the man who died when he was seven. At the same time, because the narrating act is that of a mature man relating events which occurred in his youth, the authenticating force of his discourse is strengthened.

In its narrative style, 'The Dream' is allied with the Pushkinian tradition, whereas 'Father Aleksey's Tale' and 'The Dog' have more in common with Gogol'. Thematically, it owes something to Pushkin's *The Queen of Spades* [*Pikovaya dama*, 1834]. For instance, the baron is a Mephistophelean type, with sullen, piercing eyes and a hook nose (11: 271); Pushkin's hero, Germann, has flashing black eyes, 'the profile of Napoleon and the soul of Mephistopheles.' With 'at least three crimes on his conscience' (Pushkin 1962, 3: 360, 369), Germann has something in common with the baron, whose crime is the rape of the narrator's mother. Gambling, too, is fateful for both. Still more striking are the bedroom scenes. The room where the narrator's mother is attacked is 'all hung with damask' (11: 278; A48), while in the Countess's room, which Germann surreptitiously enters, chairs and divans are all 'covered with faded damask' (1962, 3: 365; A49). In both rooms, a shrine lamp burns. The baron steals into the room of the narrator's mother through a secret door hidden behind a tapestry; Germann makes his escape through a door concealed behind a tapestry.[33] The precognitive dream is the central experience of a paranormal nature in Turgenev's story. But we sense that the mysteriousness of this world is not limited to the dream alone. Just as 'Klara Milich' studied the immutability and transcendence of attraction, so 'The Dream' presents the strange determinism of heredity, the possibility of mysterious and irrevocable bonds between people who are genetically related but who do not know each other.

These hidden bonds find channels in the ordinary phenomena of everyday life – in dreams, or in a hypnotic, dream-like state. Whatever the force that determines and shapes the narrator's dream, that activates the biological link and drives the narrator, it is not identified. It is simply postulated. It is also worth pointing out that we cannot find a motivation for the narrator's dreams in any hidden desire to find his father, since he had no inkling that the man who died when he was seven was not his real father. In any case, why these channels are open to some and not to others is an unresolved riddle; the only precondition seems to be receptiveness, which is as much a trait of the narrator of 'The Dream' as it was of Aratov.

With its focus on paranormal channels of communication, 'The Dream' outstrips all the stories that precede it. In the three tales where the paranormal is incipient, the special ability is assigned to a character who acts upon others by transmitting his or her peculiar power, such as the magnetism in 'A Strange Story' and 'The Song of Triumphant Love.' No one, including the reader, knows the source of Vasiliy's and Muzio's powers, but what makes them effective is the susceptibility of their victims: Sofya and Valeria are as receptive in their ways as the narrator of 'The Dream' is in his.[34] But 'The Dream' is notably different. Here the narrator's will is subject to an *impersonal* force of indeterminate origin which is transmitted through the uncontrollable channel of a dream.

Turgenev's rational approach in the last four tales to unexplained, mysterious phenomena, and his probing of his characters' psychologies bring Pushkin once again to mind. In both his realistic and fantastic works Turgenev seems to have synthesized the Pushkinian and Gogolian trends in Russian literature, so brilliantly exposed by Belinsky (1844, 9: 75–117). But debts notwithstanding, Turgenev transcended both, to my mind, when he wrote his innovative 'The Dream.' He resolved the indeterminacy we find in Pushkin's fantastic tales, and did so without resorting to the ambiguity of the supernatural that characterizes most of Gogol's tales. Like Dickens in 'The Signal-Man' and, as we shall see, Maupassant in 'The Horla,' Turgenev found a place for the unexplained in the natural world that even a rationalist and a realist could accept.

6

Guy de Maupassant: The Scientific Cynic

In the fantastic stories by Maupassant, many of the characters seem to have lost their bearings in reality, a state sometimes thought to signal madness or the road to it. The journal writer in 'The Hair' ['La Chevelure'] may have been driven to his extraordinary affair by an overactive erotic imagination, and perhaps the Marquis's strange experience in 'Apparition' [L'Apparition'], was provoked by the Gothic gloominess of an old château. A closer look at such narratives suggests that the fuzzy border between sanity and insanity prompts still deeper questions about reality itself: where do the boundaries of reality lie? Does it encompass more than what is so casually called real? These unknowns fascinated Maupassant, and he made them, along with some of the possible answers, the building blocks for his fantastic fictional worlds.

Maupassant's tales evolved structurally. As with Dickens and Turgenev, the transformation of Maupassant's fantastic does not proceed chronologically. What follows are analyses of narratives grouped by their treatment of the supernatural and the unknown, this last being Maupassant's own term for phenomena that are unexplained. As Maupassant developed as a writer, he presented these phenomena increasingly as part of the natural domain, but a part not yet understood. 'The Skeleton Hand' ['La Main d'écorché'], its later variant 'The Hand' ['La Main'], and 'The Apparition' comprise the first set, traditional stories that equate the unknown with the supernatural. They display features of the disjunctive and the ambiguous modes, emphasizing the event as well as its psychological and emotional impact, instead of the cognitive puzzles to which the event might give rise. 'The Hair' is included here, although it could easily be called a transitional tale. Its focus on perception and, still better, its appraisal of madness itself are first steps towards a cognitive approach to the fantastic. 'The Hair' looks ahead with its hints that sensitive individuals with heightened cognitive abilities may have access to mysterious realms. Yet it also looks backwards to the ambiguous mode, in that the epistemic questions are raised in connection with a journal written by the inmate of a madhouse.

The second group of tales shows clearly that Maupassant was advancing towards the paranormal mode. Like the stories of the first group, they foreground the way in which the character is affected by contact with the unknown: 'Magnetism' ['Magnétisme'] offers the philosopher's reaction to the unknown, while terror becomes the focus in 'He?' ['Lui?].' Neither narrator is willing to give up his standard preconceptions about reality. 'A Madman?' ['Un Fou?'], with its blend of epistemic questioning and terror and the protagonist's attempts to sketch out an explanatory system, prefigures the tales of the last set.

The idea of the unknown as something tangible crystallizes in the third group of tales. Here Maupassant's protagonists try to characterize and define the unknown. 'Letter from a Madman' ['Lettre d'un Fou'] and the first version of 'The Horla' ['Le Horla'] are texts of this sort. With the second and final version of 'The Horla,' the unknown is translated into an entity or an uncharted force in the natural domain. This fictional world structure, and the narrator's special ability to perceive the Horla, are features of the paranormal mode. Certainly 'The Horla' does not ignore the narrator's emotional trauma, but it highlights his search for an explanatory system that would account for the unknown as a 'scientific fact.' It synthesizes the predominant features of the stories written before it: madness, the supernatural, the unknown, fear, and epistemic questioning. This exquisite tale is Maupassant's deepest probe into a human psyche challenged by the conditions of an open-ended world.

I have not assembled these tales with the idea that no other way of grouping them is possible; but there are serious problems with what has always been, for Maupassant scholars, the chosen means for dealing with them. Castex (1951) assumes that Maupassant's fantastic tales coincide with the progression of his illness. And yet nothing in the chronological succession of these stories bespeaks a failing mind. Critics caught in the loop of diagnosing the writer's mind by the state of his art and his art by the state of his mind have no perspective from which to observe the stylistic and structural transformations of his tales. As Steegmuller points out, many works 'utterly unconcerned with horror' followed 'The Horla' (1972, 256). 'Le Rosier de Madame Husson'

(1887), *Fort comme la mort* (1889), 'Le Champ d'oliviers' (1890), and 'Mouche' (1890), as well as Maupassant's very coherent letters and *Chronicles* surely argue against reducing his work to symptoms. Maynial yokes together two such disparate narratives as 'He?' and 'The Horla' because they are both concerned with 'autoscopie externe,' a symptom Maupassant allegedly displayed in the last stages of syphilis. 'It consists,' he writes, 'in seeing oneself in front of oneself' (1907, 245).[1] Fodéré's opinion is, to my mind, still more far-fetched: Maupassant was addicted to narcotics and ether, and the fantastic was the outlet for his hallucinations (1947, 69). We need not belabour the issue; even if we conceded that Maupassant's stories are manifestations of advancing insanity, we would still have before us the task of studying the stylistic features of a madman's discourse and the ingenious worlds that such a mind can concoct.

THE TRADITIONAL FANTASTIC

'The Skeleton Hand' (1875)[2] and its later variant 'The Hand' are ambiguous tales centred around the possible activities of a severed hand and its dead owner. For some critics, the tale is a throwback to an earlier tradition – to the Romantics or even to the Gothic (Castex 1951, 369; Cogny 1968, 17; Besnard-Coursodon 1973, 233). The interference in the natural domain of what seems to be a supernatural being brings to mind the disjunctive mode. But plausible natural explanations are offered and the supernatural is not fully authenticated, so that both stories remain ambiguous. Maupassant's narrative handling suggests that the term 'supernatural' has no referent, that it is an interpretation imposed in ignorance on phenomena not yet understood. Since the events are not explained, these stories lay the groundwork for a deeper analysis of the unknown in other tales.

In 'The Skeleton Hand,' the events are reconstructed eight months afterwards but, unlike so many of the other stories, there is no elaborate narrative frame. The narrator's childhood friend, Pierre, has obtained a severed hand ('black, dry, very long,' 1: 3) which he will hang first on the bell-rope outside his door, then on the rope above his bed. The hand was said to have belonged to a famous Normandy criminal. A single comment by a medical student, one of those to whom Pierre shows his acquisition, foreshadows the events by alluding to the supernatural: Pierre is told to give the human relic a Christian burial 'lest its owner come back to claim it' (1: 4; B1). Two nights afterwards,

Pierre is found out of his mind with terror, bearing the marks of an attempted strangling. He is soon afterwards committed to an asylum. The narrator observes that the hand is missing from its rope, but makes no inquiries.

The event is authenticated as supernatural in several ways. The doctor who examined Pierre asserted that whoever had tried to strangle him 'must be possessed of prodigious power and have an extraordinarily thin and nervous hand' (1: 6; B2). The perforations in Pierre's neck suggest a skeletal hand of superhuman strength. Shortly before Pierre is attacked, there is another allusion to the supernatural. While the hand had hung on the bell-rope of the outer door, someone had rung it: 'Imagine, some idiot came and rang my doorbell towards midnight, no doubt as a bad joke' (1: 4; B3). During the attempt on Pierre's life, the servant reports hearing the bell ring furiously, and finds signs of a terrible struggle when he enters the room. In retrospect, the ringing Pierre has dismissed as a joke is significant, both because he is in his right mind when he reports it, and because it is repeated the night of the strangling. Even the narrator is unaccountably nervous and agitated that same night. He awakens several times with a start and imagines someone is in the room (1: 5). His empathy with Pierre, his sensing of something wrong, is an experience that borders on clairvoyance.

Natural explanations are possible: it was an intruder, and Pierre himself may have rung the bell-rope to summon help; or the doctors, called to Pierre's bedside, may have removed the hand so as not to frighten anyone, to use their own words (1: 5) – an explanation offered by the narrator. It is only during the seven months of Pierre's insanity that an explicit link is made between his state of mind and the hand. Pierre feels himself 'ever pursued by a spectre' and shouts, before dying, 'take it! take it!' ['prends-la!']. 'It's strangling me' ['Il m'étrangle'] (1:7). The use of the feminine pronoun *la* is obviously a reference to the hand; the masculine pronoun 'il,' syntactically tied to the exclamation 'prends-*la*' could refer in the context only to the 'spectre,' the man, or whatever creature came to reclaim the hand. If a common intruder were present, one would expect both pronouns to be either masculine or feminine, depending on the sex of the trespasser; in that case, Pierre's use of the verb 'prendre' would be inappropriate, for it suggests an object rather than a person. But then Pierre is insane when he makes this exclamation, and perhaps grammatical inconsistency is an expression of his hallucination.

In the dénouement, the supernatural is at least indirectly authenticated. The two grave-diggers who discover the evidence in the Normandy cemetery where Pierre is to be buried are independent witnesses. They unearth a coffin containing a large skeleton and a severed hand. The hand appears to be in a different state of decay from the bones, for some skin obviously remains. It is large, dried up (1: 7), and recalls Pierre's relic. The narrator's remark that the skeleton seemed to be looking at them and the grave-digger's observation that the corpse looked as if it wanted to 'jump at your throat' (1: 7–8) also link the hand in the coffin and the relic that Pierre possessed. But the supernatural is expressed through modalizers ('seemed,' 'would say') and so remains in the realm of potentiality.

Traditional though the motif of the avenging spirit may be, 'The Skeleton Hand' is an early sample of Maupassant's preoccupation with the unexplained. Two options are offered, one natural, the other supernatural. A third option, fully developed only in the last group of tales, is implicit. The narrator's feeling that someone has entered his room, and his uneasiness for no apparent reason, are juxtaposed with Pierre's strangulation by their occurring on the same night, possibly at the same time. It could be explained away as coincidence. Still, the narrator's experience is in some degree predictive and therefore paranormal. It is in this unelaborated moment, which subtly alludes to a mysteriousness independent of the precise nature of the events, that 'The Skeleton Hand' just touches the mode that would become increasingly important for Maupassant in his fantastic tales.

In 'The Hand' (1883), natural and supernatural explanations are less subtle: none is disauthenticated, and emphasis is placed on what the magistrate calls 'the inexplicable.'

A full-fledged storytelling situation enframes the narrating: a group of men and women are in conversation with M. Bermutier, a magistrate who recently investigated a bizarre crime. A casual comment, 'cela touche au surnaturel,' stimulates him to narrate the story of an unsolved crime, an apparently supernatural event involving a severed hand.

M. Bermutier, as his profession suggests, is clear-headed, rational, and unlikely to be led into superstitious or spurious conjectures. The severed hand belonged to the burly Sir John Rowel, who had moved to Corsica during the magistrate's tenure there.[3] When the inevitable rumours about this reclusive and heavily armed man begin to circulate, M. Bermutier makes inquiries and contrives a meeting. One of the rumours has a grain of truth; it is said that Rowel has a terrible crime to conceal, and indeed the man makes no secret of having killed an enemy, whose desiccated hand is riveted to the wall with a heavy chain (1: 1118–19). It resembles that of 'The Skeleton Hand': black, with yellow nails, singularly long, obviously the appendage of a physically powerful man (1: 1119). A year later, Rowel is found strangled to death with the index finger of the severed hand jammed between his clenched teeth. A few days after the murder, the hand is discovered on Rowel's tomb with a missing index finger (1: 1121).

The supernatural is forcefully suggested: there are signs of a violent struggle, but no evidence of an intruder. The doors and windows had not been pried, nor had the guard dogs been disturbed. Rowel had always armed himself against possible attack, even during sleep, and habitually checked that the doors were locked before retiring.

The magistrate offers a simple and rational explanation: Rowel's enemy was not dead and returned to avenge his mutilation (1: 1122). There is support for this in Rowel's having received letter after letter for several months, all of which he burnt. According to the servants, the letters had worried him and he would lash furiously at the severed hand with his riding crop, behaviour that suggests a link between the letters and the hand (1: 1121). The enemy may have placed the hand on the tomb as a sardonic gesture.

None the less, the natural explanations are made ambiguous. Though rather unlikely, someone might have forced the severed finger between the dead man's teeth; after all, Rowel was often heard to quarrel with some unseen adversary at night. It is not clear whether the hand came to life to kill him or Rowel died in a fit of fury or madness. Nor can M. Bermutier explain how a stranger could arrive on Corsica without his knowledge (1: 1122). M. Bermutier's dream, three months *after* the murder, in which it seems to him that a hand is creeping about his room, does not authenticate the earlier events, but is an imaginary reconstruction, an interpretation that springs from his disgust at and horror of the object (1: 1121). Chanady considers 'The Hand' a classic example of Todorov's 'pure fantastic' because the magistrate 'refuses to accept a supernatural explanation' (1985, 72), though on that ground alone the story might also be called Todorov's 'supernatural explained.' I agree that it is ambiguous, for the reasons given in the analysis above, but I think that we can also claim for the story a little more complexity. It takes a small step towards expanding the natural domain of the fictional world with the magistrate's insistence on the term 'the inexplicable' for phenomena we do not yet understand. It hints at the more developed explanatory strategies we will encounter in Maupassant's later fantastic stories.

In 'The Apparition' (1883) the traditional revenant is treated in a most innovative way. As Fellows remarks, Maupassant 'immediately seized upon what was to be the mainspring of his tale - overwhelming fear having as its victim one who has experienced the seemingly inexplicable' (1942, 66–7). The story is a subjective, first-person narration whose telling takes place fifty-six years after the event. The narrator-protagonist is an elderly marquis still haunted by dreams of an episode that lasted for ten minutes.

Once again, the narration is enframed in a group storytelling situation, which provides a realistic setting. A discussion of forced confinement prompts the marquis to recall what happened years before. An old friend with whom he was by chance reunited sent him to fetch some documents from his château. The friend had not lived there since the death of his wife. At the château, the marquis encounters a woman – the friend's wife, it would seem – who begs him to comb her hair, an act which he performs automatically and paralysed with fear.

Several mysteries foreshadow this encounter. In themselves, they are of little importance, but taken together they are highly significant. His friend had aged abnormally in the few intervening years, a condition the narrator attributes to sorrow (1: 781). His agitation before the marquis's visit to the château is so marked as to cause speculation about something more troubling behind his state: 'He seemed to me peculiarly agitated, preoccupied, as though a mysterious battle had been waged in his soul' (1: 782; B4). At the château, the marquis discovers that the letter requesting the gardener to open the door to him is, for some mysterious reason, sealed.[4] The gardener's reluctance to admit the marquis is strange and hints at the possibility of the room being inhabited: 'If you would wait for five minutes, I'll go ... go and see if [...]' (1: 783; B5). Above all, the narrator's friend is in such urgent need of the papers and insists on such a degree of discretion that the papers themselves become a source of mystery.

These latent secrets contrast with the narrator's rapture on his way to the château. His delight in the beauty of the day is undone when he enters the gloomy rooms where the papers are. The marquis is a courageous man, not given to attacks of nerves or flights of fancy. Even his fear of the woman, whether 'woman or spectre,' he tries consciously to repress: 'I was frantic, to the point where I didn't know what I was doing; but my inner pride, and a bit of professional pride, too, made me put an honourable face on it, almost in spite of myself' (1: 785; B6). At the start of his narrative, the marquis chooses not to explain the apparition. His encounter with what appeared to be a revenant is inexplicable unless he is mad, which he insists he is not (1: 781). Nor does he believe in phantoms (1: 784). In common with 'The Skeleton Hand' and 'The Hand,' both the natural (insanity) and the supernatural (a ghost) interpretations are unacceptable to the narrator. Yet several motifs work towards authenticating the supernatural: the woman's 'icy hair' (1: 786) evokes, and leaves, 'a sensation of atrocious cold, as if I had handled snakes' (1: 785; B7); the woman comes and goes quickly and silently through a half-open door which the narrator finds locked when he tries it; he is conscious, when she enters, of 'a rustle behind me,' 'a slight, disagreeable shiver,' and, finally, of 'a great and heavy sigh.' She has approached so quietly that he is unaware of her until she is at his shoulder (1: 784). These are features readily associated with creatures of the supernatural domain, with the disjunctive mode, and they make the narrator's adventures, in Castex's words, 'distinctly romantic' (1951, 376).

A piece of evidence heightens the strangeness of the marquis's experience: he finds a strand of the woman's hair wound round a button on his jacket. The strand deepens rather than solves the mystery by confirming that he has been near a woman. But it proves neither that the woman was alive nor that she was a ghost, although perhaps a real strand of hair suggests more strongly a creature of flesh and blood. That the marquis opts for a natural explanation is clear: he calls in the authorities to search the château, fruitlessly, as it happens, for they find no sign of a woman being confined against her will. The supernatural explanation once again surfaces. The marquis's friend is of no use; he has vanished. Under a natural interpretation, he may have fled to avoid prosecution for imprisoning his wife, though this seems unlikely, since he would hardly send anyone to the château if he wished to conceal the crime. Or, perhaps he was being cowardly in sending the marquis to face what he could not, and did not wish to be taxed with questions he could not answer. Interestingly, the marquis's final words, 'I know nothing more' (1: 787) are the exact words used by the magistrate in 'The Hand' to express the impossibility of explanation, the unresolvable mystery, and indeterminacy of the unknown (1: 1121).

'The Hair' (1884) is a first-person narrative in the form of a journal that describes the experience of an ostensibly insane man.[5] Before he was confined, the author of the journal had purchased an antique piece of furniture in which he found a lock of hair. It began to obsess him. One night, he claims, the woman from whom it had been taken materialized and became his mistress. His journal passes through two pairs of hands: those of the doctor (the lock of hair is in his keeping), and those of the enframing narrator, who reads the manuscript on a visit to the asylum. The text we read is therefore filtered through the enframing narrator who reproduces it.

'The Hair' is intertextually linked to Balzac's *La Peau de Chagrin* (1831). Balzac's Raphaël and the journal writer of 'The Hair' both wander aimlessly into antique shops where they find objects that come to determine their existence. Although less fully characterized than Balzac's 'type,' the antique dealer in Maupassant's story also penetrates uncannily his customer's psychology: 'dealers seem to divine in the fervour of one's look one's hidden and growing desire' (2: 109; B8). There is also, in 'The Hair,' the more general Balzacian notion of 'the thought that kills' ['la penseé qui tue'], which is expressed in the enframing narrator's remark that the journal writer was a man 'ravaged, eaten by thought, by a Thought [...]' (2: 107; B9). We find, too, in *La Peau de chagrin*, the sense of the past that pervades the journal writer's reflections.[6] Like Raphaël, who feels that he has been a soldier when looking at a painting by Teniers, or that he has been scalped when touching a Cherokee tomahawk, Maupassant's journal writer fancies 'that I had already lived before, that I must have known this woman' (2: 111; B10). This sensation of having already lived a life is made all the more explicit with the journal writer's quotation of two verses from Villon's 'Ballade des dames du temps jadis' (2: 111). Baudelaire's poem 'La Chevelure' is yet another intertextual link: the poet's obsessive ecstasy, the 'memories lying in that hair' and its power to evoke what is absent or imaginary (1857; 1941, 27–9), bring to mind the journal writer's lock of hair with its evocative properties.[7] By highlighting the relationship between past and present, the mysterious links between them, these intertextual references set the reader up for a strange event. The narrator's conclusion that the journal writer's state, his obsession, is caused by the unknown makes that event truly Maupassantian: 'the invisible, impalpable, elusive, immaterial Idea ate away his flesh, drank his blood, extinguished his life' (2: 107; B11).

For Todorov, 'The Hair' is ambiguous (and therefore an example of the pure fantastic): the journal writer's use of the modality 'as if,' coupled with his identifying an object with its owner, prepares us for his 'abnormal love' and for a supernatural occurrence (1970, 86). Too, since the supernatural is documented only by an asylum inmate's subjective experience, Todorov believes that the decision about the status of the events depends on whether the journal writer is or is not insane (1970, 91).

Supporting the natural explanation of madness is the doctor's diagnosis, or description, rather, of his patient as 'suffering from erotic and macabre madness,' 'a sort of necrophile,' and 'an obscene madman' (2: 107). The doctor, indeed, has the last word with his remark, 'the mind of man is capable of anything' (2: 113), a phrase with two meanings when considered with other textual evidence.

To call the story ambiguous because of the journal writer's confinement to a madhouse or even the doctor's opinion ignores important features of the narrative discourse, especially the enframing narrator's indirect authentication. He does not impose an explanation or interpretation, but asks to see the lock of hair. His experience of it is so like the 'madman's' as to stand as evidence for it. The hair possesses almost identical properties for both men. For the journal writer, it is 'thick and light' (2: 110); for the narrator, 'caressing and light' (2: 113). The enframing narrator's words for describing his own experience of touching it ('and I felt, touching it, a long shiver [frisson] run through my limbs' (2: 112; B12) are, stylistically, a variant of the journal writer's: 'I shivered, feeling its light and caressing touch on my hands' (2: 113; B13). The hair's properties stir the narrator to disgust 'as upon contact with objects that have been dragged through crimes' and to feel desire 'as one is tempted by an infamous and mysterious thing' (2: 113).

The narrator's response to the object's sensuousness, his linking it to passion through metaphors of desire, temptation, and perversion, echo the journal writer's reaction. Significantly, the journal writer is lucid enough to analyse his experience as a nexus of temptation, desire, and possession: 'What a strange thing, temptation! You look at an object and, little by little, it seduces you [...] as the face of a woman does [...] A desire to possess it takes hold of you, a soft need at first [...] that grows, becomes violent, irresistible (2: 109; B14). The parallel experiences of the enframing narrator and the 'mad' protagonist endow the hair with certain immutable, objective, and unexplained properties. These are no longer a matter of one man's idiosyncratic reaction to an object, 'to believe or not' ['croire ou pas'] (Todorov 1970, 88). 'The Hair' proposes that an object may have an inherent, if mysterious, capacity for eliciting extraordinary responses and that some individuals may be sensitive to it.[8] Indirectly, the status of insanity is interrogated: the narrator's authenticating experience implies that so-called insanity may simply be an ultrasensitivity to unexplained phenomena.

The enframing narrator belongs to the doctor's positivistic world of science, of empirical fact. As a member of that world, a person to whom the doctor confides the journal, the narrator is clearly not mad; this circumstance makes the affinity of his experience with the journal writer's all the more striking. The difference is in degree; affected though he was, he did not become obsessed, while the doctor seems to be altogether immune. If our sane but sensitive narrator can be unsettled by the hair, what does it say about the journal writer's mental state?

In the end, though, the question of the journal writer's sanity is irrelevant. The narrator's authentication shifts the focus to the possibility of an object's having an aura, some invisible remnant of its owner that allows a sensitive person to perceive or even to reconstitute the original. Of greater importance than whether the woman existed or not is the cognitive issue of perception. Without the narrator's indirect authentication of the hair's evocative qualities, the question would be moot. Because the narrator cannot be charged with insanity, the hair and its scientifically unproved properties become the story's focus. In this respect, the two possible meanings of the doctor's comment, 'the mind of man is capable of anything,' become clear, whether he intended them or not: first, the mind is capable of fabricating, of imagining, and, in the case of a mentally unbalanced person, of projecting what is imagined onto something actual; and, second, since it is capable of *anything*, it is equally able to perceive the unknown.

THE RISE OF THE PARANORMAL MODE

In 'Magnetism' (1882), the topic of the title is introduced by an enframing narrator, one of a group of men engaged in a casual after-dinner discussion of Charcot's experiments and the 'tricks' of the famous Belgian magnetizer, Donato. Significantly, Charcot's clinical hypnosis is confused with Donato's vulgarized form of hypnotism. Charcot's name provides a precise time marker, the 1880s; the widespread interest in the experiments he performed during this period lends the topic a sense of immediacy. Some of the characters have been recounting instances of 'the mystery of magnetism.' The enframing narrator characterizes these storytellers as 'sceptical, nice, indifferent to every religion' (1: 406) – though they are evidently willing to consider as possible some of the mysteries brought forward. He himself assumes a sceptic's posture; the others' willingness to believe in magnetism is for him a falling back onto superstition under the guise of science (1: 406). The narration is taken over by a secondary narrator, a young man who doubts on principle, is highly rational and resolutely materialistic. He relegates magnetic phenomena to the domain of fiction by comparing Charcot to some of Poe's narrators who go mad by reflecting on instances of madness (1: 406) – a remark that recalls Gautier's parody *Onophrius* (1833), where the protagonist is driven insane by reading Hoffmann. This secondary narrator challenges not only Charcot's conclusions, but also his assumptions, which for him smack of mysticism. Charcot has neither touched upon nor explained the unknown; he has merely encountered 'unexplained and still inexplicable phenomena of the nerves,' and described them, he goes on, in terms reminiscent of 'the clergy' (1: 406).

The narrator tries to distinguish between the physiological (which may one day be explained because its causes are material) and the mystical. One of his listeners reveals the popular, broad conception of magnetism at the time of the story's writing: 'Even so, there were miracles in days gone by' (1: 407). It was commonly thought, even late in the century, that the mesmeric (or magnetic) trance opened the door to what were called higher phenomena, such as clairvoyance, telepathy, and clairsentience (what Braid termed hyperacuity, the perception of objects hidden from view). Both the enframing and the secondary narrator object to this idea of transcendence, of immateriality, which too easily allows mysticism and superstition to overlap with what purports to be science.

The secondary narrator relates two stories which exemplify this broad conception, and then provides plausible (and natural) interpretations of both. His first, the story of a fisherman's child who awakes in the middle of the night to say that his father has died at sea, is in fact an instance of clairvoyance. Here, clearly, magnetism is understood in its most comprehensive sense, that of higher phenomena, and has little to do with Charcot's hypotheses. The second is the narrator's own, subjective experience, his passionate dream of a woman acquaintance who, in waking life, did not at all interest him. After the dream, he visits her and their passion is consummated; in all its details, the dream is realized in actuality.

His explanations for these incidents express his extreme rationalism.

In the case of the boy who dreamt of his father's death, he notes that hardly a day would pass in a fishing village without some such presentiment being announced. He makes two points: the dreams are caused by an almost obsessive fear of death; and, statistically, there must occur sooner or later a death that corresponds to the dream. His audience accepts the likelihood of this explanation, but is far from satisfied with his hypothesis for his own dream. The narrator himself hesitates and attributes his experience to the underlying and mysterious workings of the human mind: 'Perhaps it was a look she had that I had never noticed, and that came back to me that night in one of those mysterious and unconscious recollections that often show us things neglected by our consciousness, unperceived, in the face of our intelligence' (1: 410; B15). What he proposes is, of course, plausible – data stored in the mind but not readily accessible, and the unexplained mechanisms of that storage facility, memory. Maupassant here invokes Herbert Spencer's idea that our senses allow us only a limited perception of surrounding phenomena, a notion he would develop more fully in other stories. The narrator's words 'mysterious' and 'unperceived' hint at such possibilities, at phenomena that lie just beyond conscious perception and rational cognition. Indeed, those two words turn his argument on its head, because they raise more questions than they answer. His argument is faulty in another respect as well. Why did the woman respond so readily to his post-dream advances? Before his dream, she seems to have been as indifferent as he (1: 408); certainly he does not suggest that she had been interested in him before his visit. Yet she appears to have expected him, or to have had him at that moment on her mind: 'She stood up straight on hearing my name' (1: 410). The sudden understanding between them implies an expectation on her part that is not lost on the narrator, and takes him by surprise: 'suddenly our eyes met with surprising fixity' (1: 410). That she is waiting for something out of the ordinary to happen is also obvious from another of the narrator's observations: 'I stammered out some banalities that she seemed not to hear' (1: 410). So exactly does the woman's passionate response correspond to his dream that he doubts for a moment whether he is awake. Her reaction in fact suggests that this dream of an extraordinarily strong experience was in some way shared by both of them, transmitted telepathically through an unknown channel.[9] The fixed stare when their eyes meet, reminiscent of some magnetizers' attempts to hypnotize a subject, is mutual; it may be that one is trying to magnetize the other. What is significant, then, is not only that a dream creates the narrator's desire, but also that the woman apparently expected and was prepared for it. In effect, the dream is a paranormal motivation for sudden passion, the *coup de foudre* often encountered in Maupassant's non-fantastic erotic narratives. 'Magnetism' links the two parts of Maupassant's oeuvre; we may read it both as an erotic story that literalizes a metaphor (magnetism = sudden erotic attraction) and as a stage in the development of fantastic tales that allude to the human mind's paranormal abilities.

Like 'Magnetism,' 'A Madman?' (1884) also broaches the phenomenon of magnetism. The feats performed by the magnetizer Jacques Parent include not only magnetism (he hypnotizes a dog), but also psychokinesis, for he is able to will objects to move without touching them. The first-person narrator of the story has witnessed Parent's feats, but has no talents of that sort himself. His main narrative role is to mediate the account of magnetism provided in Parent's self-analysis and self-reflection. The reader is given an insider's look at this mysterious phenomenon. The act of narrating is separated from the events narrated by an unspecified period of time, for Parent has since died in an insane asylum. The self-analysis focuses on three aspects of magnetism: the feats themselves, which are the outward manifestation of the magnetizer's special abilities; the conditions usual for their deployment; and the possible causes of these conditions.

Parent's power is concentrated in his extraordinary hands and eyes: 'the eyes of someone suffering hallucinations, black eyes, so black that you couldn't make out the pupil, mobile, wandering, sick, haunted eyes' (2: 308; B16).[10] Trained on their object, they are irresistible, as we see in the dog's reaction when she tries to escape them. His hands are still more singular. They have a disquieting tic which makes them seem, even in performing the routine tasks of picking up a fork or knife, unpredictable.[11] They are 'bony, fine, a bit feverish,' and Parent tends to hide them in his pockets or under his coat. When they are exposed, he makes efforts to control them, to avoid the random, unconscious gestures typical of most people (2: 308). He moves objects simply by aiming his hand at them and drawing them towards him (2: 313).

Parent finds his power horrifying, as does the narrator, and cannot explain why he has it. It is involuntary: 'I only have to look at people to deaden their senses as if I had poured them some opium. I have only to spread my hands to bring about things ... things that are ... terrible' (2: 311; B17). Although he calls it magnetism, he cannot define the word to his satisfaction: 'I am endowed with a power ... no, a capacity ... no, a force' (2: 311; B18), and again: 'What is it? Magnetism? Electricity? Attraction?' (2: 313; B19). Certain situations seem to activate it. Parent observes that it is most obtrusive under particular atmospheric conditions, such as before a storm, when the air is filled with electricity (2: 309). That his powers are stimulated in this way recalls Mesmer's hypothetical bio-magnetic fluids emanating from space, not to mention a variety of vulgarizations of the electromagnetic forces in nature. But this allusion, though it may explain the optimal conditions for the onset of Parent's power, does not account for the power itself.

In describing the workings of his remarkable abilities, Parent touches upon questions that pervade Maupassant's fantastic works. He does not question the reality of magnetism, and cites its use by doctors, in particular Charcot (2: 310). By invoking science and Charcot's potent name, he not only gives credibility to his strange power, but also places himself outside the category of charlatan or madman. As a device, it allows the narrative to pass on from a demonstration of Parent's powers to speculation about cognitive matters. Magnetism as a field of scientific, empirical inquiry is incorporated into the fictional world. In contrast to the preceding story, this fictional account of magnetism is more closely allied with contemporary debates about the higher phenomena popularly associated with it.

According to Parent, magnetism robs a man of his soul, 'this sanctuary, this secret Me, the soul [...]' (2: 310). It is a violation accomplished by one person's will acting on and overriding that of another. Without being able to identify it, Parent recognizes that there is a channel through which magnetism operates. Using the analogy of music, whose sounds would be imperceptible without the eardrum, he posits a world of phenomena which humans are not physically equipped to perceive, once again bringing into play the notion of our sensory limitations: 'Everything is a mystery. We communicate with things only through our paltry senses, which are incomplete, crippled, so weak that they barely have the capacity to record what surrounds us' (2: 310; B20).[12]

There is in 'A Madman?' a suggestion that forces external to humans are responsible for these extraordinary powers. There is also a subtle hint that the forces may be intelligent and capable of superseding humans, whose perceptual defects render them vulnerable to being taken over. Parent realizes that the power he possesses in fact possesses him; he can exercise it at will, yet controls it only with great effort. It constantly threatens to break out, to act on its own against his will; just as he is able to subdue the will of others, his own will is in perpetual jeopardy. The power is almost fully externalized and made concrete when he explains, 'One could say another being [is] locked up inside me that incessantly wants to break out, to act in spite of me, that tosses about, gnaws at me, wears me down' (2: 311; B21).

Although this Other is not externalized, not made an autonomous being, Parent's metaphorical description of his state contains the germ of a novel explanation. It is no longer a question merely of one man exercising his will over another; in the realm of the imperceptible, there may exist entities or forces capable of usurping the human being, body, and soul. Parent recognizes the Other through the opposition of wills within himself. He is equally aware that two opposing wills cannot coexist; he concludes, therefore, 'we are two within my poor body and it is he, the other, that is often the stronger' (2: 311).

Parent's statement, by metaphorically alluding to the possibility of another, autonomous, being, is thus a tentative explanation. A different slant on Parent's sense of another self is, of course, incipient madness. He may be in an early stage of schizophrenia, where his disintegration of personality, his loss of self to an imagined Other, is not fully effected. But this interpretation in no way explains the special abilities which the narrator has witnessed and which are themselves a subject of interest to science, as Parent observes. The dubiousness of this second interpretation is signalled by the question mark in the title: there is no certainty that Parent is insane. Indeed, that he dies in an insane asylum merely casts doubt on medicine's assumptions about madness.

The narrator of 'He?' (1883) is filled with an indefinable sense of fear that drives him to marry in order not to be alone. In the most ordinary of all settings, his lodgings, the narrator experiences something he does not understand and cannot explain. Returning one evening from an outing, he discovers his door unlocked and a stranger sitting in his chair. When he approaches, no one is there.

His sense of horror is, as he describes it, a fear of fear itself (1: 870). The narrator is persuaded that although the stranger will not return, he is none the less present. He externalizes his fear to the extent that even the objects around him seem to be endowed with 'some kind of animal existence' (1: 870), rendering them unfamiliar and therefore threatening. The invisible – indefinable and inexpressible – has taken root in him and become the determining factor of his existence. Yet 'He?' is more than a study of the psychological effects of solitude. It is not, as

Castex suggests, simply a story about 'a neurotic whose mental balance succumbs ... to the horror of feeling himself alone' (1951, 376). If the narrator becomes nervous and acutely conscious of his fear, he changes very little in other respects. He was and remains coherent and rational.

The narrator states clearly that whatever he saw, it was not a revenant; he denies the possibility of life after death, and does not believe in the supernatural (1: 870). He attributes his experience first to hallucination – 'that was an unarguable fact' (1: 873), but soon realizes that his mind was singularly lucid when he saw the stranger, and finds his ability to reason incompatible with hallucination. He is convinced that his vision was not caused by a disorder of the mind, but of the optic nerves (1: 873), the deceiving eye that we will meet again in 'Letter from a Madman.' There is none of the wavering incertitude of the sort that characterizes the narrator of 'The Apparition.' When he again sees the stranger three times, he decides, 'I was feverish, I had a nightmare, how should I know? I was sick, after all' (1: 874; B22). In his rational, materialist perspective, the narrator persuades himself that the indefinable 'he' is in fact 'I'; that is, the outward projection of his own fear: 'I know very well that he doesn't exist, that it's nothing. He exists only in my anxiety, in my fear, my anguish' (1: 875; B23).

The narrator's rationalistic explanation of a psychological disturbance should satisfy him. He has not only accounted for his own experience, but has defined superstition as well: 'I had a vision, one of those visions that make the naive believe in miracles' (1: 873; B24).[13] Yet his own *ad hoc* explanations really fail to persuade this arch-positivist; he clings to them tenaciously to stave off irrationality and to preserve his system, albeit with little success: 'Yes, but it's no use, my reasoning with myself, steeling myself. I can no longer stay alone at my place because he is there' (1: 875; B25).

The narrator has not arrived at the state of questionable madness that we noted in 'The Hair'; and although irrationality has begun to consume him in spite of himself, he has not come to grips with it. He is unable to construct a new epistemology to account for the strange phenomenon, for he has not accepted the possibility of an immaterial or invisible world around him.[14]

His argument hinges on a problem of perception, the senses deceiving the mind. But if a rationalist can at all admit to a malfunction of the senses, he faces a paradox. As he is aware, there are two logical consequences of the unreliability of perceptions: if, under extraordinary conditions such as fever, the senses can misfire and show what is *not* present, they might as easily show what *is* present, though not necessarily perceptible under ordinary conditions. The lucidity of which the narrator is conscious would not then be incompatible with hallucination. Indeed, he happens upon an idea that would become increasingly important in twentieth-century fiction – that hallucination, or altered states, may heighten perception.[15] His own remark, 'the mind races at such moments' (1: 873) contains this thought in embryo. The narrator is therefore caught between two possibilites of equal weight, the one rational, the other, according to his system, irrational. He becomes an inefficient interpreter of his own sensory data.

In 'He?' a paranormal phenomenon is posited, but the rational, positivistic perceiver refuses to admit its existence. But the fear he suffers indicates a crack in his system. The only positivistic explanation (sensory deception) is weak and unsatisfactory, given the phenomenon's recurrence. It is no longer sufficient to call the narrator's fear self-propagating, for his succumbing to that fear does not tally with his extreme rationalism. His fear arises from his inability to resolve the paradox without surrendering his rationality. And yet he cannot make sense of his experience without doing so: 'I'm afraid solely because I do not understand my fear' (1: 870). Nor can he elude the paradox. The vision recurs three times, and even after a night of peaceful sleep he remains obsessed. What haunts him is not fear alone, but a question he will not face. His marriage, an attempt to dodge solitude, is not a solution to the paradox but an anodyne for fear.

THE PARANORMAL MODE

The boundaries of the real are most searchingly explored in the three versions of the story which was called, in its final version, 'The Horla.' In this cycle, Maupassant constructs a fictional world from two primary assumptions. The first is Herbert Spencer's notion that today's known is yesterday's unknown, which has led to the suggestion that there exists a latent world imperceptible to our imperfect sensory and cognitive organs.[16] The second is a fanciful elaboration of Darwin's theory of evolution and natural selection: if humans represent one stage in the evolution of species, they may be outstripped by other beings with superior faculties. Their sensory limitations would then disadvantage them, rendering them vulnerable to higher beings that are imperceptible.

The three versions make comparison profitable: 'Letter from a Madman' (1885) is a prototype of 'The Horla' both in its textual overlap and in its thematic similarity to the other two versions. It is in 'Letter from a Madman' that the cognitive basis of the three versions is openly enunciated, in a letter to the narrator's doctor. This exposition of ideas is triggered by an intertextual reference to Montesquieu: 'One organ more or less in our mechanism would have made for us another intelligence' (2: 461; B26). The narrator, by the way, has made a revealing change in Montesquieu's words, which were taken from *L'Essai sur le goût* (1783) – the original reads 'would have made for us another eloquence ['nous aurait fait une autre éloquence']' (2: 1459, n. 1). With this 'quotation,' which he claims abruptly cleared his thoughts (1: 461), the narrator constructs a possible world that consists of phenomena inaccessible to the human senses (2: 463). The sensory organs, those intermediaries between human and world, interior and exterior, I and Other, are imperfect, limiting, and arbitrary. Still fewer organs would exclude man from knowledge he already has; without the eardrum, for instance, the art of music would be non-existent (2: 453). Arguing by analogy, the narrator infers that additional organs would therefore open up a world of other things. As a consequence, the empirical concept of reality is suspect: 'Everything is false, everything is possible, everything is uncertain' (2: 463).

A second aspect of the narrator's epistemology draws implicitly on science, on its discovery of such forces as electricity and its failure to explain them fully: 'I concluded that half-glimpsed mysteries like electricity, hypnotic sleep, transmission of will, suggestion, all the magnetic phenomena, only remain concealed from us because nature has not furnished us with the organ, or organs, necessary to understand them' (2: 464; B27). In order to overcome his sensory impediments, the narrator deliberately tries to sharpen and excite his organs (2: 464).[17] To the narrator's way of thinking, this stimulation accomplished what he intended. He finally sees an invisible being: 'On the following day I locked up early, looking for ways to see the Invisible thing that was visiting me. And I saw it' (2: 465). The being is apparently intelligent, for the narrator writes that the creature understood that he had been seen (2: 466). Frightened as he is by his vision, and although the being is apparently intelligent, the narrator does not feel himself menaced. Tacitly, he recognizes that his *desire* to perceive something in the seeming void [le vide apparent] may have determined his seeing it, an inference supported by his ranking the hypothetical invisible world with the traditional supernatural: 'the supernatural is nothing other than that which remains veiled for us' (2: 464). Once his hypothesis is demonstrated he realizes, paradoxically, that he has opened a door precisely onto the supernatural and the irrational. He finds himself in an imaginary domain peopled by mythical creatures which, by his own claim, are born of nothing but fear: 'And in that mirror, I begin to see crazy images, monsters, hideous corpses, all sorts of terrifying beasts, atrocious beings, all the unlikely visions that must haunt the mind of the mad' (2: 466; B28). By recognizing the paradox and concluding that he is prey to hallucinations (2: 461) he undermines his own hypothesis and disauthenticates his experience of seeing the invisible. Perhaps most interestingly, the narrator has reversed the transformation observed in the first group of stories. There the traditional, mythological, supernatural domain was voided, made irrelevant by being amalgamated with the unknown; in 'Letter from a Madman,' the narrator's contact with the unknown, with a natural but uncharted phenomenon, leads him back into the domain of the supernatural, from which his post-positivist epistemology does not safeguard him. Obviously it could be argued that the story ought for this reason to have been included with the tales of the first group. Its fictional world structure has more in common with them. But its affinity with the 'Horla' cycle justifies its inclusion here if only for the purpose of comparison.

In 'Letter from a Madman,' the narrator devises a cognitive strategy by reflecting on philosophical sources. In the two versions entitled 'The Horla' (1886 and 1887), the strategies are formulated in response to the narrators' experiences. They search for explanations only when an anomalous phenomenon intrudes into their otherwise peaceful worlds.

The narrator of the 1886 version does not doubt his experience in retrospect; it only confirms his hypothesis that an invisible superbeing has appeared on earth with the power to dominate humankind. His vision of a new species or race is based on evolutionary principles: 'It's the one the world has been waiting for, after mankind! The one who is coming to dethrone us, to enslave us, to tame us, and perhaps to feed off us, the way we feed off cattle and boar' (2: 829; B29). Like the narrator of 'Letter from a Madman,' he implies that humans are fragile, and could easily be exterminated by superior beings. Humanity can hardly contend with a foe it cannot see. The narrator feels that when he is asleep, and most vulnerable, his 'self' is being annihilated, as though by an incubus: 'Yes, I fell into a void, into an absolute void, into a death of my entire being, from which I was abruptly, horribly, jerked by the appalling sensation of a crushing weight on my chest and of a mouth that was eating my existence' (2: 823; B30). His fear in the face of this invisible threat echoes that of the narrators of 'He?,' 'A Madman?' and 'Letter from a Madman.'[18] Indeed, the narrator has at first no name for this unseen threat; his consistent use of the pronoun 'on' is a taboo forced on him by necessity, until he coins the word 'Horla.'[19] The narrator's conception of a world invisible to the human senses transforms the supernatural into natural phenomena. All the subjects of human legend, for centuries relegated to the domain of the supernatural, are suddenly explicable. People have always sensed and had a terror of these invisible beings whose existence was announced in the form of stories about fairies and gnomes (2: 829). These creatures, products of the human imagination, reflect also our groping towards an explanation for our uneasiness, for the suspicion that much in reality affects us that we cannot perceive. The Horla is in a sense a reincarnation of mythological beings, the rebirth, in a non-supernatural form, of all the bogies of legend that 'haunted our fathers' (2: 829). Paranormal abilities, the capacity to perceive such phenomena, are the natural, rational explanation for manifestations which, for the superstitious, were supernatural.

From the narrator's point of view, the issue is primarily epistemological. He wastes little time looking for flaws in his own evidence; after all, his is an empirical experience. But he must argue for the supraindividual existence of the Horla, and like the narrator of 'Letter from a Madman,' he argues by analogy: the wind and electricity exist, although they are not visible; the microworld and distant universes exist even in the absence of special devices for perceiving them (2: 829). The Horla is not a natural force; it is an intelligent, human-like creature of substance, an organism that drinks liquids and so requires sustenance. Its materiality, if so transparent a creature can be called material, belongs to a plane of perception beyond the ken of humans.

In order to establish the Horla's reality and to authenticate his own experience, the narrator introduces external evidence. His coachman and several people in his neighbourhood have complained of the same symptoms and had the same sense of life being sucked from their bodies, an assertion which the doctor corroborates from his own investigations (2: 828). The narrator also adduces, as objective evidence, a newspaper clipping that describes a similar occurrence in Brazil, where people have been fleeing their homes to escape pursuit by invisible vampires that prey on them during sleep (2: 830). But it is the doctor's comment at the close of the narrative that invests the narrator's claims with a certain degree of authenticating force: 'I don't know if this man is mad, or if both of us are ... or whether our successor has truly arrived' (2: 830; B31).

This version of 'The Horla' is an enframed first-person narrative which is not prompted by the events themselves; the motivation for its telling is made explicit in the frame. The narrator, who is confined to a sanatorium, is asked to report to a consortium of doctors on an event which occurred a year previously. The narrative is robbed of immediacy by its use of pseudo-scientific discourse, and takes the form of a defence plea, of a speech act aimed at explaining the speaker's beliefs and clearing him of the suspicion of insanity.[20] The narrator's sanity, though, is a side issue, as it was in 'The Hair.' The focus on his mental condition only draws attention to the wonderful lucidity and coherence of his arguments. The doctor's final remarks confirm that the psychopathological explanation is problematic; he withholds judgment.

With the final version of 'The Horla' (1887) Maupassant achieved what he had set out to do in the first two versions. It is his most focused attempt to deal with the problem of interpreting extrasensory phenomena and it is his most skilful effort at elaborating a discursive pattern of multiple interpretations.

The text is a purely subjective first-person account which is not motivated by any external circumstance, in contrast to the 1886 version. Again unlike the earlier story where the narrative takes the form of a plea, here the narrative is a diary, an act of writing which is closest to confession and self-analysis. Because the narrator records his experiences in a diary, the events have immediacy; they are almost simultaneous with the act of narrating. According to Fitz, the journal is 'figuratively speaking, a mirror which the author holds at an oblique angle in order for the reader to see him, and directly in front of himself, in order to see his own image' (1972, 956). As the narrator succumbs to the Horla's will, he finds that the creature causes him to speak and write words that are alien to him (2: 934–5). Thus the journal reflects the gradual fusion of the narrator and the Horla.

The narrator's growing sense of a presence that baffles the usual sensory channels follows a pattern of gradation. The first stage is a vague uneasiness intensified by declining health and nightmares. In the next stage, the narrator feels that something external to him is devouring his vitality while he sleeps. This 'something' is fully externalized in the third stage, when the milk and water (but not the wine) that he has left out as a test, are drunk during the night – a force or a being intrudes from without, acting independently of the narrator. The fourth and climactic stage in this gradation occurs when the narrator perceives that the Horla has form and substance. Even at this stage, though, the perception is indirect, mediated by a mirror.

Castex observed this gradation and assumed that it parallels, and is therefore a sign of, Maupassant's progressing illness (1951, 387). Schurig-Geick, in contrast, sees in it only the *narrator's* growing anxiety and mental instability (1970, 51). Yet the narrator is not predisposed towards the arcane. Before he senses the Horla's presence, his life is peaceful and he has no cause for anxiety. Certainly he gives little thought to metaphysical matters, preferring to stretch out on his lawn and gaze at the sky and the water. It is only when his life is pervaded by a strange presence that he looks for an explanation. And only in that search does he formulate an epistemology to account for the unexpected and bizarre change in his rather banal existence.

The Horla's intervention makes this version a story of ontological questioning and epistemic reinterpretation. It is a story of power and survival as well, of the relationship between two beings struggling to dominate. In the 1886 version, the event is filtered through and interpreted by the narrator alone. He presents a case to the representatives of science, and the doctor deems his two interpretations possible. In the 1887 version, the narrator filters the events, but he mediates interpretations which come, rather, from three independent sources. Each of these interpretations functions for the narrator as a partial explanation, as a piece of the puzzle he will put together to form a new epistemology.

The first of these sources is a monk who argues for the existence of invisible beings by analogy with such elements as the wind, an unseen force of great potency (2: 918). The conversation takes place on Mont Saint-Michel, a place rich in legend and superstition, but still more interesting is the fact that it is a monk who makes a case for an invisible, parallel domain. His belief in mythological worlds reminds us of Comte's first stage of human intellect, the theological, which is concerned with primary and final causes.[21] The second interpretation is tendered by a Parisian scientist, the antithesis to the superstitious monk. Dr Parent conducts an experiment in hypnotism, using the narrator's cousin as subject. He demonstrates not only that the will can be suppressed and dominated, but also that a hypnotized subject can perceive the invisible. Mme Sablé is handed her cousin's calling card and told that it is a mirror. She believes she sees in this 'mirror' the narrator's image, an instance of the higher phenomena which hypnotized subjects were thought capable of perceiving. The doctor then proposes a theory whereby hypnotism is a naturalizing force: he claims that it is gradually revealing as natural the so-called mysterious phenomena that were once thought to be supernatural by those of a primitive intellect (2: 922). Once again, Comte's three stages are brought to mind. As Targe points out, the monk's story and the doctor's demonstration are, for the narrator, 'echoes of the Horla's possession' (1975, 450). Even though they are interpretations of mysterious phenomena they reflect, in a sense, the narrator's own experience of feeling himself dominated.

The third interpreter is the narrator himself, and the nature of his explanations also parallels the increasing intensity of his experience. When he is still only vaguely conscious of a presence nearby, he ascribes it to a physical disorder: 'Isn't it strange that mere indisposition, a circulatory disorder perhaps, the irritation of a nerve, a little congestion [...] can make a melancholic out of the most cheerful of men [...]' (2: 915; B32). There are shades of Scrooge's digestive metaphors in this – Marley's ghost as 'an underdone fragment of potato' – though without the humour. The narrator then wonders about his state of mind, but is not satisfied for long with the notion that he might be mad, or hallucinating. In the 10 July entry of his diary, he writes: 'I am certainly mad' (2: 920). Almost a month later, he reasons: 'I would certainly believe myself mad, absolutely mad, if I were not conscious of my state, if I didn't know it perfectly, if I were not able to probe it, analysing it with complete lucidity' (2: 928; B33). Once he is convinced that an autonomous being is usurping his soul, the narrator elaborates a theory of the paranormal. He recalls Dr Parent's experiment and likens his cousin's hypnotic state to his own: 'That's exactly how my poor cousin was possessed and dominated [...] She was subject to an alien will that had entered her, like another soul, parasitic and imperious' (2: 930; B34). When the narrator notices the physical traces left by the Horla, he develops Dr Parent's interpretation, postulating a domain that lies beyond the reach of ordinary human sensory mechanisms. His theory accounts for the special form his experience takes at its peak. He perceives the Horla negatively as the absence of his own image, which is obstructed or overlaid by an opacity between his body and the mirror. Like the narrator of 'Letter from a Madman,' his sharpened senses are already on the alert when he sees the invisible being (2:

935). Hypnotism introduces for the narrator the question of *how*, by what unknown force or channel, one person's will can dominate another's. The Horla comes to represent not only a dominant being, but the unknown force itself. The narrator's final thesis crystallizes after he reads a newspaper report about a similar occurrence in Brazil. The monk's words come to his mind – 'Do we see a hundred thousandth part of all that exists?' – and he proposes that a new race of superhuman, invisible beings has arrived (2: 934). In this way the narrator brings together all the interpretations he has heard or himself formulated. His ability to synthesize these interpretations is also, surely, a sign of his rationality.[22] This jewel in his theory is quite clearly a fanciful extension of Darwinism. From the postulates of limited human sensory mechanisms comes his notion of invisible creatures in the world and of uncharted forces acting as channels for special powers (2: 914). From this comes the narrator's vision of a new and superior race of beings – 'A new being! Why not? Surely he was bound to come! Why should we be the last?' (2: 934; B35).

An interpretation of Darwin's theory of natural selection, vulgarized in the formula 'the survival of the fittest,' leads the narrator to conclude that the reign of humans is over; as an inferior species humans will be enslaved and preyed upon (2: 934). His tragic attempt to kill the Horla illustrates the formula well, since he is engaged in mortal combat with a foe whose survival means his own annihilation. With his synthesis of interpretations, and his blending of science, pseudoscience, and mythology, the narrator establishes the Horla's existential status. He has identified it and accounted for it, and must therefore recognize it as an autonomous entity.[23]

Despite the fact that it is the narrator who mediates everything we read, the interpretations of Dr Parent and the monk and the newspaper article he draws our attention to are authenticating devices. The experiment with his cousin and the illness of his coachman also serve to authenticate. The coachman's illness mirrors the narrator's deteriorating health, while Mme Sablé's experience is an artificially induced mirror of his experience and supports it by analogy.[24] Indeed, his test with the milk, water, and wine is an attempt to authenticate the invisible (2: 920). So, in a less direct way, is the servants' quarrelling over objects that have disappeared or been broken (2: 926).

Stylistically, the narrator's discourse parallels the gradual increase in the intensity of his experience. It is also an indicator of the ways in which his theory changes. For instance, when he sees a rose apparently being picked and held suspended, his words are, 'j'ai vu' (2: 927). The absence of a grammatical object suggests that the narrator cannot yet identify what he has seen; he is simply voicing his awareness of an alien presence. During the most vivid of his experiences, when he 'sees' the Horla, he exclaims: 'je l'ai vu!' (2: 935), the grammatical object referring to a specific and individualized entity.[25] At a certain point, he accumulates nouns and related verbs, an act that represents his effort to concretize and give expression to his experience. Before he sees the Horla, he knows it by its influence: 'Someone is in command of all my actions, all my movements, all my thoughts [...]' (2: 929). Afterwards, his utterances express an aggressive desire to counter the Horla's influence by asserting his own will. It has become for him a concrete being upon which he can act: 'I would have the strength of the desperate, I would have my hands, my knees, my chest, my forehead, my teeth to strangle him, crush him, bite him, tear him apart' (2: 935; B36).

The description of the Horla itself is semantically indefinite, conveyed indirectly in similes and figurative language: 'It was as bright as day, yet I could not see myself in my mirror! [...] Then, all of a sudden, I began to make myself out in a mist at the back of the mirror, as though through a sheet of water [...] it was like the end of an eclipse' (2: 935–6; B37). The obliqueness of his language – it is almost entirely made up here of metaphors – is a mirror of his experience. The narrator has perceived the Horla indirectly. The Horla's 'opaque transparency' [transparence opaque] finds its echo in the symbol most frequently associated with it, the colour white. The narrator deduces that the creature arrived on a white Brazilian three-master and was attracted to his white house; his own experiment revealed that the Horla would drink only water (transparent) or milk (white) (2: 920).

The opening of the narrative is strongly contrasted with the dramatic events that follow. In the first episode, calmly descriptive, the protagonist is at one with nature: 'What a lovely day! I spent the whole morning stretched out in the grass in front of my house under the enormous plane tree that covers it, sheltering it and shading it completely' (2: 913; B38). Compare the style of the climactic 19 August entry, which is highly charged, dramatic, and presents the event in all its emotionality and immediacy; abrupt syntactic phrases contribute to the discursive tension: 'I'm done for!' (2: 929); 'It's he, he, the Horla [...] He is inside me, he's becoming my soul; I'll kill him!' (2: 935). Despite the affectivity of such passages, the narrator's logical coherence shows no sign of deteriorating and there is no trace of pathological semantic or syntactic distortion. The texture of his discourse speaks strongly for the narrator's sanity.[26]

In the crucial 19 August entry, stylistic contrast recurs in the narrator's description of his room. His nonchalant and impersonal tone in itemizing his furniture tells us how banal is the setting for this most remarkable experience: 'In front of me, my bed, an old oak four-poster; on the right, my fireplace; on the left, my carefully closed door [...]' (2: 935; B39). It is a bald description, preceded by a flood of verbs expressing violent action (strangle, crush, bite, tear apart). He seems to get a grip on himself until he observes that his reflection is missing, with the Horla's interposition between him and the mirror. This brings him back to the exclamatory style: 'It was empty, bright to the very depths, full of light!' Another slowly paced description follows, as the narrator describes just what he does see in the mirror: 'it seemed to me that this [sheet of] water was slowly creeping from left to right, making my reflection more distinct moment by moment' (2: 936; B40). At the end of the entry the narrator resumes his emotionally charged style, and the circle, stylistically, is closed (2: 936). Interestingly, the shift in register in the 19 August entry is signalled by different tenses of the same verb: 'and I pretended that I was writing' ['et je fis semblant d'écrire'] 'so I was pretending to write' ['donc je faisais semblant d'écrire']. The simple past and the conjunction of the first phrase mark a completed action which took place the evening before and which is being viewed from the narrating present. The second is introduced by 'donc,' which connotes here not consequence, but the picking up of the narrative thread which was retarded while the narrator itemized his furniture. The imperfect 'faisais' brings the past into the present, as though relived, and makes more immediate the event that follows – seeing the Horla. The entry as a whole is similarly enframed, opening with 'I saw him!' ['je l'ai vu!'] and closing with 'I have seen him' ['je l'avais vu'].[27]

The mirror itself, in the 19 August entry, is marked by stylistic shifts and textural density: from 'armoire à glace' to 'ma glace,' from 'grand verre limpide' to 'miroir.' 'Armoire à glace' is stylistically neutral and simply denotes one of the items of furniture in the narrator's room; 'ma glace' is personalized by the possessive pronoun. Significantly, he uses the pronoun at the moment when he is most at a loss; that is, when he notices that his reflection is missing. 'Grand verre limpide' is the narrator's poetic expression when confronting the enigma, helpless and unable to move. 'Miroir,' however, literalizes a metaphor ('au fond du miroir') for a unique effect. The narrator progresses from the mirror as an object that occupies a certain space in his room to the mirror *as* space; that is, the virtual or illusory space which we see in the mirror. It is in this *illusion* of space, paradoxically, that the invisible becomes visible. The opposition corresponds to the expressions 'glace vide' and 'verre limpide,' which serve as a prelude to his phrase 'transparence opaque.' This episode is a stylistic mise-en-abîme that mimics the larger, surrounding, episode of the narrator's encounter with the Horla.

Questions ('what's the matter with me?' ['qu'ai je donc?']; 'so close that I could perhaps touch him, seize him?' ['si près que je pourrais peut-être le toucher, le saisir?'], etc.) are a stylistic feature of Maupassant's fantastic tales and index even some of his titles. Obviously they serve a purpose, expressing his protagonists' uncertainty, their desire to make sense of bewildering events. In 'The Horla,' the questions have a very clear semantic function: the narrator's shuttling back and forth from question to answer represents his obsessive querying of a reality grown unfamiliar, his struggle to 'plug the gap' (Dentan 1976, 46) in a paranormal fictional world where the unknown intrudes and must be expected.

First-person narration, the enframed narrative, syntactic and stylistic devices signifying what can only be called shattered nerves – these are features of Maupassant's fantastic tales that he used no less frequently in his realistic works. Maupassant's entire oeuvre, MacNamara observes, is 'founded on an aesthetic of rupture,' a 'nervousness of style' to be identified with the fictional language of Realism in general (1986, 196).

Our overview of his works shows that rupture alone does not give Maupassant's fictional world its structural specificity. Rather, Maupassant enlarges the fictional world, making ordinary existence encompass more. In his non-fantastic narratives, it is generally the narrator's or protagonist's scope of standard everyday experience that is transgressed. A father might fall in love with his daughter ('M. Jocaste,' 1883) or learn that he has just committed incest in a brief encounter with the daughter whose existence he was unaware of ('Le Port,' 1889). The narrators are not thrown into a crisis by their adventures, nor is their outlook skewed, for there is no challenge to the fictional world's modal homogeneity. Nor does reality become suspect. Even in 'Le Tic' (1884), where the protagonist's trauma has left him with a visible sign, the scope of fictional reality is unaltered. He has changed; the world around him has not. Maupassant's non-fantastic stories disclose unexpected facets of the natural world and suggest that experience cannot be predetermined. The events themselves are motivated by explainable conditions, especially erotic passion, which in Maupassant's work often challenges a closed view of reality – of marriage, family, love, and the constraints society places on human relationships.

His fantastic stories query the very concept of reality. The scope of the fictional world is expanded, not merely transgressed as in his realistic works. The natural world in its narrowness and limitedness becomes suspect, seems false. Standard conceptions of the natural world are subverted and replaced with new epistemologies.

In the stories of the first group, this subversion is not complete. The fantastic is still tied to tradition – revenants appear, severed hands roam, a dead woman may or may not have been resurrected. The narrators encounter phenomena that defy their mediocre ideas about the natural world. The opposition between natural and supernatural is not erased; narrative indeterminacy simply makes the fictional world structurally ambiguous, both for the reader and for the narrators/protagonists. These stories are narrated by sceptics who shun the supernatural and yet who do not insist that reality is altogether closed. They are open-minded enough to question their preconceptions and to allow for possibility. Even so, they fail in the interpretation of their experiences and relegate them to the category of the 'inexplicable.' The enframing narrator of 'The Hair' is the only one to approach an expanded conception of reality.

The second set begins to inscribe this expanded view of reality. To be sure, the narrators remain sceptical and positivistic. Yet their experiences propel them ineluctably towards a different epistemology even while they close their minds to it. The narrator of 'He?' would rather marry into oblivion than wipe out his conception of reality. But the narrator of 'Magnetism' accepts the possibility that channels of cognition exist that are not understood. He unwittingly enlarges the scope of fictional reality in this way, making unexplained phenomena a special part of the natural domain; that is, taking them as paranormal. And the magnetizer of 'A Madman?' proposes a pseudoscientific theory to account for his mental powers: they are natural, but paranormal.

With the Horla cycle, the transformation of the traditional modes of the fantastic is completed by means of a radical shift in the outlook of the narrators and interpreters: positivistic confidence gives way to philosophical uncertainty and anxiety. The protagonists do more than report their strange experiences; they formulate a new, post-positivistic outlook to integrate their experiences into the natural world. In this, in the complexity of the narrator's epistemology and the power of Maupassant's artistry, the final version of 'The Horla' towers over all the rest. The narrator synthesizes the systems people have erected through the ages to make sense of the unknown, from the mythological to the scientific, and ends with a fictional world where the unknown finds its place in the expanded natural domain. And so one of the most memorable of mysterious characters in all of fantastic literature, the Horla, is brought into fictional existence.

Conclusion

By now it should be evident that the literary fantastic is a peculiarly plastic artistic category, even though I have concentrated on nineteenth-century literature. Movements, period styles, literary techniques spring up and are put aside, to be replaced with others according to the dictates of fashion and the prevailing philosophies. The fantastic survives these vicissitudes by allowing itself to be shaped as the times require. It adapts to a variety of genres just as it fits many period styles. This is the facet of the fantastic which has so often perplexed critics and theorists; if a literary phenomenon can be so flexible, then what is it in its own right but an element or a feature of a larger category? And if it is an element, then it is a rhetorical device, or mode of expression. For instance, a rather common approach to fantastic stories in undergraduate courses in North America is to read them allegorically, as messages. If it is claimed that the tale conveys a message, then the fantastic is understood as a device; it becomes a cloak that conceals a moral, social, or didactic message – the sugar coating that hides the bitter pill of a lesson. In such a story as Dickens's *A Christmas Carol*, all of the thematic entities (the ghosts) and events (Scrooge's flying, forays into the past/future, etc.) would become aspects of that device, vehicles or 'techniques' (an overused word with little meaning in this context) for conveying the 'moral.' What is particularly feeble about such an approach is that the decision that a narrative is allegorical (didactic, a social critique, or a moral message) is arbitrary, arrived at by fiat. In such a vicious circle, the fantastic cannot be theorized as a legitimate aesthetic and literary phenomenon.

It is easy to be led astray by apparently simple solutions. But three questions seemed to me to require answers, questions which would not arise if the fantastic were merely a device. The first is very basic, even primitive: how is it that readers, at the intuitive level, can agree about whether a given narrative is or is not fantastic? Lists of thematic phenomena – creatures and events – are attempts to define a common ground, an area of agreement. At first glance, themes may appear to be a simple and clear-cut answer to the question. But themes are culturally and historically bound and would demand, if one were thorough, a list so comprehensive as to be utterly impractical, even if it would be useful. At any rate, the fact that we can usually agree about whether a work is fantastic led me to look at the way the narratives are put together, rather than at individual thematic components. So, to answer this first question, I felt that it was necessary to describe how fantastic narratives are structured. As I wrote in the first chapter, orderly description must precede interpretations if we wish to avoid remaining on an easy, personal, intuitive level.

The second and third questions are related: why do some fantastic narratives, written perhaps centuries apart, seem much of a muchness, beyond their themes? For instance, what more do such works as Marlowe's and Goethe's versions of *Faust* have in common with the legend than just the theme of a man selling his soul to the devil? The third question is, in what do the differences lie? This is more challenging: two narratives which, on the intuitive level, seem to be very different may have identical themes. In what, then, does their difference lie? Traditional thematics cannot even come close to answering this question because, although it is capable of saying that transformations happen, it has no *theory* of transformation.

With these three questions in mind, I presented a typology of modes – *theoretical models* described in chapter 1. At the risk of sounding repetitive, I will say once again that the typology is theoretical in intention; it would utterly defeat the purpose of the modes to see them as slots into which one drops works of art. The different world structures which the modes describe are founded on the opposition of the natural and the supernatural, defined in chapter 1 as 'physically possible' and 'physically impossible.' The modal opposition itself provides a ground for that primitive intuition that certain texts are fantastic, while others are not. The typology distinguishes fantastic from non-fantastic texts, and goes still further in differentiating the fantastic from those narratives where the supernatural consists of an isolated, peripheral episode.

But the typology is designed to be something more than a theoretical model. Chapters 4, 5, and 6 take up the last two questions, showing that writers, by varying the opposition between the natural and the supernatural, have made it dynamic. They shape the fictional world by bringing to bear on it stylistic and narrative devices that are both individual and linked to the period in which they are writing. Depending on how the opposition is configured, we may find that works of different periods and widely divergent styles are similar in their fictional world structure, or that two works apparently sharing the same theme are dissimilar. The opposition, then, undergoes certain describable transformations.

In another sense also, the typology is not static. I argue throughout that the modes are not mere abstractions; they do not transcend history. Chapters 2 and 3 are attempts to link the modes to some intellectual, cultural, ideological, and aesthetic factors. The relationship, though, is not deterministic; in other words, the modes cannot be derived from the extraliterary factors. These two aspects of the modes – the configuration of the fictional world according to the way the opposition is treated, and the intellectual, etc., context in which a narrative is written – indicate a preference at certain moments in history for particular modes; and they indicate as well that the modes recur time and again. We may find the disjunctive mode as readily in the twentieth century as in the eighteenth.

Five modes, one of which is a subtype, were proposed to describe the modal opposition and its transformations. In the *disjunctive mode*, the fictional existence of both domains, supernatural and natural, is uncontested. The entities of both domains interact, but a supernatural entity is never absorbed into the natural domain, and a supernatural event is not naturalized. In the *fantasy mode*, a subtype of the *disjunctive mode*, the supernatural domain is dominant; either the natural domain is not represented at all or it is part of an enframing narrative. Supernatural beings and events are often generated by poetic language – by the literalization of poetic figures, or by poetic utterances becoming events. In the *ambiguous mode*, the supernatural domain is not fully authenticated, but neither is it disauthenticated. Various narrative strategies create unresolvable indeterminancy and ambiguity. In the mode called *the supernatural naturalized*, narrative strategies throughout the text serve to authenticate the supernatural domain, but in the conclusion (quite often in an appended epilogue), the supernatural is abruptly disauthenticated. Dream, hallucination, and mental disease are among the most popular narrative devices for disauthentication. Though disauthentication nullifies the supernatural character of the fictional beings and events, it is not sufficient reason for excluding works of this mode from fantastic literature.

While I was studying these structural transformations it became evident that something happened to the fantastic after the middle of the nineteenth century. It seemed that another domain was added which supplanted, at least for some writers, the supernatural domain. This I have called the rise of the *paranormal mode*. Further study discovered that the paranormal mode evolved in a context of intellectual crisis in the second half of the nineteenth century. Natural science in the nineteenth century was forcing people to re-examine the supernatural, indeed forcing the complacent to question some long-held beliefs. Positivist philosophy and science rejected the supernatural as a product of superstition or mysticism – in any case, as decidedly irrational. Scientists did not reject unexplained phenomena out of hand, however; it was simply a question of subjecting the unexplained to the scrutiny and methods of science. Theories began to emerge to account for phenomena once ascribed to supernatural intervention. At the same time, Darwin's theory of natural selection was giving rise to a spate of fanciful notions about the future of humankind, and spiritualism was on the rise as a popular pastime. Hypnosis, as distinct from Mesmerism (though not in the popular mind), was being studied seriously by scientists like Braid and, later, Bramwell in England, Charcot, Richet, Bernheim in France, and Bechterev in Russia. Modern theories of the mind and its latent abilities began to emerge, and a split soon occurred between those who saw in spiritualism a confirmation of the supernatural, and those who found alternative explanations in science. The latter trend, as it grew, became known as psychical research. In this context, fantastic literature underwent a radical modernization that helped it to endure in the nineteenth and on into the twentieth century.

The possible-worlds approach (and the typology of the fantastic derived from it) does not break down; quite the opposite – it allowed me to describe and explain this transformation. There is a restructuring and a renaming. Once it is seen that 'supernatural' is merely superstition's word for 'not yet explained,' it can be said that the domain of paranormal phenomena belongs within, is part of, the natural domain. It is not absorbed to the extent that it becomes an indistinguishable constituent of the natural domain – paranormal phenomena are not commonplace natural events. But they are not physically impossible;

they are extraordinary and mysterious, natural – physically possible – but latent and awaiting explanation.

I observed the emergence of this mode in the works of three writers who were all Realists, a factor which I am convinced is no coincidence. These men were anxious to breathe the atmosphere of their times, and scientific knowledge in the nineteenth century was so widely disseminated, at least in a popular form, that they could hardly fail to be exposed to it. Like many scientists and philosophers, they came to believe that reality was not the closed empirical given that the most doctrinaire of the positivists preached. Through the natural sciences, these writers sensed the mysteries still hidden in nature. In theories of evolution, in particular Darwin's theory of natural selection, they saw the possibility of humanity's growth or degeneration in an environment not fully understood and not altogether under human control. From the psychological sciences they gleaned information about the nature and hidden potentialities of the human mind and their consequences for human development. As Realists, none of them could go on rehearsing the traditional artistic treatments of the fantastic. They sought, and found, a new mode of the fantastic which they were able to cultivate along with their purely realistic works, without any violation of their artistic principles.

In the works of the three writers analysed, there are several stories which I have called transitional tales, or tales which show that the paranormal mode is incipient. Remarkable parallels can be found in these stories which lead, not always chronologically, to the paranormal mode. Only three of them, one by each writer, are what I would call fully developed instances of the paranormal mode. These are Dickens's 'The Signal-Man,' Turgenev's 'The Dream,' and Maupassant's 1887 version of 'The Horla.' And here, most interestingly, their focus is not identical, for each writer emphasizes different aspects of the paranormal mode. For Dickens, it was the epistemological questions that mattered, for Turgenev, the psychological, and for Maupassant, the philosophical.

Dickens's 'The Signal-Man' asks whether there is not some factor behind the seemingly random concatenation of events that we call coincidence. The event here is a kind of personified warning, a premonition borne out in fact, in the signal-man's death and the manner of his dying. The coincidences are too many, but other explanations elude the narrator and the reader.

In Turgenev's 'The Dream,' the paranormal experience is also private; but it is rendered in a first-person narrative. The focus shifts from epistemological questions to the psychological and existential aspects of the experience – the effects of the clairvoyant dream on the protagonist/narrator. He cares primarily for what it says about *his* existence, rather than about reality, and how it affects *him*.

Maupassant's 'The Horla' shifts the question away from private concerns and individual psychologies. The pivotal issue is the survival of the human race, for 'Le Horla' presents the terrifying prospect of humanity's confrontation with a race of beings it is physically and mentally ill-equipped to deal with. Individual epistemological and psychological anxieties give way, here, to the terror arising from a vision of humankind surrounded by an imperceptible and threatening superior race.

It might be thought that the case I have made for the emergence of the paranormal mode ties it to the nineteenth century. After all, aside from the transitional tales, only three tales were offered as examples. Does this mean that the paranormal mode simply vanished by the end of the century?

Far from being the closing chapter in the history of the fantastic, the paranormal mode was the start of a new series, by opening the way for further developments, newer trends. I consider Dickens's 'The Signal-Man' to be the precursor of a whole new trend of twentieth-century ambiguous fantastic. The paradigmatic text would be Henry James's *The Turn of the Screw*, whose ambiguity stems not so much from the unreliability of the governess as from the fact that the events are filtered through so many narrators. In Dickens's story, the signal-man's experience and the supporting evidence of the engine-driver are all mediated through a non-participating narrator. In James's novella, the mediation is more complicated: the children's and the governess's experiences are mediated by Douglas, who narrates the story to the fictional 'author' of the text we read. The reader's hesitation is quite natural and, at the same time, theoretically irrelevant. In such a complex chain of narrative transmission no authentication, no certainty about the existential status of the 'apparitions,' is possible.

Maupassant's 'The Horla' has an equally distinguished succession in modern science fiction. This is not the traditional, optimistic, technological Utopia such as Jules Verne wrote, but the frightening anti-Utopia of an earth invaded by aliens. With 'The Man from Mars' (1887) Maupassant in fact took the step that led from the fantastic to science fiction with the story of a failed Martian landing that one man alone claims to have witnessed. 'The Horla' brings into play the threat of annihilation from an unfamiliar entity, and one can see how readily the paranormal mode links up with science fiction by imagining the Horla to be an extraterrestrial. The paradigm example of this trend is H.G. Wells's 1898 *The War of the Worlds*. The Martians ultimately die, but their invasion has changed the atmosphere of the human world forever. Wells captures this alteration in words that could be applied as well to 'The Horla': 'We have learned now that we cannot regard this planet as being fenced in and a secure abiding-place for Man; we can never anticipate the unseen good or evil that may come upon us suddenly out of space' (1898, 300).

Perhaps the most interesting historical development follows upon Turgenev's 'The Dream.' This tale, I believe, was a step towards the modern fiction represented by Franz Kafka, particularly in such of his works as *The Metamorphosis* (1915) and *A Country Doctor* (1919). Kafka takes the paranormal mode to its limit. The domain of the paranormal is no longer latent; rather, it pervades the natural domain, and blends with it, so that they cannot be distinguished. In Kafka, strange events are commonplace, as regular as any other. His is an ontologically 'hybrid' fictional world, to use Doležel's term (1984). Strange events occur haphazardly, wherever, whenever, without any special reason, just as they do in a dream. Oneiric logic dominates the fictional world of Kafka's narratives, as it does Turgenev's 'The Dream': in Turgenev's story, dream turns into reality; in Kafka, reality *operates* as a dream. It is only under the oneiric logic of 'The Dream' that a corpse could disappear leaving tracks that lead nowhere; or that the narrator could follow a mysterious man to a house he knows from his dream. And it is only under the same logic, in Kafka's story, that a country doctor could be called to attend a patient who is both dying and perfectly healthy, and discover in a derelict pig-sty a carriage and a pair of horses to get him there.

These are selective links, but they are intended to show that the history of the fantastic has not yet been exhausted. The fantastic survived the impact of science and of positivist philosophy by developing a new mode, by making an adjustment that carried it into the twentieth century. That flexibility suggests it will survive as long as writers exercise their imaginations.

Notes

1: Fictional Worlds of the Fantastic

1 Doležel 1990, ch. 2, discusses at length the contributions of Breitinger, Bodmer, and Baumgarten and their importance for the emergence of a possible-worlds poetics.
2 Despite her absorption with recurrent motifs, Scarborough ignores the antiquity of those she cites; for instance, the Wandering Jew (also called Ahasuerus or Cartophilus) was already popular in mediaeval legends and folk books (Daemmrich 1987, 250–1). For a discussion of the theme and its origins see Auguet 1977. The werewolf is a creature of ancient legend, too, and was a literary theme in Ovid's *Lycaon*. According to Penzoldt, it entered English literature through the *Lais de Bisclaverat* (1965, 41).
3 For Pierre-Georges Castex (1951) and Roger Caillois (1966), fear arises from the intrusion of the strange or unreal into reality.
4 Translation of *Introduction à la littérature fantastique* (1970). Page numbers refer to the original version, followed by those of the translation.
5 Culler adroitly undermines Todorov's reliance on the reader's decision-making or 'kind of reading': 'It is not clear whether membership of a genre is determined by properties of the work which induce certain reactions on the part of readers – properties such as the presence or absence of naturalistic explanations – or whether genre is determined by the reaction of the reader, who might, for example, have missed a naturalistic explanation subtly outlined in the text' (58). Molino quite rightly notes that hesitation cannot structurally distinguish between fantastic, uncanny, and marvellous before the end of the story (1980, 21).
6 Finné does attempt to describe degrees of hesitation. He uses the vector as a model to determine degrees of tension between supernatural and natural

explanations, the lowest degree being what he calls, metaphorically, 'un souffle fantastique.' He strays from his model with Kafka's *The Metamorphosis* (1912), whose literary or didactic intention, he claims, destroys the 'souffle' and robs the fantastic of its 'gratuity' (1980, 45).

7 Schneider's characterization of the fantastic as a product of 'rupture' has a historical dimension as well: 'the fantastic could hardly appear in the Middle Ages because magic and the marvellous were daily bread' (1985, 16).

8 If the pragmatic approach is taken to an extreme, the author's intention would become the focus. For Kathryn Hume, the fantastic is produced by two impulses, fantasy and mimesis. However, in her distaste for abstraction, she falls back precariously upon the author's didactic intentions and the readers' responses (stimulated by the author's aim; 1984, 21, 125, 149. See my criticism in Traill 1988). Levy also restitutes the intentional fallacy, but in a novel and somewhat bizarre way. He claims that hesitation typifies the fantastic, but that it is the *author* who hesitates (1973, 12–13). See also Rabkin 1976, and Clayton's criticism of Rabkin (in Slusser et al., eds., 1982, 64).

9 This concept and related problems of fictionality are analysed fully in Eco 1979, Doležel 1985, 1989, and Pavel 1987. See also McHale 1987, Ryan 1991, Pozuelo Yvancos 1993, and Ronen 1994.

10 Penzoldt distinguishes between tales *of* the supernatural and the supernatural *in* tales, using the Gothic novel and Elizabethan drama as cases in point (1965, 4), an idea which might be applied to the works mentioned here. But his classification is rudimentary – purely quantitative and thematic – and does not describe macrostructural features of the fantastic.

11 The four modal systems (alethic, deontic, axiological and epistemic) are derived primarily from von Wright 1968. Their applicability to narrative worlds is taken up at length in Doležel 1978. Since I use the term 'epistemic' as well, I shall quote Doležel's definition. It refers to narrated actions which 'follow the course given by the modalites of knowledge, ignorance and belief' (1978, 544).

12 Doležel (1980) is a thorough discussion of the authentication force of the various kinds of narrators, of which I have given here merely a very brief paraphrase.

13 'Narrative transmission' is Seymour Chatman's term. The 'how' of narrative discourse is divided into two components, 'the narrative form itself – the structure of narrative transmission – and its manifestation – its appearance in a specific materializing medium, verbal, cinematic, balletic, musical, pantomimic, or whatever' (1978, 22).

14 Jackson disagrees. She believes that supernatural and natural explanations

are made redundant, and that the work foregrounds 'the impossibility of certainty and of reading in meanings' (1981, 28).
15 In his 1925 article 'The Problem of *Skaz* in Stylistics' [Problema skaza v stilistike], Vinogradov argued that Eikhenbaum's conception of *skaz*, presented in 1919, is too narrow, since it is only a 'description of the imitative-declamatory aspect in one form of the comic skaz' (1980, 43; see also Eikhenbaum 1919). Vinogradov defined it as 'a particular literary-artistic orientation towards oral monologue of a narrative type' (1980, 49).
16 Among the best known are the works of M.R. James and J.R.R. Tolkien. Contemporary Canadian authors as well have found these traditional modes attractive for a few of their stories. See Mazo de la Roche's 'Portrait of a Wife' (1928), Virgil Burnett's 'Fallowfields' (1986), and Rohinton Mistry's 'The Ghost of Firozsha Baag' (1987).
17 Thomas Pavel offers an apposite cultural explanation for this phenomenon: 'Romance versus epos and tragedy, fantastic literature versus realism, these were and still are cyclical fights between two projects, with varying chances of temporary success according to the religious context (since naive religiosity tends to favor romance), to the social milieu (with idle groups preferring fantasy and compulsive ones inclining toward truth), to the level of saturation with the opposing project. Thus *Quixote* could have appealed to a period overfed with fantasy, whereas *The Master and Margarita* exploded in a context in which realism was the sternly enforced obligation' (1987, 147).

2: Context and Intertext of the Paranormal Mode

1 Turner 1976 is devoted to a discussion of the various reactions in Victorian England to the advances in the natural sciences.
2 On the relevance to spiritualism of these beliefs and practices, see Powell 1864; Figuier 1873; Podmore 1902; Ellenberger 1970, ch. 1: 3–52; Beloff 1977.
3 See Nelson 1969 and Moore 1977 for the Fox sisters' story.
4 Moreil 1977 and Webb 1974 are devoted to discussions of Kardec and French spiritualism.
5 Two of the few discussions of Russian spiritualism in English are Berry 1985 and Berry 1988, where Home's name is consistently spelled 'Hume.'
6 Dostoevsky cites an ironic report that appeared in Petersburg newspapers in 1876. Readers were informed that Gogol's spirit had returned to dictate the second volume of *Dead Souls* to a Muscovite (1981, 22: 32, 336).
7 Petrovo-Solovovo reproduces Tolstoy's letter in full in a note (1900, 72–3).

Opinions about Home's authenticity are, not unexpectedly, contradictory: M.M. Petrovo-Solovovo discusses in the *Proceedings of the Society for Psychical Research* the rumour that Home was caught cheating in front of the French Emperor (1930, 247–65). Podmore, a psychical researcher in the 1880s who turned sceptic and historian before the end of the century, remarks (after becoming a sceptic): 'Home was never publicly exposed as an impostor; there is no evidence of any weight that he was even privately detected in trickery' (1902, 2: 230). More recently, Beloff discusses and argues against several theories of Home's dishonesty (1977, 7–10).

8 For a brief account of the analogies between animal magnetism and nineteenth-century spiritualism in England, see Oppenheim 1985, 217–24.

9 Inglis notes that the French Revolution and the Napoleonic Wars drove research into mesmerism into the background. But in 1831 a commission appointed by the French Academy accepted Puységur's reports of 'higher phenomena,' although its conclusions were repudiated in turn by still another commission (1986, 17–18).

10 Elliotson founded *The Zoist* in 1843, a journal devoted to publicizing his findings and explaining Mesmer's theory.

11 The term 'primary cause' refers to an intelligent primary cause, the regulation of nature by divine will, and assumes the purposeful intervention of God or some other supernatural entity; 'secondary cause' refers only to the discovery of laws which regulate natural processes, and relies on models of mechanistic or material causality. Supernatural and teleological beliefs therefore have to be rejected.

12 The terms 'ultramundane interference' and 'ultramundane intervention' are other terms, coined by Robert Dale Owen, who also shunned the word supernatural (1860, 6, 511).

13 Letter to Charles Kingsley, 12 April 1869.

14 Myers was one of the first members of the Society for Psychical Research, formed in 1882, which included many physicists, chemists, psychologists, and philosophers, who were notable as much for their rigour as for their intellectual curiosity. Histories of the early SPR abound; among the most useful are Podmore 1902, Podmore 1909, Gauld 1968, Oppenheim 1985.

15 Xenophanes and Anaximander, among the first to offer pre-evolutionist theories, thought that life forms sprang from mud. It was Aristotle who introduced the idea of gradation from lower to higher forms; but because the concept of species had not been formulated, he believed that each organism was derived from a preformed, separate element (see Glass et al. 1959, 6–11, 31–4). Lamarck's four postulates, which have some bearing on Maupassant's work, may be briefly summarized as follows: the relationship

between organism and environment is dynamic – organisms continually react to their environment and develop new organs in response to the needs imposed by it; the development and function of organs is in proportion to their use, becoming stronger if they are much used, deteriorating if not; the changes in the organism are then transmitted to offspring and result in the formation of new species. For a discussion of evolutionary theories before Darwin, see Glass et al. 1959, 265–91.
16 For discussions of the impact of Darwinism, and science in general, on nineteenth-century literature, Henkin 1963, Coslett 1982, Morton 1984, and Levine 1988 are particularly useful.
17 Kuhn uses the term 'paradigm' in two senses: 'On the one hand, it stands for the entire constellation of beliefs, values, techniques, and so on shared by the members of a given community. On the other, it denotes one sort of element in that constellation, the concrete puzzle-solutions which, employed as models or examples, can replace explicit rules as a basis for the solution of the remaining puzzles of normal science' (1970, 175).
18 For a discussion of the theories of Romanes, Ward, and James see Turner 1976; on James, see Le Shan 1969.
19 See in particular Oppenheim 1985. Thomson's memoirs (1936), too, shed light on his and other scientists' involvement in the SPR.

3: The Realists: Experience and Inspiration

1 Years after this review appeared, Dickens again expressed his opinion of Mrs Crowe and her beliefs in a letter to his friend Emile de la Rue: 'The spirit rapping rottenness is fading away, after having done a world of harm, and driven divers and sundry out of their five wits. There is a certain Mrs Crowe, usually resident in Edinburgh, who wrote a book called *The Night Side of Nature*, and rather a clever story called *Susan Hopley*. *She* was a Medium, and an Ass, and I don't know what else' (9 March 1854; Dexter, ed. 1938, 2: 545).
2 Dickens refers here to Mrs de la Rue, wife of his Swiss friend and correspondent Emile de la Rue. In a letter to Emile de la Rue, dated 29 February 1848, Dickens remarks: 'In the Examiner I sent you yesterday, there is a Paper about Ghosts, in which you will recognise an allusion to our patient' (quoted in Collins 1963, 5). For a discussion of Dickens's attempts to cure Mrs de la Rue through Mesmerism, see Johnson 1952 and Kaplan 1975.
3 'Rather a Strong Dose,' *All the Year Round*, 21 March 1863: 84–7.
4 For more information, see Inglis 1986, 213–14, Grant 1965, Lang 1901.
5 'The Martyr Medium,' *All the Year Round*, 4 April 1863: 133–6.

6 Brewster was a Scottish physicist devoted to exposing fraudulent mediums. He attended séances, wrote extensively on the subject, and was generally credited with having exposed Home although, as we saw in chapter 2 n. 7, opinion was divided over Home's credibility.
7 Letter to Mrs Trollope, 19 June 1855.
8 He was not, however, averse to sending Wills, his editor. One of Wills's write-ups, 'At Home with the Spirits,' can be found in *All the Year Round*, March 3, 1866.
9 Letter to Mrs Linton, 16 September 1860 (quoted in Peyrouton 1959, 810).
10 Letter to Mrs Dickinson, 19 August 1860.
11 22 June 1867: 614–20.
12 Dickens expressed himself in much the same way to a contributor to *All the Year Round*: 'I do not set myself up to pretend to know what the Almighty's laws are, as to disembodied spirits. I do not profess to be free from disagreeable impressions and apprehensions, even. But there are no reasons for calling that evidence, which is no evidence at all, or for taking for granted what cannot be taken for granted' (quoted in Goldfarb and Goldfarb 1978, 95). The Goldfarbs take this passage as Dickens's admission that communication with the dead is possible, if unlikely; but in view of Dickens's other remarks, he was more likely dismissing communications with the disincarnate, while allowing for the possibility of information being picked up paranormally through 'impressions' and 'apprehensions.'
13 Berry confirms that Lev attended both Home's séance in Paris in 1857 and a Bredive séance in St Petersburg in 1874 (1985, 87, 71).
14 13 (25) May 1875. According to Polonsky, Turgenev was by his own account a sceptic; yet Polonsky also says that Turgenev was superstitious and inclined to credit 'omens' (1889, 567–8).
15 25 February (6 March) 1875.
16 For a discussion of mimesis, see Abrams 1953, 8–14; for a critique of mimesis and pseudomimesis, Doležel 1988.
17 'On Realism in Art' was originally published in Czech in 1921. Among the more recent attempts at definition, Barthes et al. 1982, Martin 1986, and Wellek 1963 are instructive.
18 On these successive epochs, see Belinsky's 1844 review of *Tarantas* in Belinsky 1953, 6, 9: 75–117. See also Bowman 1954, Terras 1974.

4: Charles Dickens: Tradition and Transition

1 All further references to Dickens's fictional works are from the 1982–5

Oxford edition unless otherwise indicated. The volumes are not separately numbered.
2 In both 'The Bagman's Story' and 'The Story of the Bagman's Uncle,' a man rescues a woman. In the first tale, he marries her. In the second story, the woman's discourse is the cliché of the 'damsel in distress': 'I have been torn from my home and friends by these villains ... That wretch would have married me by violence in another hour' (733). The stereotyped discourse and situation bring to mind eighteenth-century heroines such as Radcliffe's Emily in *The Mysteries of Udolpho* (1794), and Richardson's Pamela (1740) and Clarissa Harlowe (1747–8).
3 This calling of attention to the question of authenticity is, in Patten's opinion, a means of ironically underscoring the naïveté of the Pickwickians, who are quite 'willing to believe fiction fact' (1967, 359). When we consider the frequency with which the Pickwickians allow themselves to be imposed upon by various sorts of nonsense, irony is not improbable. But, as Doležel points out, authentication is 'annihilated' if 'the narrator takes an ironic attitude towards his authentication authority and thus turns the narrating act into a not binding game' (1980, 22).
4 See note 13 in chapter 1.
5 For comparisons of Dickens and Gogol', see Futrell 1956 and chapter 2 of Katarsky 1966.
6 It is a setting common enough in Dickens's work. See for example 'The Holly Tree Inn' (1855), where the narrator intends to write down everything interesting that he has ever seen at inns; the adventures of the two apprentices in *The Lazy Tour of Two Idle Apprentices* (1871), and the wonderful description of Todgers, in *Martin Chuzzlewit* (1844). On the importance of inns in Dickens's work, see Matz 1922.
7 To take a few examples, Ann Radcliffe had a propensity for Italian settings (*The Mysteries of Udolpho*, 1794, *The Italian*, 1797); M.G. Lewis's *The Monk* (1796) is set in Spain, as is most of Charles Maturin's *Melmoth the Wanderer* (1820). Mary Shelley used Switzerland as a backdrop for *Frankenstein, or the Modern Prometheus* (1818), though the monster was created in Germany where his maker, Frankenstein, was a student. For a discussion of Gothic motifs (and their transformation in American and Canadian literature) see Dimić 1979.
8 There is no scarcity of pathetic fallacy even in Dickens's non-fantastic works: Edwin Drood (*The Mystery of Edwin Drood*, 1870) disappears on the night of a violent storm, Pip encounters Magwitch in a bleak churchyard (*Great Expectations*, 1861), and Lady Dedlock is haunted by her mysterious past on the gloomy ghost walk (*Bleak House*, 1853).

9 Davis's claim that Dickens 'appropriated the fairy-tale atmosphere and intended to preach a moral' (1963, 149) is symptomatic of his own tendency to preach the intentional fallacy. Even in *Hard Times* (1854) Lodge observes a rhetorical 'fairy-tale' element, used in two ways: ironically, 'to dramatize the drabness, greed, spite and injustice which characterize a society dominated by materialism'; and as a simplifying device, to encode the 'means of redemption' (1966, 162). Dibelius calls *A Christmas Carol* a 'realistic Märchen,' meaning that it is 'not without spatial and temporal determination'; it is 'not poor in detail, as is the well-known folk genre, but on the contrary fully represents contemporary life' (1926, 214). For a further discussion of the mythic in Dickens, see Pothet 1979.
10 For a typology of narrators, see Doležel 1973 and Booth 1983.
11 Daleski considers Scrooge's encounter with Marley's ghost 'a genuine uncanny experience, and it is used proleptically and in lieu of elaborate characterization to prepare for his sudden transformation' (1984, 197). But Scrooge *has* been so strongly characterised as a miser and a materialist, utterly without fancy, that his transformation, especially by supernatural means, seems remarkable indeed. However, one must bear in mind, as the narrative progresses, that Scrooge was not always so, as he himself will be made to remember.
12 For Lodge, a 'key-word' serves not merely to identify a character, but 'also to evaluate him, and is invoked at various strategic points in the subsequent action.' Using the example of Mrs Gradgrind (*Hard Times*), Lodge notes that key-words may involve 'a combination of expectancy (we know they will recur) and surprise (we are not prepared for the particular formulation)' (1966, 152).
13 See for instance Radcliffe's *The Castles of Athlin and Dunbayne* (1789) and *The Mysteries of Udolpho*. In the Gothic, Dimić observes, 'the favourite lines of action include driving the hero into solitude and fits of madness, the isolation of the heroine, who is put into places of desolation, threatened with violence, bodily injury and "a fate worse then death" ...' (1979, 145). The themes were popular beyond the Gothic, as in Richardson's *Clarissa Harlowe*, and Fielding's *Tom Jones* (1749).
14 In *Reprinted Pieces*, 661–72.
15 The story constitutes chapter 2 of 'Doctor Marigold,' in *Christmas Stories*, 453–90. It is preceded and followed by chapters entitled, respectively, 'To Be Taken Immediately' and 'To Be Taken for Life.' 'To Be Taken with a Grain of Salt' sometimes appears in collections as 'The Trial for Murder.'
16 See chapter 3, n. 6 for a comment on Brewster.
17 In *Christmas Stories*, 544–58.

18 According to Stahl, these features suggest that the narrator 'is the signal-man's ghostly alter ego, his own spirit returning across the bounds of time and death, to visit himself before the inevitable fatal accident' (1980, 99). However, apart from the backward logic of a spirit crossing the boundary of death before the person has died, Stahl's interpretation ignores the crucial events that occur after the signal-man's death.
19 The signal-man does not seem to be overwhelmed by his surroundings; the narrator himself comments that 'In the discharge of his duties, I observed him to be remarkably exact and vigilant ...' (548). Seed notes that the 'fire, desk, book, etc. are prosaic but important details, since they hint at a corresponding orderliness in the signal-man himself' (1981, 48).
20 As Levine observes, there is 'nothing chancey about Dickensian chance.' Coincidences are generally allegorical, determined perhaps by some higher intelligence or inescapable Karma that leads to retribution – for instance, the deaths of the treacherous Carker in *Dombey and Son* (1848) and of Lady Dedlock for her so-called sins in *Bleak House* – or to reward, such as the preservation of Oliver's innocence against all probability in *Oliver Twist*. However, in 'The Signal-Man,' this is not the case; the deaths are senseless, random, and without design. Such a conception of coincidence or chance, according to Levine, parallels Darwin's: 'there is no perfection ... no intelligent design, no purpose. Fact may not be converted to meaning' (1986, 269).
21 Precognition is the non-inferential prediction of future events. That the premonition assumes the form of a spectre in the mind of the signal-man would seem to be clear from the episode where he chases it into the tunnel. When he reaches out to seize its sleeve, the spectre is not there (552). It 'vanishes' because it exists only as an outward projection of his premonition and not as a discrete entity.
22 For a discussion of the precognitive paradox, see Brier and Schmidt-Raghavan, 1990). There is a parallel here with Scrooge's question to the 'Spirit of Christmas Yet to Come': 'Are these the shadows of the things that Will be, or are they shadows of things that May be, only?' (80).

5: Ivan Sergeevich Turgenev: Tentative Beginnings

1 I have translated 'Prizraki' as 'Phantasms,' rather than the customary 'Phantoms' or 'Apparitions,' since the word is less directly linked with spectres or revenants, and therefore with survival after death. It should be said, though, that Turgenev himself translated the title into French as 'Les Apparitions.'

2 First published in German in 1869.
3 Letter to Botkin, 26 November (8 December) 1863. The English phrase 'dissolving views' is Turgenev's.
4 Ledkovsky likens the Lago Maggiore singer to St Cecilia who, as we shall see, is an important symbolic figure in 'The Song of Triumphant Love.' She also notes the indebtedness of 'Phantasms' to the German Romantics, for whom St Cecilia represented the 'ideal woman' (1973, 162, n. 80).
5 Brang believes Turgenev was inspired by Schopenhauer's 'Ergänzungen zum ersten Buch' of the *The World as Will and Idea* [*Welt als Wille und Vorstellung*] – 'the picture of the earth,' as Turgenev called it (Brang 1977, 145). The bird's-eye view found in 'Phantasms' may indeed have been inspired by Schopenhauer, but the plot device is traditional. There are aerial 'tours' in Vélez de Guevara's *El Diablo cojuelo*, Le Sage's *Le Diable boiteux*, Dickens's *A Christmas Carol*, and, in the twentieth century, Bulgakov's *The Master and Margarita* [*Master i Margarita*] (written between 1928 and 1940, published only in 1966–7).
6 The letter 'A' followed by a number refers to Appendix A, where a transliteration of the Russian original is given.
7 In 'The Portrait' [Portret] (1834–42), Gogol' uses a similar stylistic technique. The portrait is first personified: 'Two terrible eyes bored into him as if preparing to devour him alive' (1973, 1: 491; pt. 1; A50); and again, 'This was no copy from nature, this was that same uncanny, lifelike look you would expect to find on the face of a corpse risen from the grave' (1: 492; pt. 1; A51). The portrait then apparently comes to life, leaping out of the frame into the room. But the narrator is not certain in the end whether he was dreaming or awake.
8 See especially Vetrinsky 1920, who considers Ellis an allegorical representation of Turgenev's own muse. The poet is driven by an ideal which is both muse and vampire; that is, inspiring and destroying him at the same time. For Žekulin, the 'vampire-like' Ellis has something in common with the necromancer Krakamiche of Turgenev's operetta *Le Dernier sorcier*, written jointly with Pauline Viardot between 1859 and 1869 (1984, 425). Scarborough calls it 'suggested vampirism' in contrast to the 'psychical vampirism' of Klara Milich (1917, 68, 163).
9 23 December 1863.
10 Waddington may have had something of the sort in mind when he speculates that Turgenev, after witnessing Home's feats in 1857, was perhaps 'fascinated by the artistic and technical aspects of the thing. It seemed possible that a medium at a séance created an illusion of reality akin to that of a work of literature' (1980, 109).

11 The term *skaz*, as we saw in chapter 1, n. 15, refers to the reproduction in a literary narrative of the stylistic and rhetorical devices and other elements of spoken language characteristic of oral storytelling.
12 Turgenev remarked on the language of this tale to the historian and journalist Mikhail Matveevich Stasyulevich: 'In a perfectly devout language is rendered a tale (actually reported to me) of a rural priest ... The tone, it seems, has been faithfully kept' (18 (30) March 1877; *Pis' ma* 1966, 12: 127; book 1; A52).
13 Later critics did not find it wanting. One of the earliest was Chekhov, who praised its 'remarkable language' (quoted in Brang 1977, 151). Henry James appreciated the story, and named it among several in which 'nothing could have more of the simple magic of picturesqueness' (1908, 219). Originally the story was a genuine *skaz*, for Turgenev told it in various forms over a period of years before it appeared in print (Turgenev 1965a, 9: 501–2, 497).
14 'Trezorushka,' with its colloquial diminutive, is a *skaz* name. But because the French word 'trésor' is used as a root, the name becomes a humorous mix of two styles, 'high' and 'low.'
15 In the seventeenth century the Schismatics [raskol'niki] (also called 'Old Believers' [staroobryadtsy]) broke away from the official Church to create a sect of their own because they objected to the changes being made in Scriptures and Church service books under Peter's reforms. As Vinogradov notes: 'The new, European influences disturbed the semantics of Church Slavonic by shaking the ideological and mythological bases of its conceptual structure ... The judgments of the Old Believers are very indicative of the mythological process of a *real* perception of church phraseology' (1969, 21).
16 Byalyy points out the widespread conviction that Schismatic prophets and holy fools possessed mysterious but very real powers (1962, 215).
17 When the creature makes its second appearance, Porfiry Kapitonych's servant Fil'ka uses the word 'navazhdenie' (9: 126), which we aready met above and which means in Russian folk and Christian mythology 'the evil power.' The narrator grows accustomed to the supernatural dog, but a visiting neighbour reacts negatively, calling Porfiry Kapitonych 'doomed,' or 'possessed,' [oglashënnyy] and the dog a 'filthy thing' [pakost'] (9: 127). The first Schismatic the narrator addresses thinks the devil theory is nonsense and proposes his own: 'only, what do you mean, the evil power? It is a phenomenon, or a sign; but you won't be able to understand it; it's not up your alley' (9: 130; A53). Porfiry is then sent through the network of Old Believers to Prokhorych.

18 Gruzinsky argues (with regard to 'The Song of Triumphant Love') that Turgenev was familiar with Charcot's theories (1918, 219). Initially, Charcot proposed that hypnosis was an 'induced form of hystero-epilepsy' (Inglis 1986, 285; see also Ellenberger 1970, 13–45). And indeed, Mr X subtly refers to this in his final conjecture about Vasiliy: 'perhaps epilepsy has conquered him' (10: 185; A54).

19 Turgenev was clearly aware that young women were active in this revolutionary movement and that some were even arrested (Byalyy 1962, 217; Muratov 1980, 20, 26). The topic resurfaces in a somewhat different guise in *Virgin Soil* [*Nov'*] (1877). About Sofya, Turgenev wrote to Avdeev: 'such people lived and as such have the right to be rendered by art' (13 (25) January 1879; 1964b, 8: 172; A55). To Annenkov, he wrote contemptuously of the kind of mummery Vasiliy practised, and described a case from real life, that of a former Russian Minister, Count Bobrinsky: 'I had always known him for a dull-witted, inwardly faltering and unintelligent man, but they say he has been made into a preacher, almost a prophet; they say he has – in England, in the English language – even seduced various workers and artisans onto the path of truth' (16 (28) March 1876; 1966b, 11: 234; A56).

20 Levitation was not associated with the Orient alone. Early Christian churches took a dim view of it, believing that invisible demoniac hands were lifting the possessed person. Palmer and More cite versions of the story of Simon Magus, a reputed sorcerer whom the Apostle Peter challenged to a show of magical skills; as Simon was levitating over Rome, Peter ordered the demons to release him, and he fell to the earth (1936, 28–41). Later Church opinion was divided over whether levitation was beatific or demoniac. Inglis cites the case of the sixteenth-century Teresa of Avila who would levitate uncontrollably while praying (1986, 160). Muzio, however, is in control of what appears to be a learned ability.

21 The contrast between the high-minded innocence of Fabio and Valeria and the dark negative forces which seem to rule Muzio is symbolized by the bay and oleander trees under which they sit on the night of Muzio's return, though it may not have been deliberate on Turgenev's part (13: 57; ch. 3). From ancient times the bay laurel was associated with noble deeds and poetry, as seen in its Latin name *Laurus nobilis*. The beautiful *Nerium oleander*, in contrast, is one of the deadliest of plant species, with over 50 toxic compounds, including two cardiac glycosides.

22 Before Valeria retires on the night of her dream, Muzio displays his talent for hypnotism, a scene which led Gershenzon (1919, 107–9) to compare the story to Bulwer-Lytton's *A Strange Story* (1862), where Margrave, with his remarkable powers, masters Lillian, spirits her away, and then thwarts her

husband's attempts to find her. Muzio's magnetic power is implied elsewhere: Valeria observes his 'piercing and curious eyes' [pronzitel'nykh i lyubopytnykh glaz] (13: 61), and appears to be drawn irresistibly to his open arms in their final nocturnal encounter (13: 69). Gruzinsky notes a strong resemblance between the couple's somnambulism and Charcot's experiments in hypnotic states (1918, 219). Even Muzio's diamond-tipped bow scattering its 'ray-like sparks' has a potentially hypnotic force.

23 Disregarding the story's ambiguity and fantastic features, Pustovoit naturalizes Valeria's experience with Muzio, leaping to the conclusion that Valeria does not love her husband and that Muzio's return reawakens her passion. Pustovoit does support his contention with one unarguable, if isolated, textual fact: Valeria married Fabio at her mother's wish, and herself claimed no preference for either man (1957, 130; Turgenev 13: 55). However, one has to ignore a great many other facets of the tale in order to arrive at a purely psychological explanation for Valeria's submission to Muzio.

24 See Ledkovsky (1973, 62) and Turgenev (1967a, 13: 585) for brief comparisons with Villier's story, which begins 'L'Amour est plus fort que la Mort.' The phrase is apparently taken from *Canticles (Song of Solomon)*, but the wording in the Authorized King James Version is 'for love is strong as death' (8: 6).

25 Bruce was one of Peter I's advisers; after Peter's death, he retired from service and devoted himself to a passionate study of the sciences. Eventually he gained a reputation for sorcery and soothsaying (Turgenev 1967a, 13: 588).

26 Turgenev does not suppress the realistic narrative strain when the fantastic is introduced with Aratov's nightmares. Ledkovsky points out that the story's 'mysterious plot of love beyond death, into whose fabric are woven the fantastic motifs of premonition, visionary dreams, magnetism and ghosts, develops against a perfectly commonplace, plausible background.' She calls this technique 'neutralization' (1973, 112).

27 Quoting a passage from *Parerga and Paralipomena*, Ledkovsky observes the interesting correspondence between Aratov's experience and Schopenhauer's views on the conditions that favour supernatural visions: 'When visions occur the inner eye projects the figures into places where the outer eye does not perceive anything: into dark corners, behind curtains becoming transparent all of a sudden and in general into the darkness of the night ... Only the dark, quiet and lonely midnight will be the time for the appearance of ghosts' (1973, 111).

28 The sentence '*He must decide my fate*' may also be translated '*it must decide*

my fate.' The masculine pronoun 'on' in the Russian original may apply either to the word 'day' or to a man.
29 Turgenev's 'Faust' (1856), like 'Klara Milich,' is concerned with bonds that linger after death.
30 10 (22) January 1877.
31 'Mechta' is perhaps best understood as the waking dream that occurs in a state of reverie [mechtanie], while 'son' is the dream of sleep. I have translated both 'mechtanie' (the state) and 'mechta' (the dream that occurs in that state) as either 'reverie' or 'musing.' The person who spends his time musing is both 'dreamer' and 'visionary.'
32 This textual indeterminacy is reinforced by the use of indefinite pronouns, as Brang notes (1977, 173), and by indefinite verbs and adverbs that designate both the secrets the narrator senses and the mysterious forces which drive him: 'I *seem* to hear' [mne chudilos'], '*some* far-off cries, *some* senseless, mournful complaints ... *somewhere* beyond a high wall ... ' [kakie-to dalëkie vopli, kakie-to smolkaemye, zaunyvnye zhaloby ... gde-to za vysokoy stenoy ...]
33 *The Queen of Spades*, however, exemplifies the ambiguous mode, as discussed in chapter 1.
34 Ledkovsky finds several parallels between 'The Dream' and 'The Song of Triumphant Love': Muzio, like the baron, is dark and enigmatic and, in his own way, seems to have violated a woman. Both characters are accompanied by mysterious, dark men and both are, ostensibly, murdered. In 'The Dream,' the mother is 'numb with terror' and unable to resist the rapist; in 'The Song of Triumphant Love,' Valeria is made a somnambulist with magic and wine, and cannot resist her seducer. 'The Song of Triumphant Love' could be the prehistory of 'The Dream.' If Valeria were to bear a son, he might well dream of his 'real father,' and perhaps meet him one day, just as the narrator of 'The Dream' meets his (1973, 57–9). Brang also notes similarities between the two (1977, 179).

6: Guy de Maupassant: The Scientific Cynic

1 Ignotus considers Maupassant's genius 'the product of an illness,' but redeems (and perhaps undoes) his point by arguing that if Maupassant 'had not ended up a lunatic, his excursions into occultism and the phantom world would not even strike us as pathological ... He was as interested in the abnormal as any normal person might be ...' (1966, 231). More recently, Schasch, rigorously Freudian in approach, has tried to associate Maupassant's art with his mental health by pedantically combing the author's

'biographical facts in relation to his work, in order to reconstitute "the fundamental underlying complexes"' (1983, 22).
2 All references to Maupassant's stories are from the two-volume 1974/1979 Pléiade edition published by Gallimard. Square brackets distinguish my omissions of text from Maupassant's own ellipses, which are a frequent and important aspect of his style.
3 More than one mimetic critic has seen in the name Rowel a thinly disguised allusion to Swinburne's friend Mr Powell (in spite of their different pronunciations), who apparently reminded Maupassant of Edgar Allan Poe. From Swinburne, they inform us, Maupassant obtained an actual severed hand (Steegmuller 1972, 31; Godfrey 1987, 82).
4 The gardener himself is a mysterious figure for several reasons: he is obviously not tending the estate and gardens, which are run-down and overgrown; he has been handed a letter which he seems to *pretend* to read (either there is nothing written or the man is illiterate); and, perhaps most significantly, he stumbles over the word 'death' as though it is not quite apt. Fellows sees a strong tie between Maupassant's 'The Apparition' and Lecomte's *Courrier de Paris* (1852), and shows how the hackneyed, Gothic setting of Lecomte's story has been transformed, in Maupassant's tale, to create greater suspense and psychological penetration (1942, 67).
5 There is a certain irony in the doctor's comment about the madman's journal ('Moreover, he has written his journal, which shows us as clearly as can be the sickness of his mind. His madness is there made tangible, so to speak'; 2: 107; B41): the patient's journal is used as evidence of his madness. Ironically, if the events he describes are not authentic experiences, then his text is fictional – and evidence of nothing but its own fictionality and the writer's creative imagination. Those of Maupassant's contemporaries and critics who judge(d) his state of mind by his fictional texts, and vice versa, commit the doctor's error, and the same irony applies.
6 Describing Raphaël's response to the past as it is represented in the antiques he is examining, the narrator of *La Peau de chagrin* writes: 'He clung to all joys, seized upon all sorrows, grasped at all forms of existence, so liberally sprinkling the shadows created by these plastic and empty representations of nature with his own life and feelings that the sound of his footsteps rang in his soul like a distant sound from another world ...' (1831; 1979, 10: 72–3; B42).
7 I am indebted to Peter W. Nesselroth for this observation.
8 Le Huenen's remark, in the context of *La Peau de chagrin*, is pertinent to 'The Hair': 'What is specifically fantastic in this strange story is less the object itself which is, after all, only an ass's skin, but the contract, the pact, the rela-

tion of ontological coincidence which is suddenly established between the object and the character' (1980, 51). In 'The Hair,' the fantastic is linked with the subject's very special relationship with the object; but still more important are his peculiar sensitivity and the possibility that the object – though a mere lock of hair – in itself possesses supernatural properties.

9 It is not unimportant, I think, that before the narrator dreams about the woman, he sees her in a vision while quite awake: 'I distinctly saw, saw as if I were touching her [...] and suddenly I discovered in her a heap of qualities that I had not noticed at all [...]' (I: 409; B43).

10 We see this power of the eyes to fascinate in Maupassant's non-fantastic story 'Un Portrait' (1888), with its explicit reference to Baudelaire's 'L'Amour du mensonge' (1857; 1941, 110–11). Looking at the portrait of a woman, Maupassant's narrator calls attention to the ability of the eyes to captivate: 'They [the eyes] drew me irresistibly, as it were, threw me into a strange, new and powerful turmoil [...]' (2: 1054; B44).

11 In Maupassant's story 'Le Tic' (1884), Juliette's father has a similar, unpredictable hand tic which is associated, however, with a trauma, and not with exceptional powers. The tic shows how Maupassant could ascribe different functions to the same motif.

12 Vial claims that this passage is reminiscent of Sir John Lubbock, the naturalist who, in his studies of ants and other insects, theorized that sounds and sensations perceptible to insects and other animals may be imperceptible to humans, who lack the special organs adapted for the purpose (1954, 130–1; see also Lubbock 1882 and 1888).

13 In 'Conte de Noël' (1882) as well, a doctor, M. Bonenfant, claims to have witnessed a miracle, yet denies all belief in the supernatural. That the 'miracle' in question is, by his own definition, an instance of auto-suggestion implies that there is a perfectly natural explanation for what the superstitious consider miraculous or supernatural. The credulous blacksmith's wife brings upon herself a state of 'possession,' just as she unconsciously allows herself to be cured by a mock exorcism, because she is predisposed to believe in miracles.

14 Indeed, even his views on love are materialist. Women are 'charming' and 'inconsequential'; not a means to transcendence, but a matter of satisfaction and experiment, much like eating and a change of menu.

15 In Maynial's opinion, Maupassant's use of chloroform and ether taught him that perception can be artificially heightened: 'A remarkable intoxication courses through the flesh, the hearing is fine-tuned, sounds are amplified, and visions linked to the last memories of the conscious state haunt the subject's imagination' (1907, 229).

16 In his *Chronicle* 'Adieu mystères' (1881), Maupassant remarks on the progress of science: 'Each day they [scholars] tighten their boundaries, enlarging the frontiers of science; this frontier of science is the boundary of the two camps. On this side is the known that was yesterday's unknown; beyond is the unknown that will be tomorrow's known' (1980, 1: 313).
17 We may note the Lamarckian basis for the narrator's attempts to stimulate his organs. In Lamarck's theory, new needs stimulate the growth of new organs, which develop in proportion to the amount of use they are subjected to. See Chapter 2, n. 15.
18 Before his first confrontation with the Horla, the narrator is reading Musset's poem 'La Nuit de mai' (2: 826). Comparison reveals a semantic similarity between this poem and the text 'The Horla.' In Musset's dialogue between poet and muse, the poet has the sense that he is surrounded by something frightening: 'Qu'ai-je donc en moi qui s'agite/Dont je me sens épouvanté?/Ne frappe-t-on pas à ma porte?/Pourquoi ma lampe à demi morte/M'éblouit-elle de clarté?/Dieu puissant! tout mon corps frissonne./ Qui vient? qui m'appelle? – Personne' (Musset 1852, 305; see also the notes in Maupassant 1979, 2: 1591, 1618).
19 For a survey of this much-discussed word, its possible origins and meanings, see Forestier's editorial notes in Maupassant 1979, 2: 1620–1. Among the least far-fetched are, perhaps, the descriptive 'hors-là' and the anagram of 'choléra' ('ce Horla'). A somewhat tenuous link between cholera and the invisible threat called Horla may be found in Maupassant's 'La Peur' (1884): 'Cholera is another matter, it's the Invisible, it's a scourge of yore, of times past, a sort of evil spirit that returns and astonishes us as much as it terrifies us because it belongs, it seems, to a bygone age' (2: 204; B45). For a more recent discussion of the word, see Schaffner 1988.
20 The enframing narrator's description of the man who will report to the doctors recalls, once again, Balzac's 'pensée qui tue': 'He was extremely thin, cadaverously so, the way some insane people are when a thought eats away at them, because sick thoughts devour the flesh more than fever or consumption do' (2: 822; B46).
21 A useful comparison can be made with Maupassant's 'La Légende du Mont Saint Michel' (1882) (1: 679). For Comte's three stages of human intellect, see chapter 2.
22 Calling the narrator 'Wissenschaftler' and 'child of his time,' Döring suggests that his scientific rigour in appraising his situation and his use of scientific terminology and methodology confirm his sanity (1984, 57–8).
23 Vax fails to see that the narrator's scientifically based epistemology is a step forward in the development of the fantastic, and claims that 'The Horla'

looks backwards: 'We are no longer in the determined world of science, but in the enchanted world of magic. Or rather magic fatality regains its lost prestige by borrowing the mask of scientific determinism' (1960, 113).
24 Dentan calls the cousin's hypnotic adventure 'a fine example of *mise en abyme*,' and quotes Ricardou, for whom *mise en abyme* 'multiplies what it imitates or, if one prefers, underlines it in repeating it' (1976, 54).
25 This stylistic device, which Jakobson called 'repetition with variation,' is a general feature of Maupassant's narrative style.
26 Todorov's classification of 'psychotic discourse' is particularly useful here for confirming the narrator's sanity. Paranoic discourse, according to Todorov, reveals the subject's inability to distinguish between fiction and truth. Schizophrenic discourse is characterized by violations of the conditions of reference; since 'all parts of a discourse refer to the same fact,' the discourse is incoherent and often contradictory. Each segment of the enunciation is, moreover, isolated: 'even the simple recall of a preceding part of the discourse is exceptional' (1976, 51–4). The narrator of 'The Horla' seeks new and concrete means to describe a novel and by no means concrete phenomenon. If his discourse is marked occasionally by hesitations and ellipses – that is, by frustrated speech – the narrator none the less follows a coherent line of argumentation and never loses a sense of the real world around him. Further discussions of the discourse of madness may be found in Alexandrescu (1973), Consoli (1979), Kristeva (1979), and Samarin (1976). More generally, the representation of madness in literature has been studied by Foucault (1972), Felman (1978), and Gilman (1988). Trautwein believes that 'The Horla' leaves the narrator's state indeterminate, because the sanity/insanity issue is never resolved. The reader is therefore left with a sense of disquiet that challenges a naïve, unambiguous conception of reality (1980, 225).
27 Bessière notes in 'La Nuit' a stylistic feature which we can apply as well to 'The Horla.' Observing the frequency of perfect and imperfect tenses in a narrative that purports to be immediate, present, she writes: 'It points to the falseness of the text and assures the cohesion, at the expense of coherence, of contrary elements (past and present, illusion and reality) ... The improbable is not born of any questioning on the hero's part, nor of the flaunting of the supernatural ... it arises from the play of the stylistic signs that give the text two postures of conflicting reality' (1974, 175). I would simply remark that the use of these tenses points not to the *text*'s falseness, but to the protagonist's growing recognition that what he had considered *reality* is false.

APPENDIX A

Russian Original (Transliterated)

1 chërt by pobral eti gluposti s vertyashchimisya stolami! ... tol'ko nervy rasstraivat' (9: 77; ch. 1).
2 mne pochudilos', kak budto v komnate ... (9: 77; ch. 1).
3 Vot do chego mozhno dovesti sebya (9: 77; ch. 1).
4 luna stoyala nizko na nebe i pryamo glyanula mne v glaza. Belyy kak mel lezhal yeë svet na polu ... (9: 77; ch. 1).
5 Ne odno nebo zardelos' – ves' vozdukh vnezapno napolnilsya kakim-to pochti neestestvennym bagryantsem: list'ya i travy, slovno pokrytye svezhim lakom, ne shevelilis'; v ikh okameneloy nepodvizhnosti, v rezkoy yarkosti ikh ochertaniy, v etom sochetanii sil'nogo bleska i mertvoy tishiny bylo chto-to strannoe, zagadochnoe (9: 80; ch. 3).
6 ya kak budto popal v zakoldovannyy krug (9: 80; ch. 3).
7 Chto takoe Ellis v samom dele? Prividenie, skitayush-chayasya dusha, zloy dukh, sil'fida, vampir, nakonets? Inogda mne opyat' kazalos', chto Ellis – zhenshchina, kotoruyu ya kogda-to znal ... (9: 109; ch. 25).
8 Da uzh ne vo sne li ya vsë eto vizhu (9: 97; ch. 17).
9 U vas yavlyayushcheesya sushchestvo obyasneno kak upyr'. Po moemu by ne nado etogo obyasneniya (Turgenev 1967b, 12: 61; book 1).
10 No ne khochu ya verit', chtoby gospod' stal sudit' yego svoim strogim sudom ... (11: 304).
11 Sovsem slovno pomolodel i stal na prezhnego pokhozh Yakova. Litso takoe tikhoe, chistoe, volosy kolechkami zvilis' – a na gubakh ulybka (11: 304).
12 ya ni na kakom chelovecheskom litse ne vidyval bolee grustnogo, vpolne bezuchastnogo, – kak govoritsya, – 'ubitogo' vyrazheniya (11: 291).
13 bez vsyakikh seminarskikh ili provintsial'nykh zamashek i oborotov rechi (11: 292).
14 No yesli dopustit' vozmozhnost' sverkhestestvennogo, vozmozhnost' yego

vmeshatel'stva v deystvitel'nuyu zhizn', to pozvol'te sprosit', kakuyu rol' posle etogo dolzhen igrat' zdravyy rassudok? (9: 123).

15 Anton Stepanych ... sluzhil v kakom-to mudrënom departamente i, govorya s rasstanovkoy, tugo i basom, pol'zovalsya vseobshchim uvazheniem (9: 123).

16 Ya poklonilsya v zemlyu – i tak uzh i ne podnimayus': takoy v sebe strakh k tomu cheloveku oshchushchayu i takuyu pokornost', chto, kazhetsya, chtó by on ni prikazhi, ispolnyu totchas zhe! (9: 131).

17 on poluchil mesto nadziratelya nad kazënnymi magazinami, mesto vygodnoe, dazhe pochëtnoe i ne trebovavshee otmennykh talantov: samye magaziny sushchestvovali tol'ko v predpolozhenii i dazhe ne bylo s tochnost'yu izvestno, chem ikh napolnyat (9: 124).

18 sosed moy – byl uma obshirnogo! Teshchu svoyu, mezhdu prochim, tak obrabotal chudesno: veksel' yey podsunul; znachit, vybral zhe samyy chuvstvitel'nyy chas! ... A ved' eto kakoe delo – teshchu-to skrutit', a? (9: 127).

19 Nikto iz nas nichego ne nashëlsya otvetit' – i my po-prezhnemu prebyvali v nedoumenii (9: 139).

20 chelovek nesomnenno obladal znachitel'noy magneticheskoy siloy; deystvuya, konechno, neponyatnym dlya menya sposobom na moi nervy, on tak yasno, tak opredelënno vozbudil vo mne obraz starika, o kotorom ya dumal, chto mne, nakonets, pokazalos', chto ya yego vizhu pered glazami (10: 173-4).

21 k prezhnemu zadumchivo-izumlënnomu vyrazheniyu prisoedinilos' drugoe, reshitel'noe, pochti smeloe, sosredotochenno-vostorzhennoe vyrazhenie. Detskogo v etom litse uzhe ne ostavalos' ni sleda (10: 183).

22 ya ne osuzhdal yeë, kak ne osuzhdal vposledstvii drugikh devushek, tak zhe pozhertvovavshikh vsem tomu, chto *oni* schitali pravdoi, v chëm *oni* videli svoë priznanie (10: 185).

23 no tak kak voobshche v priëmakh Mutsiya, vo vsey yego povadke proyavlyalos' nechto chuzhdoe i nebyvaloe (13: 58; ch. 3).

24 etot malaets prinës velikuyu zhertvu – i zato obladaet teper' velikoyu siloy (64).

25 samoe upotreblenie kotorykh kazalos' tainstvennym i neponyatnym (13: 57; ch. 3).

26 kazalos' yey tyazhëlym i odarënnym kakoy-to strannoy teplotoy (13: 57).

27 i almaz na kontse smychka brosal na khodu luchistye iskry, kak by tozhe zazhzhënnye ognëm toy divnoy pesni (13: 59; ch. 3).

28 krov' yeë tikho i tomno volnovalas', i v golove slegka zvenelo ... (13: 60; 4).

29 bledno, kak u mertvetsa ... ono pechal'nee mërtvogo litsa (13: 61, ch. 4).

30 yego sukhie guby obozhgli yeë vsyu ... Ona padaet navznich', na podushki ... (13: 60; ch. 4).
31 ona pripodnimaetsya na krovati, oziraetsya ... Drozh' probegaet po vsemu yeë telu ... (13: 60-1, ch. 4).
32 ona lyubila napevat' starinnye pesni, pod zvuki lyutni, na kotoroy sama igrala (13: 54; ch. 1).
33 mramorny satir, s iskazhënnym zloradnoy usmeshkoy litsom, prikladyval k svireli svoi zaostrënnye guby (13: 63; ch. 6).
34 lunnyy do zhëstkosti yarkiy svet oblival vse predmety (13: 65; ch. 7).
35 yego zhëstkie ruki obvivayut stan Valerii (13: 60; ch. 4).
36 ona neskol'ko raz s osobennoy nastoychivost'yu posmotrela na nego svoimi tëmnymi, pristal'nymi glazami (13: 86; ch. 4).
37 v nego chto-to vnedrilos' ... chto-to zavladelo im (13: 107; ch. 11).
38 ona netronutaya – i ya netronutyy ... Vot chto dalo yey etu vlast'! (13: 120; ch. 14).
39 Otkuda vzyalis' eti volosy? U Anny Semënovny byla takaya pryad', ostavshayasya ot Klary; no s kakoy stati bylo yey otdat' Aratovu takuyu dlya neë doroguyu veshch'? Razve kak-nibud' v dnevnik ona yeë zalozhila – i ne zametila, kak otdala? (13: 133; ch. 18).
40 Raza dva glaza yego slipalis' ... On totchas otkryval ikh ... po krayney mere yemu kazalos', chto on ikh otkryval (13: 123; ch. 15).
41 Razve ona [dusha] ne bessmertnaya ... razve yey nuzhny zemnye organy, chtoby proyavit' svoyu vlast'? Von magnetizm nam dokazal vliyanie zhivoy chelovecheskoy dushi na druguyu zhivuyu chelovecheskuyu dushu ... Otchego zhe eto vliyanie ne prodolzhitsya i posle smerti – koli dusha ostaëtsya zhivoyu? (13: 118; ch. 14).
42 Moskva. Vtornik ... go iuniya. Pela i chitala na literaturnom utre. Segodnya dlya menya znamenatel'nyy den'. *On dolzhen reshit'* moyu uchast'. (Eti slova byli dvazhdy podchërknuty.) Ya opyat' uvidala ... Tut sledovalo neskol'ko tshchatel'no zamarannykh strok (13: 116; ch. 13).
43 mne, pravo, chudilos', budto ya stoyu pered poluzakrytoy dver'yu, za kotoroy skryvayutsya nevedomye tayny, stoyu i zhdu, i mleyu, i ne perestupayu poroga (11: 270; ch. 2).
44 kazalos', taynoe, neizlechimoe i nezasluzhennoe gore postoyanno podtachivalo samyy koren' yeë sushchestvovaniya (11: 269; ch. 1).
45 i chto-to nesëtsya za mnoyu, i nastigaet, i lovit menya (11: 287; ch. 15).
46 i pomertveli, kak u *togo* (11: 287; ch. 16).
47 Uzh ne vstal li on sam i udalilsya? (11: 288; ch. 17).
48 komnata byla vsya obita shtofom (11: 278; ch. 9).
49 polinyalye shtofnye kresla i divany (1962, 3: 365; ch. 3).

Appendix A

50 Dva strashnye glaza pryamo vperilis' v nego, kak by gotovyas' sozhrat' yego (Gogol' 1973, 1: 491; pt. 1).
51 Eto uzhe ne byla kopiya s natury, eto byla ta strannaya zhivopis', kotoroyu by ozarilos' litso mertvetsa, vstavshego iz mogily (Gogol' 1973, 1: 492; pt. 1).
52 sovershenno nabozhnym yazykom peredaëtsya (deystvitel'no soobshchënnyy mne) rasskaz odnogo sel'skogo popa ... Kolorit, kazhetsya, sokhranen verno (18 (30) March, 1877; *Pis'ma* 1966, 12: 127; book 1).
53 a tol'ko kakoe eto navazhdenie? Eto yest' yavlenie, a libo znamenie; da ty etogo ne postignesh': ne tvoego polëta (9: 130).
54 razve paduchaya yego slomila (10: 185).
55 podobnye lyudi zhili, stalo byt', imeyut pravo na vosproizvodenie isskuistvom (13 (25) January 1879; 1964b, 8: 172).
56 ya yego vsegda znal za tupogo, vnutrenno stupannogo i neumnogo cheloveka; no iz nego, govoryat, vyrabotalsya propovednik, chut' ne prorok; on dazhe v Anglii, govoryat, na angliyskom yazyke sovrashchal raznykh rabochikh i remeslennikov na put' istiny (16 (28) March 1876; 1966b, 11: 234).

APPENDIX B

French Original

1 de crainte que son propriétaire ne vienne te le redemander (1: 4).
2 devait être doué d'une force prodigieuse et avoir une main extraordinairement maigre et nerveuse (1: 6).
3 figure-toi qu'un imbécile quelconque, sans doute pour me faire une mauvaise farce, est venu carillonner à ma porte vers minuit (1: 4).
4 Il me parut en effet singulièrement agité, préoccupé, comme si un mystérieux combat se fût livré dans son âme (1: 782).
5 Si vous voulez m'attendre cinq minutes, je vais aller ... aller voir si [...] (1: 783).
6 J'étais éperdu à ne plus savoir ce que je faisais; mais cette espèce de fierté intime que j'ai en moi, un peu d'orgueil de métier aussi, me faisaient garder, presque malgré moi, une contenance honorable (1: 785).
7 une sensation de froid atroce comme si j'eusse manié des serpents (1: 785).
8 Et les marchands semblent deviner à la flamme du regard l'envie secrète et grandissante (2: 109).
9 ravagé, rongé par sa pensée, par une Pensée (2: 107).
10 que j'avais vécu autrefois déjà, que j'avais dû connaître cette femme (2: 111).
11 Elle, l'Invisible, l'Impalpable, l'Insaisissable, l'Immatérielle Idée minait la chair, buvait le sang, éteignait la vie (2: 107).
12 et je sentis, en la touchant, un long frisson qui me courut dans les membres (2: 112).
13 Je frémis en sentant sur mes mains son toucher caressant et léger (2: 113).
14 Quelle singulière chose que la tentation! On regarde un objet et, peu à peu, il vous séduit [...] comme ferait un visage de femme [...] Un besoin de possession vous gagne, besoin doux d'abord [...] qui s'accroît, devient violent, irrésistible (2: 109).

15 C'est peut-être un regard d'elle que je n'avais point remarqué et qui m'est revenu ce soir-là par un de ces mystérieux et inconscients rappels de la mémoire qui nous représentent souvent des choses négligées par notre conscience, passées inaperçues devant notre intelligence! (1: 410).
16 des yeux d'halluciné, des yeux noirs, si noirs qu'on ne distinguait pas la pupille, des yeux mobiles, rôdeurs, malades, hantés (2: 308).
17 je n'ai qu'à regarder les gens pour les engourdir comme si je leur avais versé de l'opium. Je n'ai qu'à étendre les mains pour produire des choses ... des choses ... terribles (2: 311).
18 je suis doué d'un pouvoir ... non ... d'une puissance ... non, d'une force (2: 311).
19 Qu'est-ce que cela? Du magnétisme, de l'électricité, de l'aimant? (2: 313).
20 Tout est mystère. Nous ne communiquons avec les choses que par nos misérables sens, incomplets, infirmes, si faibles qu'ils ont à peine la puissance de constater ce qui nous entoure (2: 310).
21 On dirait un autre être enfermé en moi, qui veut sans cesse d'échapper, agir malgré moi, qui s'agite, me ronge, m'épuise (2: 311).
22 j'avais eu la fièvre, le cauchemar, que sais-je? J'avais été malade, enfin (1: 874).
23 Je sais bien qu'il n'existe pas, que ce n'est rien! Il n'existe que dans mon appréhension, que dans ma crainte, que dans mon angoisse! (1: 875).
24 Les yeux avaient eu une vision, une de ces visions qui font croire aux miracles les gens naïfs (1: 873).
25 Oui, mais j'ai beau me raisonner, me roidir, je ne peux plus rester seul chez moi, parce qu'il y est (1: 875).
26 Un organe de plus ou de moins dans notre machine nous aurait fait une autre intelligence (2: 461).
27 je conclus que les mystères entrevus comme l'électricité, le sommeil hypnotique, la transmission de la volonté, la suggestion, tous les phénomènes magnétiques, ne nous demeurent cachés, que parce que la nature ne nous a pas fourni l'organe, ou les organes nécessaires pour les comprendre (2: 464).
28 Et, dans cette glace, je commence à voir des images folles, des monstres, des cadavres hideux, toutes sortes de bêtes effroyables, d'êtres atroces, toutes les visions invraisemblables qui doivent hanter l'esprit des fous (2: 466).
29 C'est celui que la terre attend, après l'homme! Celui qui vient nous détrôner, nous asservir, nous dompter, et se nourrir de nous peut-être, comme nous nous nourrissons des boeufs et des sangliers (2: 829).
30 Oui, je tombais dans le néant, dans un néant absolu, dans une mort de

l'être entier dont j'étais tiré brusquement, horriblement par l'épouvantable sensation d'un poids écrasant sur ma poitrine, et d'une bouche qui mangeait ma vie (2: 823).

31 je ne sais si cet homme est fou ou si nous le sommes tous les deux..., ou si... si notre successeur est réellement arrivé (2: 830).

32 Est-ce étrange qu'un simple malaise, un trouble de la circulation peut-être, l'irritation d'un filet nerveux, un peu de congestion [...] puisse faire un mélancolique du plus joyeux des hommes [...] (2: 915).

33 Certes, je me croirais fou, absolument fou, si je n'étais conscient, si je ne connaissais parfaitement mon état, si je ne le sondais en l'analysant avec une complète lucidité (2: 928).

34 Certes, voilà comment était possédée et dominée ma pauvre cousine [..] Elle subissait un vouloir étranger entré en elle, comme une autre âme, comme une autre âme parasite et dominatrice (2: 930).

35 Un être nouveau! Pourquoi pas? Il devait venir assurément! Pourquoi serions-nous les derniers? (2: 934).

36 J'aurais la force des désespérés; j'aurais mes mains, mes genoux, ma poitrine, mon front, mes dents pour l'étrangler, l'écraser, le mordre, le déchirer (2: 935).

37 On y voyait comme en plein jour, et je ne me vis pas dans ma glace! [...] Puis voilà que tout à coup je commençai à m'apercevoir dans une brume, au fond du miroir, comme à travers une nappe d'eau [...] C'était comme la fin d'une éclipse (2: 935-6).

38 Quelle journée admirable! J'ai passé toute la matinée étendu sur l'herbe, devant ma maison, sous l'énorme platane qui la couvre, l'abrite et l'ombrage tout entière (2: 913).

39 En face de moi, mon lit, un vieux lit de chêne à colonnes; à droite, ma cheminée; à gauche, ma porte fermée avec soin [...] (2: 935).

40 il me semblait que cette eau glissait de gauche à droite, lentement, rendant plus précise mon image, de seconde en seconde (2: 936).

41 Il a d'ailleurs écrit son journal qui nous montre le plus clairement du monde la maladie de son esprit. Sa folie y est pour ainsi dire palpable (2: 107).

42 Il s'accrochait à toutes les joies, saisissait toutes les douleurs, s'emparait de toutes les formules d'existence en éparpillant si généreusement sa vie et ses sentiments sur les simulacres de cette nature plastique et vide, que le bruit de ses pas retentissait dans son âme comme le son lointain d'un autre monde... (1831; 1979, 10: 72-3).

43 j'ai vu distinctement, vu comme si je la touchais [...] et soudain je lui découvris un tas de qualités que je n'avais point observées [...] (1: 409).

44 Ils [les yeux] m'attiraient, en effet, d'une façon irrésistible, jetaient en moi un trouble étrange, puissant, nouveau [...] (2: 1054).
45 Le choléra c'est autre chose, c'est l'Invisible, c'est un fléau d'autrefois, des temps passés, une sorte d'Esprit malfaisant qui revient et que nous étonne autant qu'il nous épouvante, car il appartient, semble-t-il, aux âges disparus (2: 204).
46 Il était fort maigre, d'une maigreur de cadavre, comme sont maigres certains fous que ronge une pensée, car la pensée malade dévore la chair du corps plus que la fièvre ou la phtisie (2: 822).

Bibliography

Abrams, M. H. 1953. *The Mirror and the Lamp.* New York: Oxford UP.
Ackerknecht, E.H. 1948. '"Mesmerism" in Primitive Societies.' *Ciba Symposia* 9: 826-31.
Afonin, L.N. 1966. '"Pesn' torzhestvuyushchey lyubvi."' In Izmailov and Nazarova, eds. 1966/67. Vol. 2. 209-13.
Albérès, R.M. 1962. *Histoire du roman moderne.* Paris: Alban Michel.
Alexandrescu, S. 1973. 'Le Discours étrange.' In Chabrol, ed. 1973. 55-95.
Allén, Sture, ed. 1989. *Possible Worlds in Humanities, Arts and Sciences: Proceedings of Nobel Symposium 65.* Berlin and New York: de Gruyter.
Anchev, Angel. 1984. *I.S. Turgenev: Poetika i estetika.* Sofia: Nauka i izkustvo.
Andreski, Stanislav. 1974. *The Essential Comte: Selected from Cours de Philosophie Positive.* London: Croom Helm.
Annenkov, P.V. 1880. *Zamechatel'noe desyatiletie.* Eng. trans. *The Extraordinary Decade.* Trans. I. Titunik. Ann Arbor: University of Michigan Press. 1968.
Appleman, Philip, William A. Madden, and Michael Wolff. 1959. *1859: Entering an Age of Crisis.* Bloomington: Indiana UP.
Artinian, Artine. 1969. *Maupassant Criticism in France, 1880-1940.* New York: Russell and Russell.
Asako, Keïko. 1983. 'Turgenev et Maupassant.' Actes du Congrès du Centenaire 1883-1983. *Cahiers,* no. 7. Paris: 45-51.
Auerbach, Erich. 1953. *Mimesis: The Representation of Reality in Western Literature.* Princeton: Princeton UP.
Auguet, Roland. 1977. *Le Juif errant: Genèse d'une légende.* Paris: Payot.
Azouvi, François. 1980. Introduction to Jean-Jacques Paulet. *L'Antimagnétisme.* 1784. Rpt. Geneva-Paris: Slatkine. 1-5.
Baguley, D. 1987. 'An Essay on Naturalist Poetics.' *Essays in Poetics* 12, 1: 41-56.

Balzac, Honoré de. 1976–1981. *La Comédie humaine*. Paris: Gallimard.
Bancquart, Marie-Claire. 1976a. *Maupassant: conteur fantastique*. Paris: Minard.
– 1976b. Introduction to Guy de Maupassant. *Le Horla et autres Contes cruels et fantastiques*. Paris: Garnier. i–xlv.
Barnes, Barry, and Steven Shapin, eds. 1979. *Natural Order*. Beverly Hills: Sage.
Baronian, J.B. 1978. *Panorama de la littérature fantastique de langue française*. Paris: Stock.
Barrucand, Dominique. 1967. *Histoire de l'hypnose en France*. Paris: Presses universitaires.
Barthes, Roland, L. Bersani, P. Hamon, M. Riffaterre, and I. Watt. 1982. *Littérature et réalité*. Paris: Seuil.
Baudelaire, Charles. 1857. 'La Chevelure.' In *Les Fleurs du Mal*. Paris: Cluny. 1941.
Baudelaire. 1857. 'L'Amour du mensonge.' In *Les Fleurs du Mal*. Paris: Cluny. 1941.
Baumer, Franklin L. 1965. *Intellectual Movements in Modern European History*. New York: Macmillan.
Beckford, William. 1786. *Vathek*. Oxford: Oxford UP. 1983.
Beer, Gillian. 1983. *Darwin's Plots: Evolutionary Narrative in Darwin, George Eliot and Nineteenth Century Literature*. London: Routledge and Kegan Paul.
Belinsky, Vissarion. 1844. *Tarantas* [Review]. *Polnoe sobraniy sochineniy*. 9: 75–117.
– 1953–56. *Polnoe sobraniy sochineniy*. 12 vols. Moscow: Akademia nauk.
Bellemin-Noël, Jean. 1972. 'Notes sur le fantastique.' *Littérature* 8: 3–23.
Beloff, John. 1977. 'Historical Overview.' In Wolman, ed. 1977.
Bergson, Henri. 1886. 'De la simulation inconsciente dans l'état d'hypnotisme.' In *Mélanges*. Ed. André Robinet. Paris: Presses universitaires de France. 1972. 333–41.
– 1901. 'Le Rêve.' *Bulletin de l'Institut psychologique international*. In *Revue de Philosophie* I: 486–9.
Berry, Thomas E. 1985. *Spiritualism in Tsarist Society and Literature*. Baltimore: Edgar Allan Poe Society.
– 1988. 'Mediums and Spiritualism in Russian Literature during the Reign of Alexander II.' In Mandelker and Reeder, eds. 1988.
Besnard-Coursodon, Micheline. 1973. *Etude thématique et structurale de l'oeuvre de Guy de Maupassant*. Le Piège. Paris: Nizet.
Bessière, Irène. 1974. *Le Récit fantastique*. Paris: Larousse.
Blackwood, Algernon. 1929. *John Silence, Physician Extraordinary*. London: Eveleigh Nash and Grayson.

Bleiler, Everett. 1983. *The Guide to Supernatural Fiction.* Kent, OH: Kent State UP.
Bloch, George. 1980. *Mesmerism: A Translation of the Original Scientific and Medical Writings of F.A. Mesmer.* Trans. and comp. by George Bloch. Introduction by Ernest R. Hilgard. Los Altos, CA.: William Kaufmann.
Boileau, Nicolas. 1672. *L'Art poétique.* Paris: Bordas. 1972.
Bonnefis, Philippe. 1987. 'La Question du lien dans les contes et nouvelles de Guy de Maupassant.' *Modern Language Notes* 102, 4: 898–917.
Booth, Wayne. 1961. *The Rhetoric of Fiction.* Chicago: University of Chicago Press.
Boring, E.G. 1950. *A History of Experimental Psychology.* New York: Appleton-Century-Crofts. 2nd ed. Originally published 1929.
Bourget, Paul. 1888. 'Ivan Tourguéniev.' Rpt. in *Essais de psychologie contemporaine.* Paris: Plon. 1937. 185–238.
Bowman, Herbert. 1954. *Vissarion Belinsky 1811–1848: A Study in the Origins of Social Criticism in Russia.* Cambridge, MA: Harvard UP.
Bradley, Raymond and Norman Swartz. 1979. *Possible Worlds: An Introduction to Logic and Its Philosophy.* Indianapolis: Hackett.
Brandon, Ruth. 1983. *The Spiritualists: The Passion for the Occult in the Nineteenth and Twentieth Centuries.* London: Weidenfeld and Nicolson.
Brang, Peter. 1956. 'Zu Turgenevs ästhetischem Credo.' In *Festscrift für Max Vasmer zum 70 Geburtstag.* Wiesbaden: Harrassowitz. 83–90.
– 1977. *I.S. Turgenev: Sein Leben und sein Werk.* Wiesbaden: Harrassowitz.
Bridges, J.H. 1915. *Illustrations of Positivism.* London: Watts.
Brier, B. 1974. *Precognition and the Philosophy of Science.* New York: Humanities Press.
Briggs, Julia. 1977. *Night Visitors.* London: Faber.
Broad, C.D. 1953. *Religion, Philosophy and Psychical Research: Selected Essays.* New York: Harcourt Brace.
Brodsky, N.L. 1923a, ed. *Turgenev i yego vremya: Pervyy sbornik.* Moscow–St Petersburg: Gosudarstvennoe izdatel'stvo.
– ed. 1923b, *Tvorcheskiy put' Turgeneva: Sbornik statey.* St Petersburg: Seyatel'.
– ed. 1930. *V.P. Botkin i I.S. Turgenev: neizdannaya perepiska 1851–1869.* Moscow-Leningrad: Akademia.
Bromberg, W. 1959. *The Mind of Man: A History of Psychotherapy and Psychoanalysis.* New York: Harper. Originally published as *Man Above Humanity: A History of Psychotherapy.* Philadelphia: Lippincott. 1954.
Brook, G.L. 1970. *The Language of Dickens.* London: Deutsch.
Brooke-Rose, Christine. 1981. *A Rhetoric of the Unreal.* Cambridge: Cambridge UP.

Bibliography

Butt, John. 1969. 'The Serial Publications of Dickens's Novels: *Martin Chuzzlewit* and *Little Dorrit.*' In *Pope, Dickens and Others.* 149–64. Rpt. in Watt, ed. 1971. 70–82.
Bulgakov, Mikhail. 1966–7. *Master i Margarita.* Paris: YMCA Press. 1967.
Bulwer-Lytton, Edward G. 1862. *A Strange Story.* Edinburgh: Blackwood. 1866.
Burnett, Virgil. 1986. 'Fallowfields.' In Manguel, ed. 1990. 140–57.
Byalyy, G. 1962. *Turgenev i russkiy realizm.* Moscow-Leningrad: Sovetskiy pisatel'.
Caillois, Roger. 1966. *Images, Images.* Paris: Corti.
Carpenter, William. 1877. *Mesmerism and Spiritualism and c. Historically and Scientifically Considered.* New York: Appleton.
Carroll, Lewis. 1865. *Alice's Adventures in Wonderland.* London: Macmillan. 1920.
– 1872. *Through the Looking Glass, and What Alice Found There.* London: Macmillan. 1872.
Castella, Charles. 1972. *Structures romanesques et vision sociale chez Maupassant.* Lausanne: L'âge de l'homme.
Castex, Pierre-Georges. 1951. *Le Conte fantastique en France de Nodier à Maupassant.* Paris: Corti.
Cazamian, Madeleine. 1923. *Le Roman et les idées en Angleterre: l'influence de la science (1860–1890).* 3 vols. Strasbourg: Istra.
Cazotte, Jacques. 1772. *Le Diable amoureux.* Paris: Garnier-Flammarion. 1980.
Certeau, Michel de. 1987. *Histoire et Psychanalyse: entre science et fiction.* Paris: Gallimard.
Cerullo, John James. 1982. *The Secularization of the Soul: Psychical Research in Modern Britain.* Philadelphia: Institute for the Study of Human Issues.
Chabrol, Claude, ed. 1973. *Sémiotique narrative et textuelle.* Paris: Larousse.
Chadwick, Owen. 1975. *The Secularization of the European Mind in the Nineteenth Century.* Cambridge: Cambridge UP.
Chanady, Amaryll Beatrice. 1985. *Magical Realism and the Fantastic: Resolved versus Unresolved Antinomy.* New York: Garland.
Charlton, D.G. 1959. *Positivist Thought in France during the Second Empire.* Oxford: Clarendon.
Chartier, Emile [Alain]. 1939. 'Le fantastique et le réel d'après les "Contes de Noël" de Dickens.' *La Nouvelle Revue Française* 53: 817–23.
Claparède, Edouard. 1923. 'Théodore Flournoy. Sa vie et son oeuvre.' *Archives de psychologie.* Vol. 18: 1–125.
Clayton, David. 1982. 'On Realistic and Fantastic Discourse.' In Slusser et al., eds. 1982. 59–77.

Cogny, Pierre. 1968. *Maupassant: L'homme sans Dieu*. Brussels: La Renaissance du livre.
Collins, Wilkie. 1860. *The Woman in White*. London: Chatto and Windus. 1896.
Collins, Philip. 1963. 'Dickens on Ghosts: An Uncollected Article.' *The Dickensian* 59, 339: 5–14.
Comte, Auguste. 1892–4. *Cours de philosophie positive*. 5th ed. 6 vols. Paris: Au Siège de la Société positiviste. Originally published 1830–42.
Conrad, Joseph. 1917. 'Foreword.' In Garnett 1917.
Consoli, Silla. 1979. 'Le récit du psychotique.' In Kristeva, ed. 1979. 36–76.
Cornwell, Neil. 1986. *The Life, Times and Milieu of V.F. Odoevsky, 1804–1869*. London: Athlone.
– 1988. 'Critical Approaches to the Literary Fantastic: Definitions, Genre, Import.' *Essays in Poetics* 13, 1: 1–45.
– 1990. *The Literary Fantastic: From Gothic to Postmodernism*. London: Harvester Wheatsheaf.
Coslett, Tess. 1982. *The Scientific Movement and Victorian Literature*. Sussex: Harvester.
Culler, Jonathan. 1981. *The Pursuit of Signs*. Ithaca: Cornell UP.
Daemmrich, Horst S., and Ingrid Daemmrich. 1987. *Themes and Motifs in Western Literature: A Handbook*. Tübingen: Francke.
Daleski, H.M. 1984. 'Dickens and the Proleptic Uncanny.' *Dickens Studies Annual* 13: 193–206.
Danto, Arthur C. 1973. *Analytical Philosophy of Action*. Cambridge: Cambridge UP.
Darnton, Robert. 1968. *Mesmerism and the End of the Enlightenment in France*. Cambridge, MA: Harvard UP.
Darwin, Charles. 1859. *On the Origin of the Species by Means of Natural Selection*. London: Watts. 1909.
Davies, Charles Maurice. 1874. *Heterodox London; or Phases of Free Thought in the Metropolis*. 2 vols. London: Tinsley Brothers.
Davis, Earle. 1963. *The Flint and the Flame: The Artistry of Charles Dickens*. Columbia: University of Missouri Press.
Davis, Robert Murray, ed. 1969. *The Novel: Modern Essays in Criticism*. Englewood Cliffs, NJ: Prentice-Hall.
de la Roche, Mazo. 1928. 'Portrait of a Wife.' In Manguel, ed. 1990: 70–9.
Dédéyan, Charles. 1964. *L'imagination fantastique dans le romantisme européen*. Paris: Centre de documentation universitaire.
Delaisement, Gérard. 1984. *Guy de Maupassant*. Orléans: CRDP de l'Académie d'Orléans-Tours.

Dentan, Michel. 1976. '*Le Horla* ou le vertige de l'absence.' *Etudes de Lettres*, Série 3, tome 9, no. 2: 45–54.
Dessaix, Robert. 1977. 'Turgenev and Maupassant as Fantasts.' *Russian Literature* 5, 4: 325–37.
– ed. and translator. 1979. *The Mysterious Tales of Ivan Turgenev*. Canberra: Australian National University.
– 1980. *Turgenev: The Quest for Faith*. Canberra: Australian National University.
Dexter, Walter, ed. 1938. *Dickens's Letters*. 3 vols. New York: Nonesuch.
Dibelius, Wilhelm. 1926. *Charles Dickens*. 2nd ed. Leipzig: Teubner.
Dickens, Charles. [1848]. 'On Ghosts.' Rpt. in Collins 1963. 5–14.
– 1863. 'Rather a Strong Dose.' *All the Year Round*. 21 March. 84–7.
– 1863. 'The Martyr Medium.' *All the Year Round*. 4 April. 133–6.
– 1982–5. *Collected Works*. Oxford: Oxford UP.
Dimić Milan V. 1979. 'Aspects of American and Canadian Gothicism.' *Actes du VIIe Congrès de l'Association Internationale de Littérature Comparée*. Eds. Milan Dimić and Eva Kushner. Stuttgart: Bieber. Vol. 1. 143–9.
Doležel, Lubomír. 1973. *Narrative Modes in Czech Literature*. Toronto: University of Toronto Press.
– 1978. 'Narrative Worlds.' In Matejka, ed. 1978. 542–52.
– 1980. 'Truth and Authenticity in Narrative.' *Poetics Today* 1, 3: 7–25.
– 1984. 'Kafka's Fictional World.' *Canadian Review of Comparative Literature* 11: 61–83.
– 1985. 'Pour une typologie des mondes fictionnels.' In Parret and Ruprecht, eds. 1989 1: 7–23. (English in *Tamking Review* 14: 261–76.)
– 1988. 'Mimesis and Possible Worlds.' *Poetics Today* 9: 475–96.
– 1989. 'Possible Worlds and Literary Fictions.' In Allén, 1989. 221–42.
– 1990. *Occidental Poetics: Tradition and Progress*. Lincoln: Nebraska UP.
– and Nancy H. Traill, eds. *Possible Worlds and Literary Fiction*. Special issue of *Style* 25, 22.
Donovan, Robert Alan. 1962. 'Structure and Idea in *Bleak House*.' *English Literary History* 29: 175–201. Rpt. in Watt, ed. 1971. 83–109.
Döring, Ulrich von. 1984. 'Die Bedeutung der Wahrnehmung in Maupassants Phantastischer Erzählung "Le Horla."' *Zeitschrift für französische Sprache und Literatur* 94, 1: 4–65.
Dostoevsky, F.M. 1972–86. *Polnoe sobranie sochineniy*. 29 vols. Leningrad: Nauka.
Doyle, Arthur Conan. 1926. *The History of Spiritualism*, 2 vols. London: Cassell.
Druzhinin, A. V. 1865. *Sobranie sochineniy*. 7 vols. Ed. N. V. Gerbelia. St Petersburg: I. Tip. Imp. Akademii nauk.

Dugan, John R. 1973. *Illusion and Reality: A Study of Descriptive Techniques in the Works of Guy de Maupassant.* The Hague: Mouton.
Du Maurier, George. 1894. *Trilby: A Novel.* London: Osgood, McIlvaine. 1895.
Eco, Umberto. 1979. *The Role of the Reader.* Bloomington: Indiana UP.
Ehrenwald, J., ed. 1956. *From Medicine Man to Freud: An Anthology, Edited, with Notes.* New York: Dell. 1956. 256-80.
Eigner, Edwin. 1978. *The Metaphysical Novel in England and America.* Berkeley: University of California Press.
Eikhenbaum, E. 1919. 'Kak sdelana "Shinel'" Gogol'ya.' Rpt. in his *Literatura.* 1927. Rpt. 2nd ed. Leningrad: Priboy. Rpt. Chicago: Russian Language Specialties. 1969.
Eliot, T.S. 1932. 'Wilkie Collins and Dickens.' Rpt. in Ford, ed. 1961. 151-2.
Ellegård, Alvar. 1958. *Darwin and the General Reader: The Reception of Darwin's Theory of Evolution in the British Periodical Press, 1859-1872.* Göteborg: Göteborgs Universitets Årsskrift.
Ellenberger, Henri F. 1970. *The Discovery of the Unconscious: The History and Evolution of Dynamic Psychiatry.* New York: Basic Books.
Engel, Monroe. 1967. *The Maturity of Dickens.* Cambridge, MA: Harvard UP.
Esdaile, James. 1852. *Natural and Mesmeric Clairvoyance.* New York: Arno. Rpt. of 1852 edition published by H. Balliere, London.
Evans, Ifor. 1954. *Literature and Science.* London: Allen and Unwin.
Fanger, Donald. 1967. *Dostoevsky and Romantic Realism: A Study of Dostoevsky in Relation to Balzac, Dickens and Gogol.* Chicago: University of Chicago Press.
– 1979. *The Creation of Nikolai Gogol.* Cambridge, MA: Harvard UP
Fellows, Otis. 1942. 'Maupassant's *Apparition*: A Source and a Creative Process.' *The Romanic Review* 33, 1: 58–71.
Felman, Shoshana. 1978. *La Folie et la chose littéraire.* Paris: Seuil.
Fielding, Henry. 1749. *The History of Tom Jones.* Harmondsworth: Penguin. 1973.
Figuier, Louis. 1873. *Histoire du merveilleux.* 4 vols. Paris: Hachette.
Finné, Jacques. 1980. *La Littérature fantastique.* Brussels: Université de Bruxelles.
Fisher, V.M. 1919. 'Tainstvennoe u Turgeneva.' In *Venok Turgenevu.* 1919. 91–104.
– 1920. 'Povest' i roman u Turgeneva.' In Rozanov and Sokolov, eds. 1920. 3–39.
Fitz, Brewster E. 1972. 'The Use of Mirrors and Mirror Analogues in Maupassant's *Le Horla.*' *The French Review* 45: 954–63.
Flammarion, Camille. 1923. *Death and Its Mystery.* 3 vols. London: T. Fisher

Unwin. (Vol. subtitles are: 1. Before Death; 2. At the Moment of Death; 3. Manifestations and Apparitions of the Dead; The Soul after Death.)

Fleenor, Juliann E. 1983. *The Female Gothic.* Montreal and London: Eden Press.

Flournoy, Théodore. 1899. 'Genèse de quelques prétendus messages spirites.' *Annales des Sciences psychiques* 9: 199–216.

– 1983. *Des Indes à la planète Mars. Etude sur un cas de somnambulisme avec glossolalia.* Paris: Seuil. Originally published 1900.

Fodéré, Jean-Maurienne. 1947. *Maupassant: Est-il mort fou?* Paris: Gründ.

Ford, George H. 1955. *Dickens and His Readers.* Princeton: Princeton UP

– ed. 1961. *The Dickens Critics.* Ithaca: Cornell UP.

Forestier, Louis, ed. 1974/1979. *Maupassant. Contes et Nouvelles, 1875–1893.* 2 vols. Ed. Louis Forestier. Paris: Pléiade Gallimard.

Foucault, Michel. 1972. *Histoire de la folie à l'âge classique.* Paris: Gallimard.

Freeborn, Richard. 1960. *Turgenev: The Novelist's Novelist.* London: Oxford UP.

Frye, Northrop. 1957. *Anatomy of Criticism.* Princeton: Princeton UP.

– 1968. 'Dickens and the Comedy of Humours.' *Experience in the Novel: Selected Papers from the English Institute.* Ed. Roy Harvey Pearce. New York: Columbia UP. 49–81. Rpt. in Watt, ed. 1971. 47–69.

Futrell, Michael H. 1956. 'Gogol' and Dickens.' *The Slavonic and East European Review* 34: 443–59.

Gabel', M. 1923. 'Pesn' torzhestvuyushchey lyubvi: opyt analyza.' In Brodsky, ed. 1923b. 202–25.

Galdston, I. 1948a. 'Hypnosis and Modern Psychiatry.' *Ciba Symposia* 9: 845–56.

– 1948b. 'Mesmer and Animal Magnetism.' *Ciba Symposia* 9: 832–7.

Garnett, Edward. 1917. *Turgenev: A Study.* Rpt. New York: Haskell. 1975.

Gauld, Alan. 1968. *The Founders of Psychical Research.* London: Routledge and Kegan Paul.

Gautier, Théophile. 1831. 'La Cafetière.' In *La Morte amoureuse, Avatar et autres contes fantastiques.* Ed. Jean Gaudron. Paris: Gallimard. 1981.

– 1833. 'Onophrius.'

– 1840. 'Le Pied de Momie.' In *La Morte amoureuse, Avatar et autres contes fantastiques.* Ed. Jean Gaudron. Paris: Gallimard. 1981.

Gershenzon, M. 1919. *Mechta i mysl' I.S. Turgeneva* Rpt. Munich: Fink. 1970.

Gillespie, Neal C. 1979. *Charles Darwin and the Problem of Creation.* Chicago: University of Chicago Press.

Gilman, Sander. 1988. *Disease and Representation: Images of Illness from Madness to AIDS.* Ithaca: Cornell UP.

Gissing, George. 1904. *Charles Dickens: A Critical Study.* London: Gresham.

Glass, B., O. Temkin, and W.L. Strauss, eds. 1959. *Forerunners of Darwin, 1754–1859.* Baltimore: Johns Hopkins UP.
Godfrey, Sima. 1987. 'Lending a Hand: Nerval, Gautier, Maupassant and the Fantastic.' *Romanic Review* 78, 1: 74–83.
Gogol', Nikolay. 1834–42. 'Portret.' In Gogol' 1973.
– 1973. *Sochineniya.* 2 vols. Moscow: Khudozhestvennaya literatura.
Goldfarb, Russell, and R. Clare. 1978. *Spiritualism and Nineteenth Century Letters.* Cranbury, NJ: Associated University Presses.
Goldsmith, Margaret. 1934. *Franz Anton Mesmer: The History of an Idea.* London: Arthur Baker.
Gomme, A.H. 1971. *Dickens.* London: Evans Brothers.
Gose, Elliot B. 1963. 'Psychic Evolution: Darwinism and Initiation in *Tess of the D'Urbervilles.*' *Nineteenth Century Fiction* 18: 261–72.
– 1972. *Imagination Indulged: The Irrational in the Nineteenth Century.* Montreal: McGill-Queen's UP.
Grant, Douglas. 1965. *The Cock Lane Ghost.* London: n.p.
Granjard, Henri. 1954. *Ivan Tourguénev.* Paris: Institut d'Etudes slaves.
Grau, R.M. 1985. '"Persten'": Baratynskii's Fantastic Tale.' *Canadian Slavonic Papers* 26, 4: 296–306.
Greimas, A.J. 1976. *Maupassant.* Paris: Seuil.
Grisewood, H., ed. 1966. *Ideas and Beliefs of the Victorians.* 2nd ed. New York: Dutton. Originally published 1949.
Grivel, Charles. 1975. 'L'entre-jeu de la représentation: Maupassant, la Science et le Désir.' *Revue des Sciences humaines* 160: 501–11.
Grot, Nikolai. 1878. *Snovideniye kak predmet nauchnago analiza.* Kiev: Tipografia Fritza. Cited in Ellenberger, 107.
Gruzinsky, A.E. 1918. *I.S. Turgenev.* Moscow: Gran'.
Gurney, Edmund, Frederic W.H. Myers, and Frank Podmore. 1886. *Phantasms of the Living.* 2 vols. London: Society for Psychical Research. Rpt. Gainsville, FL: Scholar's Facsimiles and Reprints. 1970.
Hansel, C.E.N. 1980. *Science and Parapsychology: A Critical Evaluation.* Buffalo: Prometheus.
Haumant, Emile. 1906. *Ivan Tourguénief: La vie et l'oeuvre.* Paris: Armand Colin.
Henkin, Leo. 1963. *Darwinism in the English Novel, 1860–1910: The Impact of Evolution on Victorian Fiction.* 2nd ed. New York: Russell and Russell. Originally published 1940.
Hilgard, Ernest R. 1980. 'Introduction.' In Bloch, trans. and comp. 1980.
Himmelfarb, Gertrude. 1959. *Darwin and the Darwinian Revolution.* Garden City, NY: Doubleday.

Hogg, James. 1824. *The Private Memoirs and Confessions of a Justified Sinner.* Ed. John Wain. Harmondsworth: Penguin. 1983.
Home, Daniel Dunglas. 1872. *Incidents in My Life.* 1863. 2nd Series. New York: Holt.
House, Humphrey. 1955. 'The Macabre in Dickens.' In *All in Due Time.* London: Hart-Davis. 183–9. Rpt. in Watt, ed. 1971. 40–6.
Hull, David. 1973. *Darwin and His Critics.* Cambridge, MA: Harvard UP.
Hume, Kathryn. 1984. *Fantasy and Mimesis: Responses to Reality in Western Literature.* New York: Methuen.
Hutcheon, Linda. 1984. *Narcissistic Narrative.* New York: Methuen. Originally published 1980.
Huxley, T.H. 1913. *Life and Letters.* 3 vols. Ed. Leonard Huxley. London: Macmillan.
Huxley, Aldous. 1970. *Literature and Science.* London: Chatto and Windus.
Ignotus, Paul. 1966. *The Paradox of Maupassant.* London: University of London Press.
Inglis, Brian. 1986. *The Paranormal: An Encyclopedia of Psychic Phenomena.* London: Paladin Grafton.
Irwin, W.R. 1976. *The Game of the Impossible: A Rhetoric of Fantasy.* Urbana: University of Illinois Press.
'Is It Possible.' 1867. *All the Year Round.* 22 June. 614–20.
Izmailov, N.V., ed. 1930. *Turgenev i krug 'Sovremennika.'* Moscow-Leningrad: Akademia.
Izmailov, N.V., and L.N. Nazarova, eds. 1966/67. *Turgenevskiy sbornik: Materialy k polnomu sobraniyu sochineniy i pisem.* 3 vols. Moscow-Leningrad: Nauka.
Jackson, Rosemary. 1981. *Fantasy: The Literature of Subversion.* London-New York: Methuen.
Jackson, T.A. 1938. *Charles Dickens: The Progress of a Radical.* New York: International Publishers.
Jahn, Robert G., and Brenda J. Dunne. 1987. *Margins of Reality: The Role of Consciousness in the Physical World.* San Diego: Harcourt.
Jakobson, R. 1987. *Language in Literature.* Cambridge, MA: Harvard UP.
James, Henry. 1865. 'The Limitations of Dickens.' Rpt. in Ford, ed. 1961. 48–54.
– 1898. *The Turn of the Screw.* In *The Aspern Papers and The Turn of the Screw.* Ed. Anthony Curtis. Harmondsworth: Penguin. 1984.
– 1908. 'Ivan Turgenieff.' *French Poets and Novelists.* London: Macmillan: 211–52.
Janet, Pierre. 1892. 'Le Spiritisme contemporain.' *Revue Philosophique* 33, 1: 413–42.

Johnson, Edgar. 1952. *Charles Dickens: His Tragedy and Triumph.* 2 vols. New York: Simon and Schuster.
Jones, Louisa. 1972. 'The Conte fantastique as Poetic Fiction: Critical Definitions Then and Now.' *Orbis Litterarum* 27: 237–53.
Jung, C.G. 1902. *On the Psychology and Pathology of So-Called Occult Phenomena* [*Zur Psychologie und Pathologie sogenannter occulter Phenomälne. Eine Psychiatrische Studie*]. In Jung, C.J. 1957.
– 1957. *Collected Works.* New York: Pantheon Books.
Kafka, Franz. 1915. *The Metamorphosis.* In *The Basic Kafka.* New York: Pocket Books. 1979.
– 1919. *A Country Doctor.* In *The Basic Kafka.* New York: Pocket Books. 1979.
Kagan-Kans, Eva. 1969. 'Fate and Fantasy: A Study of Turgenev's Fantastic Stories.' *Slavic Review* 28, 4: 544–60.
Kaplan, Fred. 1975. *Dickens and Mesmerism.* Princeton: Princeton UP.
Katarsky, I. 1966. *Dikens v Rossii.* Moscow: Nauka.
Kayser, Wolfgang. 1981. *The Grotesque in Art and Literature.* New York: Columbia UP.
Kerr, Howard. 1972. *Mediums and Spirit Rappers and Roaring Radicals.* Urbana: University of Illinois Press.
Kitton, Frederick. 1900. *The Minor Writings of Charles Dickens.* London: Elliot.
Kiyko, E.I. 1966. '"Prizraki." Pomety N. B. Shcherbanya na belovom avtografe.' In Izmailov and Nazarova, eds. 1966/67. Vol. 2. 167–70.
– 1967. '"Prizraki." Reministsentsii iz Shopengauera.' In Izmailov and Nazarova, eds. 1966/67. Vol. 3. 123–5.
Kleman, M. 1936. *Ivan Sergeevich Turgenev.* Leningrad: Khudozhestvennaya literatura.
Knowles, A.V., ed. 1983. *Turgenev's Letters.* London: Athlone Press.
Kolakowski, Leszek. 1968. *The Alienation of Reason: A History of Positivist Thought.* New York: Doubleday.
Kotzin, Michael C. 1972. *Dickens and the Fairy Tale.* Bowling Green. OH: Bowling Green University Popular Press.
Kovacs, Albert. 1983. 'La poétique des *Poèmes en Prose* de Tourguéniev dans le contexte de la littérature européenne.' Actes du Congrès du Centenaire 1883–1983. *Cahiers* 7. Paris.
Kristeva, Julia. 1979. 'Le vréel.' In Kristeva, ed. 1979. 9–30.
– ed. 1979. *Folle vérité: vérité et vraisemblance du texte psychotique.* Paris: Seuil.
Kucich, John. 1985. 'Dickens' Fantastic Rhetoric: The Semantics of Reality and Unreality in *Our Mutual Friend.*' *Dickens Studies Annual* 14: 167–89.

Kuhn, Thomas. 1970. *The Structure of Scientific Revolutions.* Chicago: University of Chicago Press.
Kurlyandskaya, G.B. 1959. 'Esteticheskie vzglyady I.S. Turgeneva.' In Petrova, ed. 1959. 367–90.
– 1972. *Khudozhestvennyi metod Turgeneva romanista.* Tula: Priokskoe knizhnoe izdatel'stvo.
Ladariya, M.G. 1970. *I.S. Turgenev i klassiki frantsuzskoy literatury.* Sukhumi: Alashara.
– 1987. 'Turgenev i russkie liberaly.' In Shatalov, ed. 1987. 162–70.
Lang, Andrew. 1901. *Cock Lane and Common-Sense.* London: Longmans, Green.
Lantz, Kenneth A. 1979. *Nikolay Leskov.* Boston: Twayne.
Leblais, Alphonse. 1865. *Matérialisme et spiritualisme.* Paris: Baillière.
Ledkovsky, Marina. 1973. *The Other Turgenev: From Romanticism to Symbolism.* Würzburg: Jal-Verlag.
Le Huenen, Roland. 1980. 'La Sémiotique du corps dans *La Peau de chagrin*: le tout et le fragment.' In Le Huenen and Paul Perron, eds. 1980. 51–64.
– and Paul Perron, eds. 1980. *Le Roman de Balzac.* Montreal: Didier.
Le Shan, Lawrence. 1969. *Toward a General Theory of the Paranormal.* New York: Parapsychology Foundation.
– 1974. *The Medium, the Mystic and the Physicist: Toward a General Theory of the Paranormal.* New York: Viking Press.
Léon, Pierre et al., eds. 1971. *Problèmes de l analyse textuelle/Problems of Textual Analysis.* Montreal: Didier.
– and Henri Mitterand, eds. 1976. *L'Analyse du discours/Discourse Analysis.* Montreal: Centre éducatif et culturel.
Levin, Harry. 1966. 'What Is Realism?' In Zitner, ed. 1966. 216–21.
Levin, Samuel. 1977. *The Semantics of Metaphor.* Baltimore: Johns Hopkins UP.
Levine, George. 1981. *The Realistic Imagination.* Chicago: University of Chicago Press.
– 1986. 'Dickens and Darwin, Science, and Narrative Form.' *Texas Studies in Literature and Language* 28, 3: 250–80.
– 1988. *Darwin and the Novelists: Patterns of Science in Victorian Fiction.* Cambridge, MA: Harvard UP.
– and U.C. Knoepflmacher. 1979. *The Endurance of Frankenstein.* Berkeley: University of California Press.
– and William Madden. 1968. *The Art of Victorian Prose.* London: Oxford UP.
Levy, Maurice. 1973. 'De la spécificité du texte fantastique.' *Recherches anglaises et américaines (RANAM)* 6: 3–13.
– 1980. 'Gothique et fantastique.' *Europe* 58, 611: 41–8.

Lewes, G.H. 1875. *Comte's Philosophy of the Sciences*. London: Bell.
Lewis, Matthew Gregory. 1796. *The Monk*. Oxford: Oxford UP. 1983.
Little, Edmund. 1984. *The Fantasts*. Amersham: Avebury.
Linnér, Sven. 1967. *Dostoevsky on Realism*. Stockholm: Almqvist and Wiksell.
Lodge, David. 1966. *Language of Fiction*. London: Routledge and Kegan Paul.
Lovecraft, H.P. 1973. *Supernatural Horror in Literature*. New York: Dover.
Lowe, David. 1983. *Turgenev: Letters*. 2 vols. Ann Arbor, MI: Ardis
Lubbock, Sir John. 1882. *Ants, Bees, Wasps*. London: Kegan Paul, Trench.
- 1888. *On the Senses, Instincts and Intelligence of Animals: with Special Reference to Insects*. London: Kegan Paul, Trench.
Ludwig, Jan, ed. 1978. *Philosophy and Parapsychology*. Buffalo: Prometheus.
Lyubimov, A. 1894. *Profesor Sharko: nauchno-biograficheskiy*. St Petersburg: Suvorina.
MacNamara, Matthew. 1986. *Style and Vision in Maupassant's Nouvelles*. Berne: Lang.
Macpherson, Jay. 1982. *The Spirit of Solitude*. New Haven: Yale UP.
Maguire, Robert A., ed. 1976. *Gogol from the Twentieth Century*. Princeton: Princeton UP.
Mandelbaum, Maurice. 1964. *Philosophy, Science and Sense Perception: Historical and Critical Studies*. Baltimore: Johns Hopkins UP.
Mandelker, Amy and Roberta Reeder, eds. 1988. *The Supernatural in Slavic and Baltic Literature: Essays in Honor of Victor Terras*. Columbus, OH: Slavica.
Manguel, Alberto, ed. 1990. *Canadian Ghost Stories*. Toronto: Oxford UP.
Manlove, C.N. 1975. *Modern Fantasy*. Cambridge: Cambridge UP.
- 1983. *The Impulse of Fantasy Literature*. London: Macmillan.
Marks, R.W. 1947. *The Story of Hypnotism*. New York: Prentice Hall.
Martin, Wallace. 1986. *Recent Theories of Narrative*. Ithaca: Cornell UP.
Matejka, Ladislav, ed. 1978. *Sound, Sign and Meaning: Quinquagenary of the Prague Linguistic Circle*. Ann Arbor, MI: Michigan Slavic Contributions.
Maturin, Charles. 1820. *Melmoth the Wanderer*. London: Oxford UP. 1968.
Matz, B.W. 1922. *Dickensian Inns and Taverns*. London: Cecil Palmer.
Maupassant, Guy de. 1887. 'Le Roman.' In *Pierre et Jean*. Ed. Pierre Cogny. Paris: Garnier. 1959.
- 1974/1979. *Contes et Nouvelles*, 1875–1893. 2 vols. Ed. Louis Forestier. Paris: Pléiade Gallimard.
- 1980. *Chroniques, Etudes, Correspondance*. 3 vols. Ed. Hubert Juin. Paris: Union Générale.
Maynial, Edouard. 1907. *La Vie et l'oeuvre de Guy de Maupassant*. Paris: Mercure de France.

McCreery, C. 1975. *Psychical Phenomena and the Physical World*. London: Hamilton.
McHale, Brian. 1987. *Postmodernist Fiction*. New York: Methuen.
Meier, Stefanie. 1982. *Animation and Mechanization in the Novels of Charles Dickens*. Berne: Francke.
Mengel, Ewald. 1983. 'The Structure and Meaning of Dickens's "The Signalman."' *Studies in Short Fiction* 20, 4: 271–80.
Mérigot, Bernard. 1972. 'L'inquiétante étrangeté: note sur l'Unheimliche.' *Littérature* 8: 100–6.
Mérimée, Prosper. 1837. 'La Vénus d'Ille.' In *Colomba et dix autres nouvelles*. Paris: Gallimard. 1964.
– 1874. *Portraits historiques et littéraires*. Paris: Librairie Nouvelle.
Merrill, Lynn. 1989. *The Romance of Victorian Natural History*. New York: Oxford UP.
Mesmer, Franz Anton. 1785. *Aphorismes de Mesmer*. Paris: Bertrand. *Maxims on Animal Magnetism*. Trans. and with an introduction by J. Eden. Mt. Vernon, NY: Eden Press. 1958.
Messent, Peter B., ed. 1981. *Literature of the Occult: A Collection of Critical Essays*. Englewood Cliffs, NJ: Prentice-Hall.
Miller, J. Hillis. 1958. *Charles Dickens: The World of His Novels*. Cambridge, MA: Harvard UP.
– 1964. 'Our Mutual Friend.' Afterword to *Our Mutual Friend* by Charles Dickens. Rpt. in Watt, ed. 1971. 123–32.
– 1971. 'The Fiction of Realism.' In Nisbet, ed. 1971. 85–153.
Mistry, Rohinton. 1987. 'The Ghost of Firozsha Baag.' In Manguel, ed. 1990: 259–71.
Molino, Jean. 1980. 'Trois modèles d'analyse du fantastique.' *Europe* 58, 611: 12–26.
Moore, R. Laurence. 1977. *In Search of White Crows: Spiritualism, Parapsychology, and American Culture*. New York: Oxford UP.
Moreil, André. 1977. *La Vie et l'oeuvre d'Allan Kardec: précédées d'une étude sur le spiritisme*. Paris: Vermet.
Morton, Peter. 1984. *The Vital Science: Biology and the Literary Imagination 1860–1900*. London: Allen and Unwin.
Muratov, A.B. 1972. *I.S. Turgenev posle 'Otsov i detey' (60-e gody)*. Leningrad: Izdatel'stvo Leningradskogo universiteta.
– 1975. 'Povest' I.S. Turgeneva "Pesn' torzhestvuyushchey lyubvi."' *Studia Slavica Academiae Scientiarum Hungaricae* 21: 123–37.
– 1980. *Povesti i rasskazy I.S. Turgeneva 1867–1871 godov*. Leningrad: Izdatel'stvo Leningradskogo universiteta.

Muray, Philippe. 1984. *Le XIXe siècle à travers les âges*. Paris: Denoeul.
Musset, Alfred de. 1852. 'La Nuit de Mai [1835].' In *Poésies Nouvelles: 1835–1852*. Paris: Flammarion.
Myers, Frederick. 1903. *Human Personality and Its Survival of Bodily Death*. London: Longmans.
Nelson, Geoffrey K. 1969. *Spiritualism and Society*. London: Routledge and Kegan Paul.
Nerval, Gérard de. 1855. *Aurélia*. In *Oeuvres complètes*. 2 vols. Paris: Gallimard. 1966.
Nesselroth, Peter. 1969. *Lautréamont's Imagery: A Stylistic Approach*. Geneva: Droz.
Nikitina, N.S. 1966. '"Prizraki." Neokonchënnaya stat'ya M.M. Kovalevskogo.' In Izmailov and Nazarova, eds. 1966/67. Vol. 2. 171–2.
Nisbet, Ada, ed. 1971. *Dickens Centennial Essays*. Berkeley: University of California Press.
Oppenheim, Janet. 1985. *The Other World: Spiritualism and Psychical Research in England 1850–1914*. Cambridge: Cambridge UP.
Orel, Harold. 1986. *The Victorian Short Story*. Cambridge: Cambridge UP.
Os'makova, L.N. 1987. 'O poetike "tainstvennykh" povestey Turgeneva.' In Shatalov, ed. 1987: 220–31.
Ostrowski, Witold. 1966. 'The Fantastic and the Realistic in Literature.' Zagadnenia Rodzajow Literackich 11, 1: 54–71.
Ovsyaniko-Kulikovsky, D.N. 1910. *Istoriya russkoy literatury XIXg*. 5 vols. Moscow: Mir. Rpt. Slavistic Printings and Reprintings. Ed. Ch. van Schooneveld. The Hague: Mouton. 1969.
Owen, Robert Dale. 1860. *Footfalls on the Boundary of Another World*. Philadelphia: Lippincot.
Palmer, Philip Mason, and Robert Pattison More. 1936. *The Sources of the Faust Tradition*. New York: Oxford UP.
Parret, Herman, and Hans-Georg Ruprecht, eds. 1985. *Exigences et perspectives de la sémiotique. Recueil d'hommages pour Algirdas Julien Greimas*. Amsterdam-Philadelphia: Benjamins.
Passage, Charles. 1963. *The Russian Hoffmannists*. The Hague: Mouton.
Patten, Robert L. 1967. 'The Art of *Pickwick's* Interpolated Tales.' *English Literary History* 34: 349–66.
Pattie, F.A., Jr. 1967. 'A Brief History of Hypnotism.' In J.E. Gordon, ed. *Handbook of Clinical and Experimental Hypnosis*. New York: Macmillan.
Paulet, Jean-Jacques. 1784. *L'Antimagnétisme ou origine, progrès, décadence, renouvellement et réfutation du magnétisme animal*. Rpt. Geneva-Paris: Slatkine. 1980.

Pavel, Thomas G. 1987. *Fictional Worlds.* Cambridge, MA: Harvard UP.
Penzoldt, Peter. 1965. *The Supernatual in Fiction.* New York: Humanities Press. Originally published 1952.
Petrova, S.M., ed. 1959. *Tvorchestvo I.S. Turgeneva: Sbornik statey.* Moscow: Gosudarstvennoe uchebno-pedagogicheskoe izdatel'stvo Ministerstva prosveshcheniya RSFSR.
Petrovo-Solovovo, M.M. 1900. *Mediumicheskiya fizicheskiya yavleniya i ich nauchnoe izsledovanie.* St Petersburg: Tipografiya Demjakova.
– 1930. 'Some Thoughts on D.D. Home.' *Proceedings of the Society for Psychical Research* 114: 247–65.
Petrovsky, M.A. 1920. 'Tainstvennoe u Turgeneva.' In Rozanov and Sokolov, eds. 1920. 70–97.
– 1921. 'Kompozitsiya novelly u Mopassana.' *Nachala* 1: 106–27. Eng. trans. in *Essays in Poetics* 12 (1987), 2: 1–21.
Peyrouton, N.C. 1959. 'Rapping the Rappers.' *The Dickensian* 55, 327: 19–30, 75–89.
Pierssens, Michel. 1986. 'Littérature et tables tournantes.' *Critique.* no. 473: 999–1015.
Piksanov, N.I. 1923. 'Istoriya "Prizrakov."' In Brodsky, ed. 1923a. 164–92.
Podmore, Frank. 1902. *Modern Spiritualism.* 2 vols. London: Methuen.
– 1909. *From Mesmer to Christian Science.* 1963. New York: University Books.
Poe, Edgar Allan. 1837. *The Philosophy of Animal Magnetism, by a Gentleman of Philadelphia: Together with the System of Manipulating Adopted to Produce Ecstasy and Somnambulism – The Effects and the Rationale.* Philadelphia: Merrihew and Gunn. Republished with an introduction by J. Jackson. Philadelphia: Patterson and White. 1928.
– 1982. *The Tell-Tale Heart and Other Writings.* Toronto: Bantam.
Pothet, Lucien. 1979. *Mythe et tradition dans l'imaginaire dickensien.* Paris: Lettres modernes.
Polonsky, Ya. 1889. *Na vysotakh spiritizma.* St Petersburg: Skorokhodov.
Polyakova, L.I. 1983. *Povesti I.S. Turgeneva 70-kh godov.* Kiev: Naukova Dumka.
Porter, Katherine H. 1972. *Through a Glass Darkly: Spiritualism in the Browning Circle.* New York: Octagon.
Postman, L., ed. 1962. *Psychology in the Making: Histories of Selected Research Problems.* New York: Knopf.
Potocki, Jean. 1958. *Un Manuscrit trouvé à Saragosse.* Ed. Roger Caillois. Paris: Gallimard. Originally published in Polish, 1847.
Powell, J.H. 1864. *Spiritualism: Its Facts and Phases.* London: Pitman.
Pozuelo Yvancos, José María. 1993. *Poetica de la ficción.* Madrid: Sintesis.

Pritchett, V.S. 1954. 'The Comic World of Dickens.' In *The Listener*, 3 June: 970–3. Rpt. in Watt, ed. 1971. 27–39.
Pumpyansky, L.V. 1929. 'Gruppa tainstvennykh povestey.' In I.S. Turgenev. 1923–34. Vol. 7. 5–24.
Pushkin, Aleksandr. 1834. *Pikovaya dama* [*The Queen of Spades*]. In Pushkin 1962.
– 1962. *Sochineniya.* 3 vols. Moscow: Gosudarstvennoe izdatel'stvo.
Pustovoit, P.G. 1957. *Ivan Sergeevich Turgenev.* Moscow: Izdatel'stvo Moskovskogo universiteta.
Puységur, Armand Marie Jacques Chastenet, Marquis de. 1807. *Mémoires pour servir à l'histoire et à l'établissement du magnétisme animal.* Toulouse: Privat. 1986.
Rabkin, Eric S. 1976. *The Fantastic in Literature.* Princeton: Princeton UP.
Rachmühl, Françoise. 1983. *Le Horla et autres contes fantastiques. Analyse critique.* Paris: Hatier.
Radcliffe, Ann. 1789. *The Castles of Athlin and Dunbayne.* London: Limbird. 1826.
– 1794. *The Mysteries of Udolpho.* 1st ed. London: Robinson.
– 1797. *The Italian.* Oxford: Oxford UP. 1984.
– 1826. *Gaston de Blondeville.* 1st ed. London: Colborn.
Raim, Anne-Marie. 1986. *La Communication non verbale chez Maupassant.* Paris: Nizet.
Reed, John R. 1981. 'The Occult in Later Victorian Literature.' In Messent, ed. 1981. 89–104.
Reizov, B.G., ed. 1986. *Istoriya i teoriya literatury.* Leningrad: Nauka.
Rescher, Nicholas. 1974. *Studies in Modality.* American Philosophical Quarterly. Monograph Series. Monograph no. 8. Ed. Nicholas Rescher. Oxford: Basil Blackwell. 1974.
– 1975. *A Theory of Possibility: A Constructivist and Conceptualistic Account of Possible Individuals and Possible Worlds.* Oxford: Basil Blackwell. 1975.
– 1987. *Forbidden Knowledge and Other Essays on the Philosophy of Cognition.* Dordrecht. Boston, Lancaster, Tokyo: Reidel.
Richardson, Samuel. 1740–42. *Pamela, or, Virtue rewarded.* Harmondsworth: Penguin. 1980.
Richet, Charles. 1881. 'The Simulation of Somnambulism.' *Lancet* 1: 8–9; 51–2.
– 1884. *L'Homme et l'intelligence. Fragments de philosophie.* Alcan: Paris. 295, 543.
– 1923. *Traité de métapsychique.* Paris: Alcan.
– [1926]. *Our Sixth Sense.* London: Rider.
Richter, Anne. 1984. *Le Fantastique féminin.* Brussels: Jacques Antoine.

Riffaterre, Michael. 1983. *Text Production.* New York: Columbia UP. Trans. Terese Lyons. Originally published in French, *La Production du texte.* Paris: Seuil. 1979.

Ronen, Ruth. 1994. *Possible Worlds in Literary Theory.* Cambridge: Cambridge UP.

Roscau, Manuela. 1976. 'Modèle actantiel et modèle logique – Lecture d'une nouvelle fantastique de Maupassant: "Le Horla."' *Revue roumaine de linguistique* 13, 2: 627–36.

Rosen, G. 1948. 'From Mesmerism to Hypnotism.' *Ciba Symposium* 9: 838–44.

– 1963. 'History of Medical Hypnosis: From Animal Magnetism to Medical Hypnosis.' In Schneck, ed. 1963.

Routh, Harold V. 1937. *Towards the Twentieth Century: Essays in the Spiritual History of the Nineteenth.* Cambridge: Cambridge UP.

Rozanov, I.N., and Y.M. Sokolov, eds. 1920. *Tvorchestvo Turgeneva.* Moscow: Zadruga.

Ryan, Marie-Laure. 1991. *Possible Worlds, Artifical Intelligence, and Narrative Theory.* Bloomington and Indianapolis: Indiana UP.

– 1992. 'Possible Worlds in Recent Literary Theory'. *Style* 26, 4: 528–53.

Samarin, William J. 1976. 'The Functions of Glossolalic Discourse.' In Léon and Mitterand, eds. 1976. 37–42.

Sarbin, T.R. 1962. 'Attempts to Understand Hypnotic Phenomena.' In Postman, ed. 1962. 745–85.

Scarborough, Dorothy. 1917. *The Supernatural in Modern English Fiction.* New York: Octagon. 1967.

Schaeffer, Jean-Marie. 1989. *Qu'est-ce qu'un genre littéraire?* Paris: Seuil.

Schaffner, Alain. 1988. 'Pourquoi "Horla" ou Le Passage du miroir.' *Les Temps modernes* 499, février: 150–64.

Schapira, Charlotte. 1987. 'La Technique du récit englobé dans les contes de Maupassant.' *Neophilologus* 71, 4: 513–22.

Schapiro, Leonard. 1978. *Turgenev: His Life and Times.* Oxford: Oxford UP.

Schasch, Nahissa. 1983. *Maupassant et le fantastique ténébreux.* Paris: Nizet.

Schlobin, Roger C. 1982. *The Aesthetics of Fantasy Literature and Art.* Notre Dame, IN: University of Notre Dame Press and Harvester Press.

Schneck, J.M. 1961a. 'Charcot and Hypnosis.' *Journal of the American Medical Association* 176, 1: 157–8.

– 1961b. 'Jean-Martin Charcot and the History of Experimental Hypnosis.' *Journal of the History of Medicine and Allied Sciences* 16: 297–305.

– 1963. *Hypnosis in Modern Medicine.* Springfield, IL.: Charles C. Thomas. 3rd ed. Originally published 1958.

Schneider, Marcel. 1985. *Histoire de la littérature fantastique en France*. Paris: Arthème Fayard.
Schopenhauer, Arthur. 1851. 'Essay on Spirit Seeing and Everything Connected Therewith.' *Parerga and Paralipomena*. 2 vols. Oxford: Clarendon. Vol. 1: 227–309. 1974.
Schurig-Geick, Dorothea. 1970. *Studien zum modernen 'Conte fantastique.' Maupassants und ausgewählter Autoren des 20 Jahrhunderts*. Heidelberg: Winter.
Seed, David. 1981. 'Mystery in Everday Things: Charles Dickens' "Signalman."' *Criticism* 23, 1: 42–57.
Sère, Cesare. 1988. *Introduction to the Analysis of the Literary Text*. Bloomington: Indiana UP.
Shatalov, S.E. 1979. *Khudozhestvennyy mir I.S. Turgeneva*. Moscow: Nauka.
– ed. 1987. *I.S. Turgenev v sovremennom mire*. Moscow: Nauka.
Shaw, George Bernard. 1981. Preface to *Heartbreak House*. New York: Garland. Originally published 1919.
Shcherbina, V.P. 1987. 'Turgenev i razvitie realizma.' In Shatalov, ed. 1987. 37–105.
Shelley, Mary. 1818. *Frankenstein, or the Modern Prometheus*. Toronto: Bantam. 1981.
Shklovsky, Viktor. 1929. *O teorii prozy*. Moscow: Federatsiya.
Shor, R.E. 1968. 'Periodical Literature on Hypnotism and Mesmerism.' *American Journal of Clinical Hypnosis* 10: 265–6.
Short, Wilfrid M., ed. 1912. *Arthur James Balfour as Philosopher and Thinker*. London: Longmans, Green.
Slusser, George E., Eric S. Rabkin, and Robert Scholes, eds. 1982. *Bridges to Fantasy*. Carbondale: Southern Illinois UP.
Spencer, Herbert. 1862. *First Principles*. London: Williams and Norgate.
Spilka, Mark. 1963. *Dickens and Kafka*. London: Dobson.
Stahl, John D. 1980. 'The Source and Significance of the Revenant in Dickens's "The Signalman."' *Dickens Studies Newsletter* 11: 98–101.
Stalnaker, Robert C. *Inquiry*. Cambridge, MA: MIT Press. 1984.
Starobinski, Jean. 1970. *La Relation Critique*. Paris: Gallimard.
Stebbins, Robert Ernest. 1965. *French Reactions to Darwin: 1859–1882*. Ph.D. thesis. University of Minnesota.
Steegmuller, Francis. 1972. *Maupassant: A Lion in the Path*. 2nd ed. Freeport: Books for Libraries Press. Originally published 1949.
Steiner, Rudolf. 1973. *The Occult Movement in the Nineteenth Century and Its Relation to Modern Culture*. [*Die okkulte Bewegung im neunzehnten Jahr-*

hundert und ihre Beziehung zur Weltkultur] Trans. D.S. Osmond. London: Rudolph Steiner Press.
Stevenson, Robert Louis. 1886. *The Strange Case of Dr. Jekyll and Mr. Hyde.* Harmondsworth: Penguin. 1983.
Stevick, Philip. 1967. *The Theory of the Novel.* London: Collier Macmillan.
Stewart, Garrett. 1974. *Dickens and the Trials of Imagination.* Cambridge, MA: Harvard UP.
Stoehr, Taylor. 1965. *Dickens: The Dreamer's Stance.* Ithaca: Cornell UP.
Stone, Harry. 1979. *Dickens and the Invisible World.* Bloomington: Indiana UP.
Stříbrný, Zdeněk. 1987. *Dějiny anglické literatury.* 2 vols. Prague: Academia.
Sucksmith, Harvey P. 1970. *The Narrative Art of Charles Dickens: The Rhetoric of Sympathy and Irony in His Novels.* Oxford: Clarendon. 1970.
Sullivan, Edward D. 1962. *Maupassant: The Short Stories.* London: Arnold.
– 1972. *Maupassant the Novelist.* Port Washington, NY: Kennikat. Originally published 1954.
Sullivan, Jack. 1978. *Elegant Nightmares: The English Short Story from Le Fanu to Blackwood.* Athens: Ohio UP.
Swift, Jonathan. 1726. *Gulliver's Travels.* Harmondsworth: Penguin. 1985.
Targe, André. 1975. 'Trois apparitions du *Horla*.' *Poétique* 24: 446–59.
Tatar, Maria M. 1978. *Spellbound: Studies on Mesmerism and Literature.* Princeton: Princeton UP.
Terras, Viktor. 1970. 'Turgenev's Aesthetic and Western Realism.' *Comparative Literature* 22: 19–35.
– 1974. *Belinsky and Russian Literary Criticism: The Heritage of Organic Aesthetics.* Madison: Wisconsin UP.
– 1985. *Handbook of Russian Literature.* New Haven: Yale UP.
Thakur, Shivesh. 1976. 'Telepathy, Evolution and Dualism.' In Thakur, ed. 1976.
– ed. 1976. *Philosophy and Psychical Research.* London: Allen and Unwin. 195–210.
Thalmann, Marianne. 1964. *The Romantic Fairy Tale: Seeds of Surrealism.* Ann Arbor, MI: University of Michigan Press.
Thomson, Sir John Joseph. 1936. *Recollections and Reflections.* Toronto: Macmillan.
Tinterow, M.M., ed. 1970. *Foundations of Hypnosis: From Mesmer to Freud.* Springfield, IL.: Charles C. Thomas.
Todorov, Tzvetan. 1970. *Introduction à la littérature fantastique.* Paris: Seuil.
– 1975. *The Fantastic: A Structural Approach to a Literary Genre.* Trans. Richard Howard. Ithaca NY: Cornell UP. 1975.
– 1976. 'Le Discours psychotique.' In Léon and Mitterand, eds. 1976. 49–55.

- 1978. *Les genres du discours*. Paris: Seuil.
Traill, Nancy H. 1988. Review of Kathryn Hume, *Fantasy and Mimesis* (New York: Methuen. 1985), *Style* 22, 1: 147–50.
- 1991. 'Fictional Worlds of the Fantastic.' In Doležel and Traill, eds. 1991. 196–210.
- 1992. 'From Demons to Dreams: Turgenev's Fantastic Tales.' In *Poetics of the Text. Studies in Slavic Literature and Poetics*. Edited and introduced by Joe Andrew. Amsterdam: Rodopi. 125–37.
Trautwein, Wolfgang. 1980. *Erlesene Angst Schauerliteratur im 18. und 19 Jahrhundert*. Munich: Hanser.
Trofimov, I.T. 1967. '"Klara Milich." "Pesn' torzhestvuyushey lyubvi." Stat'i A. M-va o proizvedeniyakh Turgeneva.' In Izmailov and Nazarova, eds. 1966/67. Vol. 3: 165–7.
Trollope, Anthony. 1880. *The Duke's Children*. Oxford: Oxford UP. 1989.
Turgenev, I.S. 1923–34. *Sobranie sochineniy*. 12 vols. Moscow-Leningrad:
- 1959. *Literary Reminiscences and Autobiographical Fragments*. Ed. and trans. David Magarshack. London: Faber.
- 1960–8a. *Polnoe sobranie sochineniy*. 15 vols. Moscow-Leningrad: Nauka.
- 1961–8b. *Pis'ma*. 13 vols. Moscow-Leningrad: Nauka.
- 1962c. *Sobranie sochinenii*. Moscow: Gosudarstvennoe izdatel'stvo khudozhestvennoy literatury.
- 1979. *The Mysterious Tales of Ivan Turgenev*. Ed. and trans. Robert Dessaix. Canberra: Australian National University.
- 1986. *Perepiska I.S. Turgeneva*. 2 vols. Moscow: Khudozhestvennaya literatura.
Turner, Frank Miller. 1976. *Between Science and Religion: The Reaction to Scientific Naturalism in Late Victorian England*. New Haven: Yale UP.
Ullmann, Stephen. 1957,. *Style in the French Novel*. Cambridge: Cambridge UP.
Vax, Louis. 1960. *L'Art et la littérature fantastiques*. Paris: Presses universitaires.
- 1965. *La Séduction de l'étrange: Etude sur la littérature fantastique*. Paris: Presses universitaires.
Venok Turgenevu: Sbornik statey 1818–1919. 1919. Odessa: Ivasenko.
Vetrinsky, C. 1920. 'Muza-vampir.' In Rozanov and Sokolov, eds. 1920. 152–67.
Viatte, Auguste. 1928. *Les Sources occultes du romantisme*. 2 vols. Paris: Champion.
Vial, André. 1954. *Guy de Maupassant et l'art du roman*. Paris: Nizet.
- 1973. 'Le lignage clandestin de Maupassant conteur "fantastique."' *Revue d'histoire littéraire de la France* 6: 993–1009.
Villiers de L'Isle-Adam, Jean-Marie. 1883. *Contes cruels*. Ed. Pierre Citron. Paris: Garnier-Flammarion. 1980.

Vinogradov, Viktor. 1925. 'Problema skaza v stilistike' [The Problem of *Skaz* in Stylistics]. In Vinogradov, 1980.
- 1969. *The History of the Russian Literary Language from the Seventeenth Century to the Nineteenth*. [*Ocherki po istorii russkogo literaturnogo yazyka XVII–XIX vv.*] Trans. Lawrence L. Thomas. Madison: University of Wisconsin Press. Originally published 1934.
- 1980. *O Yazyke khudozhestvennoy prozy*. Moscow: Nauka. Originally published 1930.

von Wright, Georg H. 1968. *An Essay in Deontic Logic and the General Theory of Action*. Amsterdam: North Holland.

Waddington, Patrick. 1980. *Turgenev and England*. London: Macmillan.

Wagenknecht, Edward. 1957. *The Man Charles Dickens*. Norman: University of Oklahoma Press. Originally published 1929.

Wallace, A.R. 1881. *On Miracles and Modern Spiritualism*. New York: Arno Press. 1975.

Wallis, Roy. 1979. *On the Margins of Science: The Social Construction of Rejected Knowledge*. Keele, UK: University of Keele Press.

Watson, R.I. 1971. *The Great Psychologists: From Aristotle to Freud*. Philadelphia: Lippincott. 3rd ed. Originally published 1919.

Watt, Ian, ed. 1971. *The Victorian Novel: Modern Essays in Criticism*. London: Oxford UP.

Webb, James. 1974. *The Occult Underground*. La Salle, IL: Open Court.

Wellek, René. 1963. *Concepts of Criticism*. New Haven: Yale UP.

Wells, H.G. 1898. *The War of the Worlds*. London: William Heinemann.

Wilkinson, Ann Y. 1967. '*Bleak House*: From Faraday to Judgment Day.' *English Literary History* 34: 225–47.

Willi, Kurt. 1972. *Déterminisme et liberté chez Guy de Maupassant*. Zurich: Juris Druck.

Wills, William Henry. 1866. 'At Home with the Spirits.' *All the Year Round*. March 3. 180–4.

Wilson, Edmund. 1959. 'Turgenev and the Life-Giving Drop.' In Turgenev, 1959. 9–59.

Wolman, Benjamin B., ed. 1977. *Handbook of Parapsychology*. Jefferson, NC: McFarland.

Woodward, James. 1973. 'The Symbolism and Rhythmic Structure of Turgenev's "Italian Pastiche."' *Die Welt der Slaven* 18: 368–85.

Wynne, Brian. 1979. 'Physics and Psychics: Science, Symbolic Action, and Social Control in Late Victorian England.' In Barnes and Shapin, eds. 1979. 167–86.

Žekulin, Nicholas. 1984. 'Humour in Turgenev's Operetta *Le Dernier Sorcier*.' *Russian Literature* 16: 421–36.

- 1985. *Turgenev: A Bibliography of Books 1843–1982*. Calgary: University of Calgary Press.
Zgorzelski, Andrzej. 1984. 'On Differentiating Fantastic Fiction: Some Supragenological Distinctions in Literature.' *Poetics Today* 5, 2: 299–307.
Zilboorg, G., and G.W. Henry. 1941. *A History of Medical Psychology*. New York: W.W. Norton.
Zitner, Sheldon P., ed. 1966. *The Practice of Modern Literary Scholarship*. Glenview, IL: Scott.
Zola, Emile. 1880. *Le Roman expérimental*. Paris: Garnier-Flammarion. 1971.
Zweig, S. 1932. *Mental Healer: Franz Anton Mesmer, Mary Baker Eddy, Sigmund Freud*. [*Die Heilung durch den Geist*]. Trans. Eden and Cedar Paul. New York: Viking Press. Originally published 1931.

Index

Absurd, the: definition of, 15
Alethic opposition, 9, 13; as a modality, 12; as part of Georg von Wright's modal system, 144n. 11
Allegory, 75; allegorical readings, 135, 151n. 20
Ambiguity, 4–5, 13, 110; and narrative transmission, 14
Ambiguous mode. *See* Modes
Animal magnetism. *See* Magnetism; Mesmerism
Authentication force, 58, 62, 144n. 12; effect of irony on, 149n. 3

Balzac, Honoré de: *La Peau de chagrin*, 113, 157nn. 6, 8, 159n. 20; *Père Goriot*, 5; *Séraphita*, 11
Beckford, William: *Vathek*, 12
Bergson, Henri, 30
Bessière, Irène, 6, 7; on Musset's 'La Nuit,' 160n. 27
Braid, James, 138; hyperacuity, 25, 116
Brewster, Sir David, 36, 62, 148n. 6
Brontë, Charlotte: *Jane Eyre*, 8, 16
Brooke-Rose, Christine, 6, 7; and James's *The Turn of the Screw*, 13

Bruce, Jacob: sorcerer, 95, 155n. 25
Bulgakov, Mikhail: *The Master and Margarita*, 145n. 17, 152n. 5
Bulwer-Lytton, Edward G, 34; *A Strange Story*, 154n. 22

Canadian literature: the fantastic in, 145n. 16
Carroll, Lewis: *Alice in Wonderland*, 17; *Through the Looking Glass*, 17
Chambers, Robert: *Chambers's Journal*, 30, 31
Charcot, Jean, 25, 40, 95, 115–16, 119, 138, 154nn. 18, 22
Chatman, Seymour, 144n. 13
Christianity, 21, 25; and Darwin's theory of evolution, 30–1; and 'Father Aleksey's Tale,' 79–82; and 'Song of Triumphant Love,' 94
Clairvoyance, 17; in Dickens, 59, 61, 63, 67; in Maupassant, 108, 116, 140; Mesmer's attitude towards, 24, 31, 34; and Puységur, 24
Coincidence, 18, 36, 38–9, 49, 66, 68, 70, 109, 140, 151n. 20
Collins, Wilkie: *The Frozen Deep*, 8; *The Woman in White*, 60

Comte, Auguste: *Cours de philosophie positive*, 26, 27, 29, 159n. 21; 'The Three Stages of Human Intellect,' 26, 127, 128
Communication: alternative channels of, 28, 30, 74, 100, 104; with the dead, 21, 25, 35, 36, 39, 148n. 12

Danto, Arthur, 18, 32
Darwin, Charles, 21, 30–2, 122, 129, 138, 139, 151n. 20; and T.H. Huxley, 28; 'natural selection,' in Maupassant, 40, 122, 124, 129. See also Evolution
Dickens, Charles, 11, 20, 22, 25; and folk narrative, 49–50, 51, 58, 72; humour in, 55–6; language in, 55–6, 150n. 12; on spiritualism, 35–9, 74, 75, 76, 77, 104, 105, 135, 139, 147nn. 1, 2, 148n. 12. Fiction: 'The Bagman's Story,' 11, 47–9; 'The Baron of Grogzwig,' 50, 57–8; *Bleak House*, 44, 46, 55, 149n. 8, 150n. 9, 151n. 20; *A Christmas Carol*, 50–6, 64, 72, 75, 128, 135, 150nn. 9, 11, 151n. 22, 152n. 5; *Dombey and Son*, 151n. 20; *Great Expectations*, 58, 149n. 8; *Hard Times*, 55, 150nn. 9, 12; Jack Bamber's 'Tales,' 47, 49, 50, 57; *The Lazy Tour of Two Idle Apprentices*, 149n. 6; *Little Dorrit*, 46; *Martin Chuzzlewit*, 149n. 6; 'Mr H.'s Own Narrative,' 58, 64–7, 72; *The Mystery of Edwin Drood*, 29, 58, 149n. 8; *Nicholas Nickleby*, 46; *Oliver Twist*, 151n. 20; *Our Mutual Friend*, 56, 58; *Pickwick Papers*, 16, 46, 47, 56, 64, 72, 149n. 3; 'The Signal-Man' (in *Mugby Junction*), 38, 46, 67–72, 73, 104, 139, 140, 151nn. 18, 19, 20, 21; 'The Story of the Bagman's Uncle,' 49–50, 56–7; 'To Be Read at Dusk,' 58–61; 'To Be Taken with a Grain of Salt,' 58, 61–4, 65, 67, 72, 76, 150n. 15

Disjunctive mode. See Modes.
Doležel, Lubomír, 3, 143n. 1; on fictionality, 144n. 9. See also Authentication force
Dostoevsky, Fyodor Mikhailovich, 23, 34, 78, 145n. 6
Du Maurier, George: *Trilby*, 60

Evolution, 28–32; early theories of, 146n. 15. See also Darwin, Charles; Lamarck, Jean; Spencer, Herbert; Wallace, Alfred Russell

Fantastic, the: ability to cut across genres, 7; durability of, 18, 20; historicity of, 10, 20, 140–1; and period styles, 7, 10. See also Modes; Narrative Worlds; Realism
Fantasy, 6–7, 74, 144n. 8, 145n. 17
Fantasy mode. See Modes
Fictionality, 78, 144n. 9, 157n. 5
Fictional world, 8, 9, 10, 144n. 9. See also Narrative Worlds
Flammarion, Camille, 29, 32, 40
Frye, Northrop: 'humours,' 55; use of the term 'mode,' 10

Gautier, Théophile: 'The Coffee Pot,' 48; 'The Mummy's Foot,' 47; *Onophrius*, 116
Genre theory: problems with, 7–8, 10, 15
Gogol', Nikolai, 44, 76, 103, 104; and *skaz*, 15, 82; 'Evenings on a Farm Near Dikan'ka,' 50; 'The Nose,'

14–16; 'The Overcoat,' 84; 'The Portrait,' 152n. 7; 'A Terrible Vengeance,' 12; 'Viy,' 11
Gothic, the, 3, 4, 144n. 10, 149n. 9; conventions of, in Dickens, 46, 50, 51, 57–8, 59–60, 64, 68, 72; —, in Maupassant, 105, 107, 157n. 4; —, in Turgenev, 76, 77

Hesitation, 4–5, 9, 16, 140, 144n. 8; degrees of, 5, 143–4n. 6
Hogg, James: *The Private Memoirs and Confessions of a Justified Sinner*, 14
Home, Daniel Dunglas, 22, 41, 145–6n. 7, 148n. 6, 152n. 10; Dickens on, 36–7
Huxley, Thomas Henry, 27–8, 33
Hyperacuity. *See* Braid, James
Hyperesthesia. *See* Bergson, Henri
Hypnosis, 25, 30, 40, 86, 95, 115, 127–8, 138, 154nn. 18, 22. *See also* Magnetism; Somnambulism; Charcot, Jean; Mesmer, Franz Anton

Insanity: discourse of, 160n. 26; fictional status of, 18, 66, 105, 107, 108, 112, 114–15, 118, 120, 157n. 5
Intentional fallacy, 144n. 8, 150n. 9
Intertextuality, 34; in Dickens, 50, 58; in Maupassant, 113, 123, 158n. 10; in Turgenev, 79, 80, 84, 89, 90, 95–6, 156n. 34

Jackson, Rosemary, 6–7, 10, 144–5n. 14
Jakobson, Roman, 43, 160n. 25
James, Henry: on Turgenev's *The Dog*, 153n. 13; *The Turn of the Screw*, 5, 13–14, 34, 140

Kafka, Franz: *A Country Doctor*, 141; *The Metamorphosis*, 141, 143–4n. 6
Kuhn, Thomas, 32, 147n. 17

Lamarck, Jean, 30–1, 40; his four postulates, 146–7n. 15, 159n. 17
Language, figurative, 12, 17, 48, 59, 118. *See also* Dickens, Charles; Maupassant, Guy de; Turgenev, Ivan Sergeevich
Le Sage, René: *Le Diable boiteux*, 12, 152n. 5
Levitation, 91, 154n. 20
Lewis, Matthew Gregory: *The Monk*, 12, 149n. 7

Magnetism, 23–4, 25, 83, 86–8, 98, 116, 118–19, 146n. 8. *See also* Mesmer, Franz Anton
Marvellous, the, 3, 4, 6, 15, 24, 143n. 5, 144n. 7
Maupassant, Guy de, 20, 34, 35, 74, 80, 85, 104, 139, 140–1; attitude towards spiritualism, etc., 39–41, 42; language (style) in, 108, 130–2, 157n. 2, 160nn. 25, 26; as realist, 43–5. Essays: *Chronicles [Chroniques]*, 'Adieu mystères,' 159n. 16; 'An Emperor,' 40; 'The Fantastic,' 40, 44; 'Par-delà,' 40–1; 'Le Roman,' 44. Fiction: 'The Apparition,' 80, 105, 111–12, 121; 'Le Champ d'Oliviers,' 107; 'Conte de Noël,' 158n. 13; *Fort comme la mort*, 107; 'The Hair,' 80, 105–6, 112–15, 121, 126, 133; 'The Hand,' 105, 109–11, 112; 'He?,' 106, 120–2, 133; The 'Horla' cycle, 106; —, 'Letter from a Madman,' 123–4, 125, 128; 'Le Horla' (1886), 124–6; 'Le Horla' (1887), 18, 39, 104, 124,

126–34, 139, 140–1, 159–60n. 23; 'M. Jocaste,' 132; 'A Madman?,' 40, 106, 118–20, 133; 'Magnetism,' 40, 106, 115–18, 133; 'The Man from Mars,' 40, 140; 'Mouche,' 107; 'La Peur,' 159n. 19; 'Le Port,' 132; 'A Portrait,' 158n. 10; 'Le Rosier de Mme Husson,' 106; 'The Skeleton Hand,' 105, 107–9, 'Le Tic,' 132, 158n. 11
Maturin, Charles: *Melmoth the Wanderer*, 149n. 7
Mediums, 21, 22, 23, 25, 28, 36, 41, 147n. 1, 152n. 10. *See also* Home, Daniel Dunglas
Mérimée, Prosper de: 'La Vénus d'Ille,' 14
Mesmer, Franz Anton, 23–5, 36, 40, 119
Mesmerism, 60, 86, 116, 138, 147n. 2. *See also* Magnetism
Mimesis, 3, 43, 144n. 8, 148n. 16
Modal enhancement/incapacity. *See* Danto, Arthur
Modal system, 9; Georg von Wright's, 144n. 11
Modes: ambiguous mode, 10, 13–16, 48, 76, 77, 78, 97, 98, 105, 137, 139; antirationality of, 10; in Dickens, 42–3, 46, 58–9, 62, 64, 67, 70–3, 139; disjunctive mode, 11–12, 20, 76, 105, 107, 112; fantasy mode, 12–13, 17; in historical context, 10, 21, 29, 30, 32, 33, 34–5, 42, 138; in Maupassant, 106, 115, 122, 132, 139–40, 141; paranormal mode, 11, 17–18, 138; supernatural naturalized, 16–17; in Turgenev, 74, 75, 76, 78–9, 85, 89, 94, 99, 104, 139–40, 141; typology of, 8–20, 136–8. *See also* Narrative worlds

Musset, Alfred de, 159n. 18, 160n. 27
Myers, Frederic, 28, 32
Mystery story: in Dickens, 46–7, 59, 65–6, 71–2; Viktor Shklovsky's definition of, 61

Narrative transmission: and ambiguity, 14; in Dickens, 49. *See also* Chatman, Seymour.
Narrative worlds, 136, 144n. 11; natural/supernatural domains, 8–9, 11, 136–8; —, oppositional dynamism of, 9–10, 11, 16, 19–20, 137; —, reinterpretation of, in paranormal mode, 17–18, 21, 125, 127–8, 133, 134, 138–9
Natural selection. *See* Darwin, Charles
Nerval, Gérard de: *Aurélia*, 14
Nodier, Charles: *Inès de las Sierras*, 16

Paranormal mode. *See* Modes
Penzoldt, Peter, 4, 144n. 10
Possible-worlds semantics, 3, 8–11, 138–9; Raymond Bradley and Norman Swartz, 8; 'Physically possible,' 'physically impossible,' 8–9, 136. *See also* Modes
Podmore, Frank, 28, 31, 146n. 7
Positivism, 26–8, 29, 32, 138, 139, 141. *See also* Comte, Auguste
Potocki, Jean: *Manuscrit trouvé à Saragosse*, 16
Precognition, 17, 31, 100, 151n. 21; paradox of, 71, 151n. 22
Pushkin, Aleksandr: *Evgeny Onegin*, 96; *The Queen of Spades*, 14, 103, 156n. 33; and Turgenev, 44, 103, 104
Puységur, Marquis de, 24

Radcliffe, Ann, 3, 16–17; *Gaston de Blondeville*, 16; *The Castles of Athlin and Dunbayne*, 150n. 13; *The Italian*, 16, 149n. 7; *The Mysteries of Udolpho*, 16, 149nn. 2, 7, 150n. 13
Realism, 7, 10, 43–4, 132, 145n. 17
Rescher, Nicholas, 8–9
Richet, Charles, 26, 29, 32, 39, 41, 135; mental metapsychics [métapsychique mentale], 29; veridical hallucination, 63
Romantics, the, 3, 7, 10, 46, 47, 76, 107, 152n. 4

Scarborough, Dorothy, 4, 143n. 2, 152n. 8
Schismatics, the, 153n. 15
Shklovsky, Viktor. *See* Mystery story
Skaz, 15, 145n. 15, 153n. 11; in Turgenev, 79, 82, 84, 103, 153nn. 13, 14
Somnambulism, 24, 37, 38, 41, 93, 95, 154–5n. 22
Spencer, Herbert, 28–9; impact on Maupassant, 40–1, 117, 122
Spiritualism, 21–33, 35, 46, 62–3, 64, 73, 138. *See also* Dickens, Charles; Maupassant, Guy de; Turgenev, Ivan Sergeevich
Supernatural naturalized. *See* Modes
Swift, Jonathan: *Gulliver's Travels*, 12–13

Telepathy, 17; and Puységur, 24, 30, 34, 63, 116, 117; term coined by Frederic Myers, 28
Thematics, 4–5, 135, 136
Todorov, Tzvetan, 4–6, 7, 9, 12, 14, 16, 110; on allegorical readings, 14; and Gogol's 'The Nose,' 14–15; and Maupassant's 'The Hair,' 113–14; on psychotic discourse, 160n. 26. *See also* Genre theory; Hesitation.
Turgenev, Ivan Sergeevich, 20, 22, 34, 35, 39, 43, 44, 105; attitude towards spiritualism, 41–2; language, 79, 82, 89, 92, 93, 99, 153nn. 12, 13, 14, 17. *See also Skaz*. Essays: *Literary Reminiscences*, 44. Fiction: 'The Dog,' 75, 82–5; —, as a *skaz*, 82, 103, 153n. 14; 'The Dream,' 42, 74, 75, 98, 99–104, 139–40, 141; —, language in, 99, 103; —, reception of, 99; 153n. 13; —, and 'The Song of Triumphant Love,' 156n. 34; 'Father Aleksey's Tale,' 75, 79–82, 86, 100; —, as a *skaz*, 79, 82, 103; 'Faust,' 74, 156n. 29; 'Klara Milich,' 75, 95–9; 'Knock! ... Knock! ... Knock! ...,' 74; 'Phantasms,' 41–2, 74, 75–9, 97; 151n. 1; —, and the disjunctive mode, 76, 77, 78; *Smoke*, 74; 'The Song of Triumphant Love,' 75, 89–95, 99, 104; —, and the Renaissance novella, 89–90, 94; *Spring Torrents*, 74–5; 'A Strange Story,' 75, 85–9, 104; 'An Unhappy Girl,' 74; *Virgin Soil*, 99
Villiers de l'Isle Adam, Comte Jean-Marie: 'Véra,' 80, 34, 95, 155n. 24

Wallace, Alfred Russell, 26, 31
Walpole, Horace, 3, 9
Wells, Herbert George: *The War of the Worlds*, 141

Zola, Emile: 'Angéline or the Haunted House,' 16

www.ingramcontent.com/pod-product-compliance
Lightning Source LLC
Chambersburg PA
CBHW071200070526
44584CB00019B/2863